THE IMMORTAL IN YOU

Michael Augros

The Immortal in You

How Human Nature
Is More than Science Can Say

IGNATIUS PRESS   SAN FRANCISCO

Cover art and design by Enrique Javier Aguilar Pinto

© 2017 by Ignatius Press, San Francisco
All rights reserved
ISBN 978-1-62164-153-7
Library of Congress Control Number 2016947668
Printed in the United States of America ∞

For Amy,
anima mea.

And we, who are we anyhow?

—Plotinus, *Enneads*

Since a soul can know all things, in a way it is all things, and thus it is possible for the completeness of the universe to exist in one thing.

—Thomas Aquinas, *On Truth*

CONTENTS

PROLOGUE

More than Science Can Say

Modern science can say countless true things about you—about what sort of creature you are, about how you and your parts work, about where you came from. But the very success of modern science can tempt us to believe that its questions are the only questions, that its answers the only answers, that there is no more to say about you or the natural world than what science can say. Since the infancy of modern science, certain thinkers and writers have succumbed to this temptation and taken it upon themselves to tell us that science is simply the whole truth about us.

Bertrand Russell was one of the most eloquent of them. He began one of his essays, "A Free Man's Worship", by recounting the story of how the demon Mephistopheles reimagined "the history of the Creation" for Dr. Faustus.[1] In this devil's version of events, God got bored with the praise of the angels since they could hardly be expected to say anything bad about him after he had given them eternal life. They were like a bunch of dull, toad-eating brown-nosers. The thought occurred to him how much more entertaining it would be to obtain undeserved praise from those to whom he gave only suffering and a death sentence. God therefore made man mortal. And man, painfully conscious of his own impending doom, out of his own trustful nature invented the idea that God's purpose must be somehow good for him. Man decided to believe that God had sentenced him to death only because he had somehow deserved it of God, and that God, being so good, would not abandon man to this just punishment, but would save him and give him eternal life. God smiled at this, and when man had renounced all joys for himself in order to please and appease God, the good God sent another sun

---

[1] "A Free Man's Worship" was originally published in 1903.

crashing into man's sun, and annihilated the world and man with it. After reciting this disturbing story, Russell says:

> Such, in outline, but even more purposeless, more void of meaning, is the world which science presents for our belief.... That man is the product of causes which had no prevision of the end they were achieving; that his origin, his growth, his hopes and fears, his loves and his beliefs, are but the outcome of accidental collocations of atoms; that no fire, no heroism, no intensity of thought and feeling, can preserve an individual life beyond the grave; ... that the whole temple of man's achievement must inevitably be buried beneath the debris of a universe in ruins—all these things, if not quite beyond dispute, are yet so nearly certain that no philosophy which rejects them can hope to stand. Only within the scaffolding of these truths, only on the firm foundation of unyielding despair, can the soul's habitation henceforth be safely built.[2]

To take a more recent author who thinks along similar lines, here is a passage from the late historian of science William Provine:

> Modern science directly implies that the world is organized strictly in accordance with mechanistic principles. There are no purposive principles whatsoever in nature. There are no gods and no designing forces that are rationally detectable.... Modern science directly implies that there are no inherent moral or ethical laws, no absolute guiding principles for human society.... When I die I shall rot and that is the end of me. There is no hope of life everlasting.... There is no ultimate meaning for humans.[3]

There are plenty of people around today saying the same sorts of things. Nor do you have to read obscure books or journals to find them. You can just go to college (as long as it is not a particularly religious college). Or you can simply read the news. In an article in the *New York Times*, University of Washington psychology professor

---

[2] Bertrand Russell, "A Free Man's Worship", quoted in *Why I Am Not a Christian, and Other Essays on Religion and Related Subjects*, ed. Paul Edwards (New York: Simon and Schuster, 1957), pp. 106–7.

[3] William Provine, "Evolution and the Foundation of Ethics", *MBL Science* 3, no. 1 (Winter 1988): 27–28.

David Barash described how he kicks off every school year by giving his students what he calls "the Talk". The Talk is about how evolution and religion don't mix. The first clash comes with the existence of a divine being, as one might expect. Living things don't require a supernatural creator, he explains to his students, since life, though "wonderfully complex", is an "entirely mechanical phenomenon". Barash continues:

> A few of my students shift uncomfortably in their seats. I go on. Next to go is the illusion of centrality. Before Darwin, one could believe that human beings were distinct from other life-forms, chips off the old divine block. No more. The most potent take-home message of evolution is the not-so-simple fact that, even though species are identifiable (just as individuals generally are), there is an underlying linkage among them—literally and phylogenetically, via traceable historical connectedness. Moreover, no literally supernatural trait has ever been found in Homo sapiens; we are perfectly good animals, natural as can be and indistinguishable from the rest of the living world at the level of structure as well as physiological mechanism.[4]

So the message is not new, but it is not going away, either. And it is newly aggressive, pervasive, and persuasive. It is also rather bleak in outlook. According to it, you are in no way exceptional or spiritual. You are just a mortal, just an animal—indeed, just a machine, no more than a temporary association of molecules that will one day disband in order to become other things. Great consequences attend this view of human nature. If you are thoroughly mortal, you should not entertain hopes of perfect happiness, or of reunion with lost loved ones. If you do not differ from your nearest primate relatives in any sharp and significant way, it would be ridiculous to believe that a divine being (if such a being exists) would take any special interest in you.

One possible recourse for those with religious beliefs running contrary to this stark message is to call into question the science upon which it is supposedly based. Evolution draws a good deal of fire, for example, both because its central tenets conflict with certain interpretations of Genesis and because it is not yet a fully worked-out

---

[4] David Barash, "God, Darwin and My College Biology Class", *New York Times*, September 27, 2014.

science. In this book, I will not take that approach, nor will I criticize it. I will simply offer another kind of response entirely to the idea that you are nothing but what modern science can say. Whatever deficiencies do or do not plague the current orthodoxies of evolutionary biology, a much broader and less noticed error underlies the thinking of those who would reduce you to your molecules. The error is the assumption that if you were somehow exceptional, if there were something immortal or spiritual in you, then modern biology would tell us all about it.

The Russian cosmonaut Yuri Gagarin was the first person to go out into space, having orbited Earth in 1961. Not long afterward, Soviet leader Nikita Khrushchev said in a speech at a gathering of the Central Committee of the Communist Party of the Soviet Union that "Gagarin flew into space, but didn't see any god there."[5] Let us suppose that Khrushchev was not joking, but took this to be a serious blow to belief in the existence of God. Even if there happened to be some reason to doubt that Gagarin ever really flew into space, that would not be the sole or chief thing wrong with Khrushchev's statement. The main problem with it is the tacit assumption that if God exists, then one would see him once one got above the clouds. Similarly, even if today's biological science were fraught with misconceptions, ambiguities, or slight evidence for its claims, these could not be the only thing wrong with saying that modern biology has never found any supernatural trait in Homo sapiens. Who expected it to? If you have an immortal soul, should you expect it to show up as a white spot somewhere on an X-ray or on a picture produced by an MRI scan? Should the trait of immortality be encoded somewhere in your genome? Of course not. Yet such are the tools and terms of biology. And they are quite excellent for their purposes, too. Only, they don't function very well as detectors of immortality, or finders of souls, whether such things exist or not. To the degree that biology restricts itself to terminology that is fully reducible to that of chemistry and physics, of course its methods will be inept for determining whether you have a soul and what its nature might be.

All the data, vocabulary, principles, and methods of modern science, deep and far-reaching as these may be, are yet too narrow to

5 "Yuri Gagarin", accessed February 7, 2017, https://en.wikipedia.org/wiki/Yuri_Gagarin.

include everything we can know about ourselves. To prove this assertion of mine is one of the purposes of this book. As a preview of things to come, consider the following indications that my thesis is the truth.

First, the idea that you stand at some unremarkable point along a continuum of animals, like a particular shade of gray somewhere between black and white, might not clash with any particular facts about the fossil record or your DNA, but it clashes pretty violently with any ordinary experience of you. The difference between chimp DNA and your DNA is relatively slight, and therefore wildly disproportional to the difference between chimp intelligence and yours. Imagine spending the rest of your days entirely in the company of chimps, never to see another human being as long as you live, and you will perceive the vast gulf separating human from chimp, even if you are unable to articulate the nature of that difference. When Hamlet wanted to express his disappointment in humanity, contrasting the greatness of what a human can and should be with what human beings all too often are, he delivered his famous "What a piece of work is a man!" speech. Now imagine it slightly altered:

> What a piece of work is a chimpanzee! how noble in reason! how infinite in faculty! in form and moving how express and admirable! in action how like an angel! in apprehension how like a god! the beauty of the world! the paragon of animals!

If this lofty description strikes you as somehow true of human beings, but as a staggering impropriety in the case of chimps, then it simply cannot be the whole truth about us that we are "perfectly good animals". Nor is this a display of egotism or species pride. It is an honest response to significant differences separating us from the other members of Animalia. Nor again is Shakespeare playing on our religious beliefs, but on a quite ordinary grasp of what a human being is. If modern science is blind to any radical differences between us and the beasts, that is not because there is no such difference, but because mainstream science, due to certain limitations in its methods and purposes, misses it.

A second indication that biology, chemistry, and physics cannot paint the complete picture of you comes right out of the words of those who say the opposite. If we say that you are made of atoms, or that you have and use a brain that obeys the laws of physics and chemistry, or that you are an animal, we will agree with what science says about you; we will in no way be forced to deny that you are also something more—for example, that you are a being capable of moral choices, good and bad. If we go a step further and say that you are *nothing but* atoms, or that your actions are the products of *nothing more than* the laws of physics and chemistry, or that you are *merely* an animal, we are no longer just agreeing with what science says; we are adding negative claims besides, ones that science cannot in any way prove. More than that, once we add this "nothing but" to every positive thing that science says about you, we will be forced to draw some awkward conclusions about you—for instance, that you are not a moral entity. Right and wrong, just and unjust, and other such terms will become quite meaningless, or else names for illusions. Some materialist thinkers have tried to save morality by deriving it from natural impulses in us that natural selection supposedly fine-tuned for the good of our species. But why should we obey these commandments of natural selection? And what would it mean for us to obey, if we have no free will anyway? Provine and many others like him are much more clear-sighted. If you are nothing but an animal, or nothing but a collection of atoms, and certainly if you have no free will, there will be no objective measure or meaning to human goodness and wickedness. That is the true consequence of the materialist's picture of you. And that consequence is patently absurd. No one truly believes this doctrine, although many think they believe it, since it follows from other things they do believe. Who, besides rapists (and not even all of them), believes that rape is neither better nor worse than any other human behavior? When it comes to living their lives, materialists wish to act uprightly and expect to be treated fairly, as well as want to see punished those who do injustices to them and their loved ones. They get righteously indignant about things. They think (or think they think) in one world, and live (and really think) in another one entirely. This intellectual schizophrenia is a symptom of a bad theory, the theory that you are "nothing but" molecules, "nothing but" neurons, "nothing but" an animal. It is reminiscent of Greek philosopher Zeno's supposed refutations of the existence of motion, which were extremely clever, and yet even he could not have believed motion did not exist when he needed to go to the bathroom.

A third indication that you are not just an animal is the very fact that you wonder or worry about whether you are just an animal. What other animal does that? There is at least that clear difference between you and the rest of the species in the kingdom. You are also capable of grasping infinity in some way, since you can see that there is no such thing as a greatest number, and you can wonder whether the universe is finite or infinite in size. Unless we think animals contemplate the infinite, we must think that the human mind differs from the animal mind in some way as the infinite does from the finite. How this capacity of your mind could differ from animal intelligence merely in degree would be very difficult to say. Intellectually, you seem to be not only bigger and brighter than any other kind of animal, but superior to all of them put together, and in another class entirely.

Such indications should broaden out our way of thinking about ourselves beyond the language of molecules and genes and leave room for the more ordinary perceptions we all share of what it is to be human. Do these more ordinary perceptions contain any secrets about your nature worth finding out? It is my contention that they do. The overarching question of this book is, what are you? It is not a trivial question, but one of the deepest we can ask. It comprises the more particular questions I have already mentioned: Do you differ in kind or only in degree from other animals, and if in kind, what is your essential difference? And how do you differ, if at all, from a machine? Are you just a bodily thing, or is there something spiritual in you? Can anything that is distinctively you survive death? Is anything in you immortal? Our ordinary insight into ourselves, carried no further than our daily occupations require, is powerless to resolve these questions. But an extraordinarily careful reflection on our ordinary experience enables us to find the answers, and they are wonderful. That is what I intend to show.

Which brings me to the methods I will employ in assisting your thought about yourself. By now you will have gathered that the mode of thinking in this book will not be that of modern science. Instead, the method will be that of philosophy. Now in many circles, philosophy has a bad name. Sometimes it is roundly deserved. Some of the worst nonsense in the world is the sort of "philosophy" that would have you lose sleep over whether there is anyone in existence besides yourself, or frighten you with the thought that you might really be just a brain in a vat and that your memories are phony implants, or get you all in a frenzy about other such absurdities that no one, not even any of their inventors, really believes. You will find nothing of that flavor in this book. I will not bother to argue against such fanciful ideas. Instead, I will take it as a principle to be applied without apology that people other than myself (such as yourself) exist, and that you and I really know this, and that other people know this too, and that anyone who tries to call this sort of thing into doubt is playing a silly mind game.

If you agree with this assessment of things, and even if you disagree, then you are already engaging in philosophy yourself. Philosophy is like thinking and breathing: not something that we can either do or not do if we like, but that we must do, and must do either badly or well, so long as we live. We are all of us philosophers, willy-nilly. Even those who pretend to despise philosophy have their reasons (i.e., their philosophical principles) for doing so. The least educated persons, the most unreflective, still think about and entertain definite views or hopes concerning life after death or the absence thereof, having as much invested in such questions as any learned academic has.

We will approach the great questions about you, then, as philosophers—certainly not as players of mind games, nor again as neuroscientists or particle physicists or biochemists, but as careful thinkers going forward from facts about you already known to you at least implicitly, facts that no one really doubts, and that no one can deny without undermining all the sciences and descending into mind games.

Why employ philosophy, and not modern science? Why not approach these questions about ourselves through the lens of particle physics or neuroscience or some such discipline? Why forgo the use of such formidable knowledge?

Certainly not because of anything wrong with physics, neuroscience, biochemistry, and the like. But plenty of authors, properly trained and credentialed in those great disciplines, are already applying those disciplines to certain questions about you. Besides, in order to answer our specific questions about you, it is both possible and desirable to overcome two limitations belonging to the particular branches of modern science. The first limitation is that these sciences reason from only some of the facts about you, while ignoring others that are extremely useful for answering our particular questions. This will become clear as we go along.

Their second limitation is that such sciences require outsiders to take many matters on faith. It is part of my unusual purpose not to ask you to place your faith in my experience of anything, or in anyone's expertise in things, but simply to consult your own treasury of experience for every conclusion I mean to draw. If I lapse into personal anecdote now and then, it is only for the sake of stimulating you to find within yourself the kinds of things that I am illustrating from my own personal history. Consequently, in these pages you will not encounter anecdotal testimony of things that lie beyond most people's powers of verification, such as accounts of people's near-death experiences. Nor will you find yourself trudging along through lengthy descriptions of the structure of your DNA or the topography of your brain. Descriptions of such things would necessarily rest on the work of specialists, not purely on data readily accessible to everyone just from being a human being. When it comes to ourselves, and to urgent questions concerning our immortality or lack thereof, it is desirable for all of us to know the truth of such matters for ourselves, so far as that is possible. Medicine, biology, chemistry, and physics all have much to contribute to our search into ourselves. Perhaps, when pursued *without* adding "nothing but" to their assertions, these disciplines have something to say in answer to the big questions this book is about. Be that as it may, it turns out those big questions are already answerable, even definitively, quite apart from the methods of modern science. It is this other path less taken that I intend to take.

Although I will make little use of modern science in building my own case, I will not ignore it. When the results of modern scientific inquiry serve to illustrate a point, or when they present important challenges to what I am saying about you and how you fit into the universe, I will introduce them accordingly. For my own conclusions, I will not argue from any authority, whether modern or ancient, but demonstrate from your own experience of being you that you are something infinitely better than a mere animal or a machine, that there is an immortal something in you, and that you are more than modern science can say.

And yet there is a kind of trust I must ask of you. I must ask you to trust yourself. Most of us say we like to think for ourselves, and that all educated people should do so, at least to some extent. That is what I will be asking you to do throughout this book. When I try to draw upon human experience, you have the right to expect that experience to be something recognizable to yourself. If it isn't, you may say I have fallen down on the job. Only do not let it worry you if we seem to be arriving at very significant results based squarely on your own knowledge of yourself. Do not doubt the conclusions simply because it is you yourself who have arrived at them!

The kind of guidance I will offer you along this journey of the mind is not my own invention. I will be following guides of my own. Although I think I have gone beyond merely trusting them and have arrived at seeing certain matters for myself—as I hope to help you to do also—it is just as well to give credit where credit is due, and to avoid being charged with pretending to original discoveries where I have made none. My guides are, in the first place, Thomas Aquinas and, in the second place, his philosophy teachers, chiefly Aristotle and Plato, and, in the third place, many of their followers and opponents (down through the ages and into the present day) who have helped me to understand them. They are the real teachers here. My only service is to express their insights in modern language, with more illustrative material than the philosophers themselves tend to provide, and to explain why their ideas are not outmoded, or outmodable, by modern science, but are perennially true.

One last introductory word, now, about the spirit of this book. Although I began by quoting from some of those thinkers with whom I disagree, this book will not focus much on them. It is not about thinkers, but about the truth of things. This book is to some extent about a bright and divinely appointed hereafter, although it is not principally about divine beings. It is about human beings. It is about you. It is about something within yourself that is discoverable to you, and which is a reason to expect another life better than any that is possible in this world. It is a pilgrimage from humble, close-to-home truths about yourself to the realization that there is a forever part of you.

Many a successful novel or movie tells a story of someone's self-discovery—Superman's, Harry Potter's, Jason Bourne's. Someone perhaps seemingly ordinary, despite all appearances, turns out in reality to be the owner of remarkable powers and to have arisen from remarkable origins, and can henceforth look forward to an even more remarkable future. Imagine yourself in similar circumstances. One fine day you learn, somehow, that your mind operates on such a high level of consciousness that it cannot be destroyed with your body, or indeed at all. It will live on forever, in one form or another, maybe without your body, or maybe in a renewed version of it. Either way, your mind will exist a thousand years from now, and another trillion after that.

This story about you is better than finding you can work magic or leap tall buildings in a single bound. Talents like that would be kids' stuff compared with everlasting life and the possibility of everlasting happiness. Besides, the story I have just outlined about you isn't fiction. It's the truth. You really do have one foot in another world, a world of immortals. To learn by what paths we may arrive at this hidden facet of your humanity, and find answers to our other questions about you, just take a little courage, buckle in, and read on.

I

Your Insider's View

Withdraw into yourself and look.

—Plotinus, *Enneads*

Ugh—That's Me

"There, do you feel that?" The nurse had tapped my foot. "Yes,"
I said. "A little more time, then," she concluded. I was lying down
waiting for an epidural to take effect in order to undergo arthroscopic
knee surgery. There were bone shards protruding from the back of
my patella and causing me pain whenever I flexed my right knee.

How did that happen? Skiing—skiing badly on bad skis. I was in
high school, so I still believed myself invulnerable, and, so believing,
dared to ski over a jump rather than around it. A nearly perfect landing on my face was followed by some spectacular tumbling to impress
the girls in my company, and all would have been well except that the
right bindings did not release. The right ski applied substantial
torque to my knee, and I was unable to stand up afterward. I was
near enough to the bottom of the trail to scooch my way down the
remainder of the mountain in a sitting position, then hobble, with
assistance from friends, back to the lodge for some hot cocoa. The
pain made it difficult to abstain from whimpering, something a teen-
age boy must at all costs avoid in the presence of other teens. Weeks
went by, and although the swelling had gone down considerably,
the pain and restricted movement persisted.

So here I was, about to experience my first epidural. I waited and
waited. Eventually I asked the nurse some question or other, and to
my embarrassment found myself giggling all through it. "I'm sorry," I
giggled again, "I don't know why I'm laughing." "Oh," she explained,

"we put a little something in your IV to help you relax." Well, if feeling completely ridiculous is the equivalent of relaxing, I must own that the "little something" was doing a bang-up job.

My hands had been folded on my chest until that point, and my elbows were beginning to feel cramped. So I laid my arms down by my sides. My hands came into contact with some odd massy stuff where my thighs ought to have been. I explored these hamlike things and thought, "Good gravy, I'm groping someone"—and then realized it was my own legs I was touching. "Excuse me," I said to the nurse, "I think I'm good to go." She brought over a large chunk of ice, and I watched her rub it up and down my left leg.

"Anything?"

"Nothing."

"You're good to go."

Bewildered, I continued to feel my legs with my hands. It was just like touching someone else's legs, or the legs of a corpse. I could not feel them—that is, I had no feeling *in* them, only a feeling *of* them with my hands. And I could not move them—that is, I could not move them with a movement from within them, but only by moving them with my hands. Ugh. They did not in any way feel like they were mine, or like they were me. "Me" now came to an abrupt stop somewhere in my midsection. Below that, it was as if something foreign had been attached.

This was the most poignant experience I had yet known of the difference between perceiving myself from within and from without. Until that day, I had always perceived my legs from within as well as from without. Now I was experiencing them as other people might have done—as my surgeon did, for instance—*only* from without.

It is often something of a cold shower to perceive ourselves as others do, purely from the outside, and without the usual context of our own outlook to complement it. If not all of us have undergone epidurals or similar medical experiences, most of us have seen ourselves on video or heard recordings of our own voices. Often we don't like what we see or hear. For one thing, we don't recognize ourselves. My voice on a recording is "wrong" because it doesn't sound as I sound to myself when I speak. My voice sounds one way, the "right" way, to my own ears partly because they are attached to me. It sounds markedly different to the ears of others unaffected by the vibrations in my head when I speak. The content of what I hear myself saying on the recording also sounds wrong. I can't believe I said *that*, and hearing myself say it on a recording makes me want to crawl under a table. I didn't really say that, did I? When I said it, there were countless subtle feelings, thoughts, associations, and images running through me that were part of what I felt I was conveying by my words, and which motivated my word choices, my tone, and my emphasis. And yet the recording stupidly plays back only the words themselves with their tone and emphasis, things now stripped bare of their essential context in me. When I hear it, I'm amazed that anyone understood me at all or could bear to listen to me talk.

Objective representations of ourselves, thus hollowed-out and potentially unsettling, do not have to be video or audio recordings. Merely hearing others repeat what we said or describe something we did, or reading ourselves quoted somewhere, can produce the same effect. When I read something I wrote more than a year ago, I sometimes find myself an insufferable bore, self-important sounding, or else unintelligible. Other times what I wrote surprises me, moves me, or makes me laugh out loud just as things written by other people do. In either case, Past-Me has become like another person from Present-Me. Enough time has elapsed that I have forgotten what was going on in my mind when Past-Me wrote this particular thing, and so I am in some degree out of sympathy with myself. I am seeing what I wrote very nearly as others see it.

Once I was walking through an airport at a brisk pace, trying to make a connecting flight. As I navigated my way through the waves of other travelers, a figure up ahead seized my attention. He looked like trouble—unshaven, shabbily dressed, a scowl on his face. His whole look said, "Get in my way and I'll stab you—don't think I won't." Better avoid him. I shifted to one side as he drew nearer, but he simultaneously shifted the same way. I did it again, and so did he. Had he spotted me? Was he after me? Then I realized with a cold shock that I was approaching an enormous mirror that covered a wall. I had not understood that I was looking at a reflection of the crowd I was in, because the mirror was too clean and too large for me to see it for what it was. The questionable character I had seen was of course myself. Was that really the impression I was making on everyone around me?

These and other like instances bring home to us that we are to ourselves the object of a kind of double experience. Unlike a stone, which I can experience only from the outside, "me" is something I can experience from the outside and from the inside, and usually I experience myself in both ways at once, so that I even have trouble distinguishing between the two sides of my experience of myself. When the two get separated somehow, when I catch a glimpse of what it is like to perceive me *only* from the outside, I am taken aback.

Two Views of You

So there are two views of you. One of these is yours alone. I will call this your *insider's view*. You can feel your hands from within them, and other people cannot do that. Other people can feel your hands only from the outside, as when they shake your hand. You can also feel what your hands feel like from the outside, when you use one hand to touch the other. This other view of you, the one available not only to you but also to outsiders, is the public view of you. We might also call it the *outsider's view*, as long as we realize that it is to a certain extent available to you as well, and not just to outsiders. You can see what your hands look like in much the same way that any other person can see your hands. You can't see the back of your neck the way an outsider can, however! Even if you can to some extent perceive yourself as others do, you can't always do it as well or completely as others can, and so it makes sense to call the second view of you the *outsider's view*. Outsiders can often have that view of you better than you can.

I am drawing attention to your double experience of you for a couple of reasons. First, it is already an interesting thing about you that there are two views of you. We can begin our reconnaissance of you by taking a closer look at the relationship between them. Second, understanding the two distinct halves of your experience of yourself is the foundation of everything else in this book. We aim to find out some very deep truths about what kind of being you are, and the first step in that direction is to appreciate the indispensability of the two halves of your view of yourself, but especially your exclusive insider's view of you, which these days gets less attention and credit than it ought to. Both views of you will be essential to our work. Sometimes they seem to disagree with each other, or at least to speak very different languages, and it becomes necessary to reconcile the two views of you. Usually they agree with each other quite well, however, and this agreement between the two will prompt the question I would like to explore in this chapter.

The agreement between the two views of you is plain in all sorts of ordinary examples. Suppose you have a cold. In the public view of you, other people can perceive that you have a cold by the usual indications. You are sneezing, coughing, blowing your nose; your eyes are red and glassy; your voice is hoarse; and so on. In your insider's view of yourself, you also perceive that you have a cold, and by means of more or less the same indications, although perceived in a different way. You can hear yourself cough or sneeze as others do, but also feel it, which others cannot. If you let them, others can see that your throat is red (you need a mirror to see that), but you can feel how scratchy and sore it is, and no one else can. The public view of you says you have a cold. Your insider's view agrees.

Whether you are playing the piano, mowing the lawn, delivering a speech, or watching TV, there will be both an outsider's way of viewing you and also your own insider's view of yourself performing the same activities. Wherever there is both a third-person and first-person experience of you, the two agree considerably. Does their agreement mean that they are simply redundant? Or does one view of you say things about you that the other does not? Does each one, in addition to what it says in agreement with the other, have its own things to say? How complementary are the two parts of your dual view of you? Can we, for example, without missing anything of importance about ourselves, ignore the kind of view each of us has from within, studying ourselves solely in light of external observations such as we have of each other, and such as we have of other creatures like horses and trees? Or is the reverse possible? Can we simply replace our outsider's view of ourselves with our insider's view, and miss nothing of importance about ourselves?

The outsider's view of you clearly says many things about you that your insider's view does not. How many cells are there in your body? Why do you need to breathe? Does your blood circulate, or does it just slosh back and forth in your veins? Your insider's view has nothing to say in answer to such questions. From your experience of being you, from that first-person perception of yourself that no one else can share, you are not aware that you have cells at all, let alone how many or what kinds. What elements are you made of? How does your body break down food? Where are your childhood memories stored? Your mere experience of being you will tell you none of these things. Once we begin to take a serious look at you from the outside, however, these questions now become answerable, particularly when we assist and enhance the outsider's view of you with special equipment. You yourself can see that your blood or skin is made up of cells by looking at a sample under a microscope. This is not your insider's view at work, however, but the public view of you that any number of other people can share.

The outsider's view of you affords important information about you that is not to be had any other way. It is an irreplaceable source of many important truths about you. That side of your self-experience is indispensable.

The Inside Scoop

That answers half the question. What about your insider's view? Does it have things to say about you that the outsider's view of you cannot say? The answer is not as obvious here as it is in the case of the outside view of you. At first your insider's view seems to be nothing more than your own personal take on things that are accessible also from the outside alone. When I have a headache, my wife knows it just by the look on my face (and yes, OK, sometimes by my grouchy tone). She does not feel it as I do, but so what? She is not missing the basic fact that I have a headache, even if she does not have full access to it in all the same (and unenviable) ways that I do.

My wife can read me pretty well, sometimes frighteningly well, but even she does not have all the information about me that I have about myself. She can never tell from her outsider's viewpoint what I dreamed about last night, or what song I'm thinking of, which are things perfectly plain to me. As long as accurate mind-reading people or machines remain the stuff of science fiction, our insider's views of ourselves will continue to be the exclusive sources for all kinds of information about ourselves. Then again, what I dreamed about last night or what song is in my head at the moment are idiosyncrasies of mine. They are distinctive facts about me of little interest to anyone else, and not particularly revealing about other individuals, such as you. If personal peculiarities are all that is exclusively available by means of the insider's view, then we could and should ignore it in the pursuit of serious knowledge about what you are, since your human nature is not a peculiarity of yours, but something you share in common with others.

Your insider's view brings much more to the table than your idiosyncrasies, however. It also grants you your only access to certain crucial pieces of information about what kind of being you are. We should expect this to be the case. What are you, after all? A human being. That means, among other things, that you are alive, that you have a number of senses, and that you can think. All these things go on inside you—living, sensing, thinking. The outsider's view provides the best and most complete look at your outside. By the same token, your insider's view should provide the best and most complete look at your inside, at your inner life.

What particular questions about you does your insider's view help answer that cannot be answered from the outsider's view of you alone? This whole book is like one long answer to that question. As a more convenient answer for now, I will offer here a couple of sample questions whose answers demand the use of your insider's view.

For instance, consider these statements:

1. Every lover is loved by everyone.[1]
2. Joanie loves Chachi.

What follows? First, since Joanie loves someone (second premise), she is therefore a lover, and therefore she is loved by everyone (first premise). Next, since everyone loves Joanie (just shown), that means everyone is a lover. Consequently, everyone is loved by everyone (first premise). So everyone loves everyone.

This charming conclusion follows inescapably from the two premises, as you see. But how do you know that conclusion follows? Not because you know it is true. In fact, you know it is false. Nor is it

---

[1] Ralph Waldo Emerson wrote, "All mankind love a lover." Essay V, *Love*, in *Essays: First Series* (1841).

because you know the premises to be true. In fact, you know the first premise is false. Nor does the conclusion follow just because it is false and one of the premises is false. "All cats are black" is also false, but that statement does not follow from the two premises above, as "Everyone loves everyone" does. So where exactly are you looking in order to see that each thing follows? Where are you getting your information about that? Not just from me, of course. If I had said that what follows is that Abraham Lincoln is alive and well, you would have said to yourself, "No, that does not follow from those premises." If I had said on the contrary that what follows is that Abraham Lincoln was assassinated, you would again have said I needed a logic lesson. It was not my telling you that something followed that convinced you that something followed. So what did convince you?

It was your insider's view of what was going on in your own mind. Statements, after all, are things of the mind, not things floating around in the world. They are not ink on paper, or sounds in the air. Such things are mere symbols of the real, living statements, which exist primarily in the mind. The relationship of premises to their inescapable conclusion is a relationship that statements have because of the way your mind works, something you can pick up by reflecting on your mind at work. The question about what follows from certain statements is really a question about how your mind works, since it is asking about a relationship between things not as they are found outside your mind, but as they are found in it, and in any other mind like yours. This doesn't mean that the rules about how your mind works are irrelevant to reality. If the premises are true, and something follows from them according to the rules by which your mind works, then that conclusion must also be true, and it will agree with reality outside your mind. Otherwise logic would not be worth learning. But the relationships between the statements as they are in your mind is not simply the same as the relationships between the facts in reality that they signify. For example,

Whatever turns blue litmus paper red is acidic.
Cherry Coke turns blue litmus paper red.
Therefore, Cherry Coke is acidic.

The premises in this case might cause me to know the truth of the conclusion, but they don't cause the conclusion to be true. The fact that some soda turns litmus red does not cause it to be acidic. It's the other way around. The fact that the soda is acidic is the reason why it turns litmus red. In reality, the relation of the premises to the conclusion is that of effect to cause, although in regard to my knowledge they have the opposite relationship—my knowledge of the premises is the cause of my knowledge of the conclusion. So the logical rule that "this follows from that" is not collapsible into the relationship "this causes that." No amount of inspecting the nature of soda or litmus will ever reveal the rules that govern human thinking. The only way for us to learn the rules that govern how our mind works is to use it and watch it at work, to reflect on it by means of our insider's view. When we see others thinking by the same rules, we know that they have the same kinds of minds that we do. All teaching presupposes this very thing, that the way that teachers got to the truth of things will work for students too.

Your insider's view is not only the exclusive means for discovering the rules of logic, but it is also a necessary means to knowing what a mind is and that minds exist at all. Your senses are in the same boat, and so are your emotions. Suppose for a moment that you have never had any experience of seeing. You were born completely blind and have always been in that condition. You have never seen a glimmer of light, a movement, a color, or a shape. You are, however, a neuroscientist, and your specialty is the neuroscience of vision. You know the physics of light and color as well as anyone in the world. You understand in exquisite detail all the electrical and chemical mechanisms from the photoreceptors in the eye to the regions of the brain that are active when people see. Do you now understand what seeing is? Do you know what people mean by the word *see*? Do you know what people mean by the word *blue*?

When people say that the sky is blue, they don't mean anything about wavelengths and frequencies, or neurons and synapses. Those thoughts generally do not occur to them at all. They are naming a quality they immediately perceive, not the result of a measuring process or an instance of a scientific principle or a piece of equipment by which their seeing takes place. *Blue* names none of those things, but just an immediately perceived quality. It is just this immediately perceived quality that is entirely left out of the objective science of color. What we call *seeing* is likewise a certain activity we are immediately aware of in ourselves when we perform it, and it is just this thing we are immediately aware of that is entirely left out of the objective, outsider's description of what is happening in the eyes and brain of a seeing person.

Here we have an example of how the two views of you somehow agree, but speak very different languages; neither language is reducible to the other, although they correspond. When you see that the sky is blue, certain things are going on in your brain. When you see that the grass is green, other things are going on in your brain. When you look back at the sky, the same things that were going on in your brain before are going on again. There is a more or less definite correlation between what you experience when you see and those things simultaneously going on in your brain that can be described even by those who have never seen anything. The two go together, your act of seeing and the objective correlatives of that act going on in you at the same time. But we can't reduce one to the other, even if they are somehow mutually dependent. No amount of description of chemical and electrical events in your eyes and brain could ever contain what *seeing* means to those of us who have experienced it, or convey it to those who have never experienced it. That meaning comes only from the direct experience of seeing, which takes place only in the insider's view, in the view of the one doing the seeing.

Could someone get you (hypothetically blind you, that is) to form some vague idea of seeing by analogy to your other senses? Maybe so. Maybe the way the blind can read braille by touch approaches vision in many ways. Maybe it conveys something to the blind person to say that *red* is warm and *green* is cool. However successful these attempts might be, they still must invoke the insider's view of the person being addressed. *Warm* and *cool* and *the sense of touch* derive their meaning from the direct experience of these things. When you attribute sight or any other sense to other people or animals, you do so because they exhibit outward signs that they possess in themselves something like the senses you experience in yourself. The eyes of a dog and its behavior when it runs are similar enough to your own eyes and your own running that you perceive that it sees. Nevertheless, its eyes and behavior could not convey anything to you of seeing in particular unless you had first experienced it in yourself.

Your insider's view is therefore an original and irreplaceable source of all your understanding of what it means not only to see, but also to hear, taste, smell, feel, and also to imagine, remember, understand, and again to desire, and to feel anger or fear or love. The only direct access you have to these kinds of internal activities is your insider's view. You quite rightly attribute the same kinds of activities to others when you see the outward signs of them. When you do, you remain continually dependent on your only direct experience of such things—namely, within yourself—in order to know what you mean. We tend to believe that we simply see that people see, without any implicit reference to our own seeing. Really, though, we never directly perceive any act of seeing but our own. In others, we see their eyes and their facial expressions and their movements, things quite different from an act of seeing, although capable of indicating the presence of such an act to those who have experienced it directly, and who are in fact experiencing it directly in themselves even while they are looking at others. In this way, it is the easiest and most natural thing in the world for us to supplement our outsider's view of others with information gleaned from our insider's view of ourselves, since others (at any rate other human beings) are indeed other selves. Our insight into outsiders, into other people and animals, obviously depends on our outsider's view of things. But it also depends on our insider's view, and the dependence is subtle enough that we easily overlook it.

Yum—That's Me

Your insider's view is clearly not a superfluous repetition of your outsider's view of yourself or of others. Without it, you could never understand what it means to see, to sense, to think, to wish, and to do most of the things that are at the very heart of what you mean by being you and living your life. The two views of you are indeed complementary, not redundant, although they agree with one another and correspond in many ways. Each view says things about you that the other does not, or not as well.

Different questions about you might nonetheless require very unequal emphasis on each of the two views. Ignoring our insider's view completely is perhaps not possible, since even the laws of logic, which we apply in all good thinking, whether about ourselves or other things, are the fruit of reflecting on our own thinking, a use of our insider's view. Once we are in possession of the rules, however, we don't need to think much about ourselves. We simply use them. When Watson and Crick discovered the double helix structure of DNA, they probably did not consult their insider's view of being possessors of DNA. It would have shed no light on the question at all, since we don't perceive our DNA in light of our insider's view. Ignoring our insider's view is therefore often legitimate, even necessary, and the information thus gathered is not false, only incomplete. According to my *Funk and Wagnall's New Encyclopedia*, which is anything but new, Albert Schweitzer was a "French Protestant clergyman, philosopher, musicologist, organist, and medical missionary, born in Kaysersberg, Upper Alsace, Germany". One can say all sorts of things about Schweitzer's medical work without mentioning that he was an organist. Conversely, one could say a lot about his accomplishments as an organist without mentioning his medical missions. Each picture of him would be true, though incomplete. It would be a silly mistake, of course, to deny that he was an organist simply because so much information can be gathered about his medical missions without knowing anything about his organ playing. He was a physician, yes, but to say he was "nothing but a physician" is wrong. In just the same way it would be a silly mistake to say that you are nothing but what can be observed about you from the outside, simply because so much outside information can be gathered about you without consulting your insider's view.

Some thinkers have rejected your insider's view as a thing of no worth or validity. Philosophers Paul and Patricia Churchland, for example, deny the existence of "propositional attitudes" such as you might express when you say "I believe that men landed on the moon," or "I doubt that everything in the *National Enquirer* is true," or "I'm afraid I might have cancer." According to them, such beliefs, doubts, fears, hopes, wishes, realizations, understandings, and the like simply do not exist. Rejecting them means rejecting the existence or trustworthiness of your insider's view, since these things are immediate facts of your internal experience. It is not much of a leap from here to the denial of the existence of you entirely.

If you try to ignore your insider's view of yourself, to exclude it from your serious thought about what you are, then you essentially become an outsider to yourself, cutting yourself off from the one direct means of experiencing what you mean by "you". Adopting this peculiar method of trying to understand yourself, you will then be constrained to think that the very existence of "you" is a mere hypothesis or even a fiction. For quite a few decades, certain modern psychologists have been willing to go as far as that. The Canadian psychologist and neuroscientist Donald Olding Hebb, for example, said that "the existence of something called consciousness is a venerable *hypothesis*: not a datum, not directly observable."[2] American neurologist Lawrence S. Kubie held that "although we cannot get along without the concept of consciousness, actually there is no such thing."[3] And the American behaviorist K. S. Lashley said that "there is not direct knowledge of an experiencing self. . . . The knower as an entity is an unnecessary postulate."[4] No one who takes the insider's view seriously can say these things. To say them, we must first adopt the postulate that the only things that are real about you are those that are observable from the outsider's standpoint, such as the things that an MRI scan or a PET scan could pick up. I will consider the general kinds of reasons behind this way of thinking toward the end of this book. For now, it is enough to notice that when people reject your insider's view of yourself, they consequently force themselves also to reject the things that such a view of you is needed to reveal. One of these things is you yourself. There is no "you", they say, no "self" to you. That is pure illusion. (Who is deceived by such an illusion? Good question!) This is a marvelous confirmation that the insider's view of you is both a true view and an indispensable one. Try to dispense with it, and you end up dispensing with yourself. That is just the sort of philosophy that gives philosophy a bad name, and that I promised not to indulge in myself.

Two objections to your insider's view are nonetheless worth considering here briefly. If we can understand why some people object to the use of your insider's view as a means to acquiring serious knowledge about you, and lay their objections to rest, then our own understanding of your insider's view will improve. Unlike a naïve

[2] Edgar D. Adrian, Frederic Bremer, and Herbert H. Jasper, eds., *Brain Mechanisms and Consciousness: A Symposium Organised by the Council for International Organizations of Medical Sciences* (Oxford: Blackwell, 1956), p. 404.

[3] Ibid., p. 446.

[4] Ibid., pp. 423–24.

beginner's understanding of it that lies open to objections of which we are not even aware, our understanding of your insider's view will take account of those difficulties. We will achieve a more nuanced understanding.

One objection accuses your insider's view of being subjective, hence an unworthy foundation of real knowledge of you. No one else can share your insider's view of you. It is permanently idiosyncratic, trapped inside you, incommunicable to others, and consequently impossible for anyone else to verify.

Not a problem. You alone have the insider's view of yourself, that's true. But guess what? I have an insider's view of myself. Although these self-experiences of ours probably differ in various ways, even as our bodies do, nonetheless they share many points of commonality too, and we can know this by describing to each other our internal experience of being human and alive. Whatever is distinctive of your view of you, whatever cannot be found in everyone else's insider's views of themselves, we will leave aside. We will also leave aside any idiosyncrasies in my insider's view. We will stick to such facts as can be ascertained by means of anyone's insider's view, where "anyone" means anyone who is in possession of all the ordinary abilities that are natural to human beings. Anyway, if at any point I begin to describe an inner world altogether foreign to you, you may complain that I have broken my promise.

The other objection is that your insider's view is not (at least not yet) open to technological enhancement, and in particular it is not subject to precise measurement. Exact science, the only sure and true knowledge of you, demands exact measurement. So the insider's view of you is at best a basis for untrustworthy guesses about yourself.

A general misunderstanding underlies this objection. Precision or exactness is not the same thing as certainty. I am absolutely sure that I am taller than my wife. That is not a very exact statement, however. So, contrary to common opinion, I can have certainty without exactness. In fact, the more exact I try to be about just how much taller I am than my wife, the less certainty I have that what I am saying is true. Am I exactly two inches taller? Instruments of measurement might help me become more sure of this, but they will never make me surer of this than I am of the less exact statement that I am taller than my wife.

Even in mathematics, the exact science of quantitative things considered abstractly, and which is famous for that thing called "mathematical certainty", does not always concern itself with the metrical relationships of things. Topology is the name of a branch of geometry that talks about the nonmetrical relationships of things. Consider this question, for example. If three closed loops are such that no two of them are linked together, does that mean it will be possible to separate them without cutting any of them? The answer would seem to be an obvious yes. If no two loops are linked, one can easily move them apart from each other without cutting them, right? Actually, that is not necessarily right. You can see this for yourself in the accompanying figure. No two of the loops are linked together. Any two of them float free of each other. Now try to imagine removing one of the loops from this grouping without cutting any of them. Impossible. When you try to pull one loop away from another, the third one stops you at a certain point. Try to lower the vertical loop out of the horizontal one surrounding it, for example, and the little loop inside will prevent you. Amazing, isn't it? Counterintuitive, wonderful, and certainly true—there can be closed loops no two of which are linked, which nonetheless form an object from which they cannot be extricated. Loops arranged in this particular way are called Borromean rings. Measuring has nothing to do with their interesting relationship. The specific sizes of the loops does not matter, so long as they are arranged in a way that forms this particular type of topological lock.

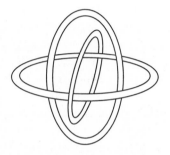

Even in mathematics, the most certain of the disciplines, we can find nontrivial and nonmetrical truths. Acquaintance with this fact demolishes the idea that nonmetrical information about you must be doubtful or trivial. It also positively inspires confidence that there will be things worth finding out about you in light of your insider's view. If the science of quantity can ignore measurement at times and still attain great certainty about truths known only to a few, much more can the science of you do the same, especially if it pays attention to your all-important insider's view.

All of us attain some degree of insight into ourselves by means of our insider's view, prior to any philosophy or science. The lessons begin in infancy. When my daughter was a baby, I was amazed at how flexible her little body was. The default position for her feet seemed to be right next to her face. Did she recognize her feet as belonging to herself? As early as six weeks and even earlier, babies smile true social smiles, a sign of recognizing, in however confused a fashion, that here is someone, and not just something. Some inchoate notions of "me", "you", and "it" are already forming in the baby's mind. This does not mean that these ideas are clear or complete. I remember watching her feet wave back and forth in front of her eyes. Her eyes followed them as if they were buzzing flies. They were attention-getting objects like any other, not yet in her control from within, not yet recognized as parts of herself. She would reach with her hand, miss. Then miss again. Then—ha!—she'd catch one of those things. Into her mouth it went (naturally). In seeing her feet, she was experiencing them as any outsider might. She also had feeling in her feet, and that was a part of her insider's view of them. Only, she did not put the two together. She did not associate, at first, the things waving in and out of her field of vision with anything in which she had feeling. Once she popped one of her feet in her mouth, however, she could connect her two experiences of it. She experienced "how this foot tastes" but also "how this foot feels when it is being tasted." She perceived her foot simultaneously from within and from without, and that dual experience of herself eventually taught her to recognize her feet as herself, just by sight. This was Self-Discovery 101.

Our simultaneous possession of inside and outside views of ourselves as intertwined and interacting aspects of one experience is not only natural and ongoing, but with us from the very start. Precisely because we all experience such things in ourselves, and from the very beginnings of our lives, it may seem at first that our insider's view has little to offer beyond common knowledge. Does it contain nothing beyond things that everyone already knows? Or, carefully examined, can it also reveal secrets of your nature known only to those who put in serious work, and think carefully? Do the basic facts it contains lead to anything deeper?

They do. We will find, if we take care to pay extraordinary attention to your ordinary experience of being you, that it goes many places very much worth getting to. We stand at the beginning of a long path that will take us through strange and wondrous truths about you.

Let's venture down it, and see what there is to see.

2

Hidden Powers

The time hath come for thee to know thyself, for the true circumstances of thy life have, heretofore, been altogether hidden from thee.

—Howard Pyle, *The Story of King Arthur and His Knights*

Captain Marvel

The secret identity of Captain Marvel was just a little boy, Billy Batson. Billy Batson had a long lost twin sister, Mary Bromfield, and guess what? She could also turn into a superhero—Mary Marvel—just by saying the magic word *Shazam!*

One could hardly avoid the inference. If someone with a name like "Mary Bromfield" (who probably sat behind me at school every day without my noticing) could just say *Shazam!* and summon a bolt of magical, power-giving lightning down upon herself, well, then, it stood to reason that I just might be able to do it, too. Sound, airtight, six-year-old logic. It was certainly worth a shot. I was as likely a candidate as the next ordinary kid, wasn't I? The thing had to be put to the test. After all, I was nobly resolved to use any powers conferred upon me only for good, never for evil. And the capital to be ventured was the mere shouting of a word.

The word did have to be shouted, though, that much was clear. And one had to mean it. Probably it had to be done outdoors, so the lightning wouldn't have to crash through the roof of my house and scare my poor mother. That complicated matters. An outdoor, public experiment meant that, in the event of a negative result, the potential for embarrassment was considerable enough. Best not to conduct the test in the backyard within earshot of Mom, or anyone else for that matter. My leash was short at age six, but I was allowed to walk around the block now and then. So it came to pass that one fine sunny morning I obtained my mother's permission to take a stroll by myself down the hill for purposes best known to myself. I rounded a bend, and my house passed out of view. So far, so good. I walked by a few more houses and found a spot where the space between them was more generous than elsewhere. Not a soul in sight. A window was open on the gable end of a nearby house, indicating the possibility of being overheard through it, but there was nothing to be done. Conditions were as good as they were going to get.

My heart thumped in my chest. My limbs went cold. I looked up into the clear blue sky. No clouds to be seen, but that hardly mattered. Billy Batson would sometimes say the Magic Word in clear weather, too, and those transformative clouds suddenly rolled up out of nowhere, gathering over him.

I nevertheless began to feel very silly and afraid that someone might be watching. Best make it quick.

"Shazam!" I had shouted it at the top of my lungs. I waited. Nothing—not a cloud, not a rumble, not a spark (ah well). Clearly I was not one of the chosen ones after all. That had been a possibility all along, I knew. I consoled myself with the thought that thousands of other boys and girls with names as ordinary-sounding as mine had probably conducted similar experiments and gotten similar results.

Not long afterward I wondered whether getting really angry might enable me to turn into a creature like the Hulk. That investigation, and a few more like it, also came to a dead end.

Eventually I gave up the search for hidden powers I never knew I had, resigning myself to the idea that human beings in general do not possess any powers above and beyond those ordinary ones (the ability to walk, for example, or the ability to talk) that we all have heard of, and which do not make any of us special.

In later years, philosophy came along and taught me to rethink this resignation of mine. I learned that although I may or may not have been right to abandon my search for superhuman powers making some human beings more special than others, I had been wrong to think that the only powers we possess are those that everyone has heard of, and wrong again to suppose that powers possessed by all of us could not prove us to be quite extraordinary beings after all, with much more to us than is ordinarily supposed.

Some human abilities we all know about and most of us possess, such as our five familiar powers of sense. Other abilities lie deeper beneath the surface, more hidden in us, and when brought to light, they tell us more about what we are than most people ever discover. I don't mean anything like ESP or telekinesis. I have in mind ordinary, natural, human abilities. Nothing extraordinary, supernatural, or superhuman. It is possible for us to go through life unaware of some of our noblest abilities. And it is right for us to marvel at them when they come to our attention.

Many years ago, my son Max sustained his first (relatively) real injury, a nasty cut on his finger. How it happened, I cannot recall. What I remember is that the pain and the bleeding dismayed him, and he worried he would just have to live with it for the rest of time. To make matters worse, he had recently learned from some cartoon on PBS that infections can set in when we get cuts. What a strange and pathetic moment that was for me. My crying, slightly damaged son was entirely unaware that his body came equipped with a way to deal with such eventualities. I explained to him that his body was made of tiny parts called *cells* that could reproduce themselves and generate fresh skin to close up the wound, good as new. As to the possibility of infections from tiny bugs, well, "Have no fear," I said. "You come equipped with an immune system, an army of microscopic infection killers in you, like nano-bots and nano-scientists who hunt down the bugs and destroy them." I will never forget the look on his face when I told him such an "ordinary" thing. He could hardly have been more pleased if I had just told him he was really Captain Marvel.

Of course my Max was a boy of five or so. Can we grown-ups become generally educated and still possess powers of which we are unaware?

We absolutely can. In this chapter we will make our first foray into your inner nature by paying close attention to your insider's view, and before we are done we will have discovered a remarkable and almost impossible-sounding power you probably never knew you had. We will not be jumping into the deep end quite yet, however. The profound question about whether you possess any nonmaterial powers must wait. The hidden power we are about to uncover might well lie hidden in your brain. In fact, it is my own view (and that of Aquinas and Aristotle) that it does. It is nonetheless a remarkable power, one that few people realize they possess, and the discovery of which will illustrate what kind of insight your insider's view into yourself makes possible. The power I have in mind will also shed a little light on your insider's view itself.

You Have Powers

The first step in the right direction is a simple matter of vocabulary. Throughout this book I will be talking about various *powers* of yours. That is not exactly ordinary English. Presumably you would admit that you are the possessor of many abilities—the ability to walk, talk, see, hear, imagine, understand, and so on. *Ability* is the plain English word, not *power*. So why the fancy word *power*? Unless we are talking about electric power or political power, the word sounds either old-fashioned or else superhuman, like Sherlock Holmes boasting of his powers of deduction, or Superman losing his powers in the presence of kryptonite.

For our specific purposes, however, it will be a good idea to use both words, and not altogether interchangeably. Examples will illustrate why this is so. My son Max has the ability to read the entire eye chart at the optometrist's, and I have no such ability. Is it right to conclude that he has a special "eye-chart-reading ability" that I simply lack? Not really. This ability of his is really nothing else than a part of his ability to see, and I also have the ability to see, only his is much more refined than mine. My daughter, Evelyn, has the ability to bend over and put her hands flat on the floor without bending her knees. I have no such ability! It would be a mistake, though, to infer that she has a special floor-touching ability, that she performs this amazing feat by something in her that is completely absent in me. She can bend over and touch the floor, thanks to her flexibility, her ability to move her body around. I also have that ability, only she has that same kind of ability to a greater degree than I do.

Examples such as these show that sometimes when people say that you possess the ability to do some particular thing, whereas I do not have that ability, they really mean we share some basic kind of ability, only you happen to have it to a greater degree than I do. When we speak of people's "intellectual ability", for example, we often have in mind not only their ability to understand anything at all, but also a specific degree to which they are able to understand.

Our purpose is to learn more about your human nature, about what you are as opposed to who you are as an individual. Consequently, we will not need to focus on any idiosyncrasies of yours (regarding which I could hardly be of any use to you). Rather, we will concern ourselves with those things about you that are common to human beings as a kind. This means we must pay fresh attention to the kinds of abilities you possess, without worrying about the special degree to which you possess them. We must focus, for example, on the simple fact that you have an intellect, without bothering about your IQ.

In order to make it clear that we will be talking about the fundamental kinds of abilities in you as opposed to any measure of their capacities or applications, it will be useful to employ a special term. Philosophers have long used the term *powers*. You have various powers, such as your five sense powers and your power to understand, called your intellect, and a self-moving power enabling you to move your body, and so on.

Another property of the word *ability* that sometimes leaves explorers of human nature reaching for another word is that it applies equally well to innate abilities and acquired ones. We speak not only of the ability to hear or see, but also of the ability to read French, the ability to play the piano, the ability to drive a stick shift. These latter examples are not inborn abilities belonging to all healthy and mature individuals. They are more like acquired habits, add-ons to one's inborn abilities. The natural powers in us that precede any habits we might acquire deserve a special name distinct from *abilities*, to bring out their naturalness. To that end, we may call them *powers*.

As you read about your *powers* in the coming pages of this book, you will now know what I mean—not that you have superpowers, but that you possess certain natural abilities that differ from one another in kind, and not merely in degree.

A Sensible Place to Start

The special power in you that we are about to get acquainted with is a sense power. Why start there? Why not start with your powers of growth or digestion instead?

The reason has to do with our special method for getting to know you better. We aim to discover certain things about you with the assistance of your insider's view, which reveals more about your senses and other knowing powers than it does about your vegetative functions. From within, you can directly experience your own acts of seeing, hearing, smelling, imagining, remembering, and the like. Other people cannot directly experience these things in you as you can yourself. Your acts of growing and healing from a wound or illness are another story. You can see that you are growing or healing pretty much the same way anyone else can verify these things about you. You measure yourself and see you are taller. You look at the scratch you got last week and see that it is smaller. Your friends can experience these things about you in the same way that you can. These things about you come to light primarily in the public, outsider's view of you. You might also feel growing pains in yourself that no one else can feel, or feel less pain in your scratch, or feel better than you did yesterday. Those perceptions belong to your insider's view. Only they are not exactly perceptions of your acts of growing and healing. Your sense of feeling better is not itself the work of getting better, but just a change in the way you feel that results from having gotten better (that is why it is possible to feel better even when you are not really better). As opposed to your more vegetative activities, such as healing from a wound, your acts of seeing and hearing fall directly within your insider's view. You can experience your acts of sensation themselves, and in a direct way that no one else can.

Another reason to begin our investigation into your nature with your sense powers is that your acts of sensing and understanding are much more distinctive of you than your vegetative functions are. All animals and even fungi perform vegetative functions. None of them can learn geography, economics, or music theory. Your cognitive activities should therefore tell us more about what you are as distinguished from the other living beings in the world.

Then why not start with your intelligence? Why start with your powers of sense? They are not most distinctive of you. Other animals have sense powers, too, after all.

While it is true that your intelligence is most distinctive of you, and will reveal the deepest and most astonishing secrets of your human nature, it is also more hidden and difficult to grasp than your sense powers. You sense things like coffee mugs, but you understand things like truth—and it is easier to get a grip on a coffee mug than on truth. Observing the rule that we should begin with what is easier for us to grasp, we will start our investigation into you by looking into your sense powers, and work our way up to things like your imagination and intellect.

So it makes sense to begin our investigations with your senses. How, then, should we begin investigating your sense powers? With a detailed study of the physiology of your eyes and ears? With imaging techniques to show us what parts of your brain are responsible for seeing and hearing? Methods such as these familiarize us with the details of the organs of sense, and would presumably tell us something about how they operate. They clearly stress the outsider's view of you, however, contrary to the program I promised to follow.

Rather than look into your organs of sense in detail, we will instead follow another path more accessible to your insider's view. We will approach your sense powers by starting from the objects that define and distinguish them. What is an *object*? The word *object* derives from the Latin verb *obicio*, meaning "to throw before, cast, offer, present, expose". The participial form *obiectum* means a thing presented to something else, laid before it, put in its way. Our word *object* retains this sense even in everyday English. If I am the object of ridicule, it means I am the target of the ridicule, exposed to it, presented to and laid before those who would ridicule me. Just as the object of ridicule is the thing ridiculed, so the thing understood is the object of understanding, and the thing desired is the object of desire. Generally, the things that lie before your various powers as the targets with which they are concerned, or which provoke them into operation, are called their *objects*.

Your senses have their own objects, the specific things that are their concerns, their targets, what they are about. Something seen is an object of sight, a visual object. Something heard is an object of hearing. By looking into the objects of your senses, we will be able to discover a sense power in you that is generally possessed but not generally known.

Five Senses—One World

Our search for a hidden power in you begins with this question: Why do you have one world of sense experience when the world of sensible things is brought to you through many different senses? How can you have five different senses without experiencing five different worlds of sense?

To assure ourselves that we are asking a real question, let us take a moment to verify the facts it presupposes. We human beings are naturally capable of developing at least five distinct sense powers: sight, hearing, smell, taste, and touch. I say "at least five" because someone might say that touch is really many senses, not one. Your sense of hot and cold is called touch; so is your sense of pleasure and pain. Your sense of pressure is also called touch, and so is your sense of how your body is positioned, and your sense of balance, and maybe others beyond these. Are these just different jobs performed by a single sense of touch? Or are they the jobs of many distinct senses irreducible to one another? Probably it is not quite exact to say you have "a sense of touch", but more accurate to say you have *several* senses of touch, so that *touch* names a whole family of related senses.

In any case, you are the possessor of many distinct sense powers. And yet your sense experience does not consist in five disconnected sensory worlds. Security guards often keep watch over a whole building by watching several monitors displaying the live feed from many different security cameras. Monitor 1 displays the feed from Camera 1 in the lobby, and Monitor 2 displays the feed from Camera 2 in the hallway, and so on. Your sense experience of the world does not present itself to you like that. It does not consist in five or more distinct, compartmentalized views of the world. Instead, your senses seem to coalesce or cooperate in presenting to you a single, coherent, integrated experience of the world.

How can this be? How can the world outside you enter your inner world through five different entryways without becoming divided into five compartments? If you enter a house through the front door that leads into the living room and you stay there, and I enter through the back door into the garage and stay there, then we will be apart, not together. Your diverse senses are like the different rooms in a house into which people can enter. Sight, for example, sees but does not hear anything. Hearing hears, but sees nothing. So why don't those of us with both sight and hearing experience two compartmentalized worlds in ourselves, a "sight world" and a "hearing world"? If a camera records video only, and a tape recorder records audio only, there will only be two separate recordings, not a single audiovisual one.

The unity of your sense experience of the world is especially clear when two or more of your senses perceive the same thing. Think of a child's wooden block. If you grasp such a block in your hand, you can both feel and see its shape at the same time. You do not experience two different blocks, a "touch block" and a "sight block", cut off from each other, leaving you free to believe that these are two distinct blocks. Instead, you are perfectly aware that there is just a single block. Somehow you know that the "touch block" is the same as the "sight block". By what power in you are you aware of this?

Could it be by your sense of touch? Hardly. Touch has nothing to say about the matter. Touch is blind. It does not of itself know anything about colors, about light and darkness, or about other objects unique to the sense of sight. Your sense of touch is entirely in the dark about seeing and about colors since these things cannot be felt. Consequently, touch knows nothing at all about the cube's visible presentation, not even that such a presentation exists. And what is completely ignorant of the visible side of things cannot possibly inform you that "the block you are *seeing* is the same as the block you are *feeling*."

Your sense of sight is equally incompetent to perform this unifying task. Your sense of sight by itself knows nothing of feeling or of purely tangible qualities such as hardness or hot and cold. (You can see signs of hot and cold, such as steam or frost or sun or snow, or even infrared imagery, but in all these cases you are really seeing colors, not temperatures themselves.) Consequently, sight alone cannot perceive that the child's block it sees is also the block that is being felt, since *felt* is meaningless to your vision considered just in its own proper capacity.

There can be no doubt that you perform the act in question. You know that the block you are feeling and the block you are seeing are one and the same block. Only you do not do this by sight—nor by touch, much less by hearing, smell, or taste. So how do you do this?

One possible answer readily comes to mind. If sight alone cannot do the job, and neither can touch alone, then sight and touch together must be doing it. Your eyesight, after all, must be partly responsible for your perception that the "sight block" and "touch block" are one and the same. Without your eyesight, you could not perform that feat. The same goes for your sense of touch. Well, then, if neither alone can do the job, and each one is needed to do it, why not say both together are doing it, and be done? If you and I are simultaneously lifting a table that is too heavy for either of us to lift alone, then of course it is just you and I together that are lifting the table. No mystery there. Why not say, then, that it is touch and sight together that know the "visible block" and the "tangible block" are one and the same?

This answer is tempting, but will not suffice. In the case of the table, no one person is lifting both ends of the table. That's all right, because lifting the two ends of a table does not have to be a single effort of a single power. As long as both ends get lifted by someone, whether by the same person or by two different people working together, the whole table gets lifted. Lifting a table can either be one act of lifting both halves or two simultaneous acts of lifting each half. But knowing the relationship between two things is not like lifting the two ends of a table. Knowing a relationship is a single act of knowing one thing about two things, not two simultaneous acts of knowing each of them. Suppose you know how old the physicist Stephen Hawking is, but you have never heard of Rupert Klausmann. I am in the opposite condition. I know of Klausmann, and how old he is, but have never heard of Stephen Hawking in my life. Since one of us knows the age of Hawking, and the other of us knows the age of Klausmann, is there also an act of "knowing Klausmann is older than Hawking" too? There is no such act. Such an act would be something over and above the two separate acts of knowing the ages of the two gentlemen in question. It would be one act of knowing the one relationship between two things, not two acts of knowing two things. Consequently, it would have to be the work of one knowing power, and of one person. Seeing a connection or relationship is a single act, but one that cannot happen without seeing both of the connected things at once.

Your sense powers are no exception to this rule. You know the "tangible block" by one power, and the "visible block" by another power. If these bits of information are in no way brought together by a single power in you but remain wholly compartmentalized and disconnected in your separate powers, then you will not perceive the identity of the tangible block with the visible one. That is a single act of knowing one thing about two things, and consequently must be the work of a single power, not two.

But of course you do perceive it. There must therefore be a single power in you that is able to know both the visible block and the tangible block. Is this just your mind? Your intellect? You are intellectually aware of this identity of the visible block with the tangible one, which is why you can form and assent to the truth of the statement "The block I am feeling is the same as the one I am looking at." Nonetheless, your intellect is not your ultimate source for this information. What reason, after all, can you give for thinking the tangible and visible blocks are one and the same? You cannot prove it. It is a fact of immediate experience. When you pick up the wooden block in your hand and realize that the shape you see and the shape you feel are the very same individual shape, that is not an abstract intellectual awareness, as when you realize that *a three-sided plane figure* is the same thing as a *triangle*. It is a concrete awareness about an individual thing right here in your hand. You do not hypothesize, conceive, or think about the sameness of the visible shape with the tactile shape. You experience it. You sense it.

We now employ a little process of elimination. You sense that the wooden shape that you see with your eyes is the very same one that you feel in your hand. By what power? Not by sight—nor by touch, much less by hearing or one of the other familiar senses. Nor do you sense the unity of the sight-block with the touch-block merely by two senses together, since there must be a single power in you that has all the information in order for you to perceive the connection. Nor again do you recognize the sameness of the sight-block and the touch-block in a purely intellectual way. Therefore you perceive it by a single power of sense that is distinct from all your more familiar sense powers. Although it is a sense power, and not just your ability to grasp abstract truths, it has no external organ, but is instead a more hidden, internal power.

Your Universal Sense

What have we discovered? A hidden sense power that all of us have and all of us use all the time but few of us notice. By means of it, you perceive the sameness of certain objects shared by more than one sense, such as the shape of a block, which is both felt and seen.

This sense of yours has other jobs, too. It also notices the differences between the objects of your many senses, the objects they do not share. Suppose you see the blue sky and at the same time smell the odor of a skunk. Even if you had never smelled that smell before, and had no idea that it came from a skunk, you would know that the blue and the odor were not the same quality. Even if you thought the sky was the thing that stank, you would perceive that its color and its stinkiness were not the same quality in it, just as you immediately perceive that the color of a wine and its flavor are not the same sensible property in it. How do you know that these things are different? The difference is a matter of perception, not of general definitions and concepts. You perceive the difference by a sense power of some kind—not by sight, since it knows nothing of flavors; nor by taste, since it knows nothing of colors. As before, the two distinct senses working at the same time will not suffice, either, since it is impossible to perceive a relationship, such as a difference or contrast, unless one thing perceives both things that are different or contrasted. Your perception of the differences between the input of your diverse senses is therefore the work of another sense power, one that listens to what all your five senses have to say, and weaves their reports back into a single world of experience, keeping distinct things distinct and perceiving the sameness of things that are the same.

This remarkable power would sound almost impossible if we did not actually experience it at work in ourselves. It must perceive both visible qualities and tangible ones, or else you could not perceive that the cube you are seeing is the same as the one you are holding and feeling. It must perceive both flavors and sounds, or else you could not perceive the difference between flavor and sound. Since you can compare and contrast all the objects of all your five external senses, this internal sense must perceive the objects of all five—an astonishing power, really, a sense perceptive not only of colors, but also of flavors and textures and sounds.

What shall we call this power? We might call it an *associative sense*. Or we might call this perceptive jack-of-all-trades by another name that it suggests for itself. Each of your external senses is restricted to a definite domain of objects, as taste is restricted to flavored things and sight to colored things. Sight can see nothing but what has color or at any rate lightness and darkness, and it sees things other than colors, such as shapes, only by reason of variations in color. Touch can perceive nothing but what has tangible qualities such as hardness, and feels things other than these, such as shapes, only by reason of variations in the tangible qualities of things. Sight cannot know hardness, and touch cannot know color. Each of these senses is therefore "particular", limited to certain particular sensible qualities. As opposed to the particular senses, the hidden, sense-integrating, connective sense in you that knows all the objects of your external senses is not at all particular. It is instead universal, and we might with justice call it your *universal sense*.[1] It is like all five senses in one.

The functioning of your universal sense depends on your external senses. For example, it cannot know the shape of a cube apart from your seeing or feeling it. If your external senses are all shut down, then so is your awareness of the sameness or difference among their objects, since they are not bringing any objects in at all. The universal sense discerns the sameness and differences of the objects of all the senses, but only by listening to those senses and learning from them, not by enjoying any independent access of its own to sensible objects. It speaks a language common to all five senses, we might say, and in this way can listen to all of them and compare all of them.

Your universal sense is able not only to listen, but also in some way to "speak" to your particular senses. It can inform one particular sense based on what another one has to say. When you walk, for example, what you see while you are walking informs the way that you move yourself. The data of your sense of sight must somehow direct your use of your sense of touch if it is indeed by your sense of sight that you avoid bumping into things, and if it is by your sense of touch that you immediately govern your own motions. The opposite is true as well—your sense of sight learns things from your sense of touch. Early in life you learned that the same things appear larger as you approached them and smaller as you withdrew from them. You first sensed your moving toward or away from things by touch, say by crawling on the floor, but then you simultaneously saw how they

---

[1] Thomas Aquinas called it the *sensus communis*, or the "common sense". Since that expression already has another meaning in English unrelated to the sense power we are now discussing, and since by "common" Aquinas meant "general" or "universal" anyway, I have taken the liberty of adjusting the name. See Thomas Aquinas, *Summa Theologiae* I, q. 78, a. 4.

"grew" and "shrank", and learned that this is how your sense of sight represents motion toward and away from things. Your visual sense of distance developed with the help of your sense of touch through the intermediary work of your universal sense, which connects the two senses. None of this would be possible if you had only touch and sight separately, with nothing to connect the two. You would not be able to perceive that the objects you see around you are the same as the ones you encounter by touch as you move along.

Your diverse senses are like different teachers, telling you about the world around you. If they said things completely unconnected to one another, you would be unable to form a unified view of the world. Taken by themselves, the external senses are like five unrelated voices. Together as they cohere in your universal sense, they interrelate and become integrated. They harmonize. By means of the universal sense, the common root of the senses, one sense can learn from another how to unify not only its objects with those of another sense power, but even its own objects. Any single shape, for example, has an infinity of different "looks" as you move around it.

Part of what helped you "learn" to see a cube as one solid shape, despite its ever-shifting appearance as you move in relation to it, is that it always *feels* the same. You can grasp it in one hand and never change the feel of it in your grip, but rotate it and watch its look vary correspondingly with the various forces you feel yourself exerting upon it. Were it not for the sense of touch, vision could never (or not very well or very easily) learn to see a single shape, despite its infinite variety of visual appearances. Such correlations of sight with touch actually complete your senses of sight and touch. The two senses inform each other, learn from each other, in the common root to which they all report back: your universal sense. For instance, this power in you is the sensory polyglot that can perceive the visual relevance of tactile data, and thus teach vision how to see better.

Implied in all the other jobs of your universal sense is the perception of the acts of your five familiar senses. You sense not only the things in the world, but also your own sensing. You perceive and distinguish not only colors and flavors, but also your seeing of colors and your tasting of flavors. Evidently you possess many diverse sense powers. To what power in you is this evident? How do you perceive that you both see and hear, for example, and that these are not the same kind of activity in you? None of the familiar five can be responsible for this perception, since each of those senses, just in its own proper functioning, is entirely ignorant of the other four. Yet you perceive yourself to perceive, and you sense your own acts of sensation. Nor is this some kind of intellectual or conceptual knowledge. It is not by some kind of argument that you know yourself to be the possessor of many diverse senses, nor is it by the mere definitions of touch, hearing, sight, and the like. It is a datum of immediate, perceptual experience. This experience is the work of your universal sense, the one sense that can listen to all five external senses.

Our first advance in understanding your inner nature is now complete. The chief fruits of our labor are these:

1. There is, within you, a single sense power that includes within itself the perceptive power of all five of your external senses. It perceives visible qualities—audible ones, tangible ones. Who would think this possible, prior to the kinds of observations we have made? How can a sense power be both auditory and visual at once? An act of comparing and distinguishing sounds from colors, or hearing from seeing, is nevertheless both auditory and visual, an act performable only by a power speaking a higher language that captures both kinds of sensible objects and both kinds of sensation.

2. Sometimes one knowing power in you is fed or informed by other knowing powers in you, even though it does not infer or reason from their input, but only perceives. Your universal sense receives all its input from your external senses, but it does not reason or infer by putting together statements, but immediately perceives things among the objects of the particular senses that they miss.

3. Some cognitive powers we can hardly fail to notice, such as our five senses. Others, such as our universal sense power, lie deeper within us and do not proclaim themselves much, although we can discover them by methodical consultation of our internal experience.

4. That is in itself another lesson. Careful consultation of your insider's view can take us from common knowledge of you to new and uncommon knowledge of you.

5. We have also uncovered at least one root of your insider's view of yourself. When you perceive yourself from within, you are perceiving your thoughts, feelings, desires, and perceptions. Your universal sense is what enables you to perceive and distinguish your diverse sense perceptions. Therefore your insider's view is brought to you, in part, by your universal sense.

6. As a final and general observation, we are already beginning to see that there is a magnificent harmony of powers in you. You are a marvelously unified being, not a collection of powers.

Other internal sense powers lie hidden in you besides your universal sense, and a great deal more could be said about them, both in light of your insider's view of them, and again in light of the empirical science of the brain. But we have seen enough of them for our purposes. Our basic training is done. We must push on, now, to another kind of power in you, one that is more commonly acknowledged, but more difficult to understand, and deeper.

3

Introducing: Your Intellect

Sense is of the particular; reason is of the universal.
— Aristotle, *Physics*

Dreams of an Electric Shark

When I was a kid, cartoon watching was confined mainly to Saturday mornings, since that was the only time cartoons aired on the major networks whose broadcast signals were powerful enough for our old rabbit ears to pick up. I would sit and watch from dawn to noon, persevering through several shows I did not care for much, just because watching cartoons was obviously better than turning off the TV and going outside.

Some do-gooder must have taken notice of this nationwide ritual of my generation, and seen the educational opportunity it presented. What more teachable moment than the ad space between shows when kids everywhere across the land sat staring, listening, waiting eagerly for the next cartoon? So it was that I, grateful member of this captive audience, soaked in every installment of the *Schoolhouse Rock!* series and other bits and pieces of semieducational content that now stand crystallized in my memory in places where noneducational cartoons might have been. Thanks to these intrusions of school into cartoon time, I still know the Preamble to the Constitution by heart (although I can't recite it, only sing it), and also my multiplication tables up to twelve times twelve.

One such injection of education between cartoons took the form of a kid-friendly version of current events. It was called *In the News*. Most of the time it was boring. But one day, one shining, magnificent, unforgettable day, *In the News* featured a piece on the most glorious thing ever conceived by human thought: *a robotic shark*. That's right, a remote-controlled robot *and* a shark, all in one. There on my TV screen, I saw the blessed inventor on a beach somewhere. He was working the remote control, a box outfitted with toggles, switches, knobs, antennae—you know, all the stuff that dreams are made of— and meanwhile out in the water a conspicuous black fin dodged now this way, now that, entirely at his command. It was as if the sun had risen in my mind for the first time, a choir of angels singing in the background. Of course I knew what I had to do. I had to build my own electric shark.

I cannot recall whether the version appearing on *In the News* was a mere fin mounted on a motor, or something more extravagant. But I intended to build a full-scale shark body, indistinguishable from a living shark to all but the highly trained eye of a shark scientist. More than that, I decided on the species. It would be a hammerhead, just for that extra dose of cool to kick it over the top.

Where to begin? I needed a workable blueprint. I set myself to the task immediately (I mean immediately after the morning cartoons were all done, and I had decided that even I could not watch competition bowling). Clearly the main thing was to get the body shape right. I found a nature book containing pictures of the hammerhead. Just the thing. Next I needed to get the mechanicals in order. Some plans drawn up by Professor Calculus in a *Tintin* book provided the necessary details.

By that evening, I had produced what was no doubt a fully executable diagram, so awesome did it look. Moved by a spirit of due diligence, I nonetheless thought it a wise precaution, before moving into the construction phase, to run it by the local expert. I brought the drawing to my father while he was sitting in his usual after-dinner spot on the couch with a very dull book in his hands.[1] I pushed the drawing between his nose and his book, and asked him whether he thought the thing would work. He glanced over it with a strange, pinched sort of look on his face, as though he were about to sneeze but was determined not to. Then he began sniffing or snorting. Poor Dad's allergies must have been acting up. My mother was on hand, and let fall some stern word with a sharp look at my

---

[1] For my father's account of what transpired, see the corrigendum at the end of this book.

father, as good as to say that allergies were not to be tolerated when he was being consulted on a matter of such high priority. I tended to agree, but felt sorry for him nonetheless. The fit left him, and he sat up straighter and adjusted his glasses to take a closer look. He pointed to a couple of key features and asked questions that, I fear, exposed some of his ignorance of the business, but overall his sense of it was fairly satisfactory. When he declared it construction-ready I was very much encouraged.

Most of the necessary parts already lay in my secret stores in a space beneath the stairs to the basement. There, in my "laboratory", the bewitching and imagination-firing mechanical parts of old vacuum cleaners, radios, mixers, sump-pump motors, and other cannibalized household appliances filled many a box and jar. I recruited my faithful friend and fellow second grader, Matt, who assisted me each day after school.

It was a mercy of my boyhood that I tended to lose interest in a project just before I fully grasped the impossibility of carrying it through. That way, new understanding came without any sense of failure. By the time I could see that an electric shark such as I had imagined swam in waters too deep for me, I had already abandoned it in favor of still grander impossibilities. It did puzzle me, though, before I had given up the work, that the electric shark problem was proving rather intractable. No matter how many drawings I made or how many old parts I screwed together, I seemed no closer to a functioning model. What was missing from my conception? What elusive adjustment would make the difference between a mere picture and a truly operational design?

Eventually it occurred to me that even when I was *looking* at a functioning design, I did not actually see what its functionality consisted in. One day I watched fans spinning and belts turning in the idling engine of my father's car with its hood propped up. Here was a functioning design all right, and I even got to observe it while it was functioning. But I still did not understand its functioning—I saw the interacting parts, and that they were interacting, but did not see the nature of their interaction. What was moving what, and why? Was this bit moving that one, or was it the other way around? And what did the movement of these things here have to do with the motions of those other things there under the hood?

So it began to dawn on me that seeing the things in a relationship is not the same as seeing the relationship itself. When I had imagined my electric shark, I was picturing the things that I wished would interact in various causal relationships, but I did not succeed in imagining such relationships, nor did I ask myself whether the things I had imagined could really support such relationships.

I had imagined. I had not really understood.

A Question for the Man on the Street

This foible of my youth, suggestive of some distinction between the powers of intellect and imagination, brings us back to our real subject—namely, you. We have so far seen something of your sense powers, and even learned of an inner sense in you, your "universal sense". In order to deepen our understanding of your inner nature, we must now turn from your sense powers to your mental ones.

Your mental abilities most of all distinguish you from other kinds of living things. Dogs can smell many things better than you can, and eagles can see many things better than you can. But you can outthink all the dogs and eagles put together—so much so, you might feel insulted if someone tried to praise you by saying you are smarter than any dog he'd ever met. If we humans have a peculiar excellence, it lies in thinking, and in the other acts that go with thinking and follow from it, such as deliberating, choosing, planning, and the like. Hence our new focus on your mental abilities. There is something distinctively human in them, or at least in the degree to which we possess them.

Stop the proverbial man on the street and ask him: "Do you have a mind? Any intelligence?" If he is not offended and is uncommonly willing to see where your questions are going, he will surely own up to having a mind. Now ask him, "Do you also possess an imagination?" He cannot deny it. He recognizes these powers in himself, and uses them all the time. Now a further question: "Is your mind the same thing as your imagination, just another name for it? Or are they two distinct mental powers?"

What will he say? Are "mind and imagination" like "vision and eyesight", two names for the same thing? Or are they like "vision and hearing", two distinct powers? Or are they instead related as the general to the specific, as "sense power and vision"? I am not entirely sure myself what the man on the street would say to this. Perhaps not everyone would give the same answer. Probably the majority of people would suspect that mind and imagination are two different powers, but they would struggle to say just how they differ. Some people, including some famous philosophers, have said that *mind* and *imagination* are in fact just two words for the very same thing. Experiences such as the one I had with my electric shark, and other experiences of your own, I am sure, suggest there is some distinction between intellect and imagination. And yet such experiences leave us with only a vague sense that there might be some difference. Without taking things any further, we must remain in some doubt about whether there is a real difference between these powers, and about the nature of that difference.

Our business in this chapter is to decide this question that the man on the street might not be able to answer. Suppose by a stroke of good fortune our particular man on the street happens to be a fairly reflective person, and he has taken the view that his mind and his imagination differ in name only. "*Imagination, mind,* call it what you will," he says, with a little flourish and a bow. What evidence might he offer in support of his view?

Quite a bit, actually. At least three reasons might incline him to believe that our imaginations and our minds (or intellects) are in fact the very same thing.

1. First of all, both *imagination* and *mind* name a knowing power with no external organ, and both name powers that can contemplate their objects even when those objects are physically absent. You cannot see or touch an elephant when there is none in the neighborhood, but you can imagine or understand or think about one whenever you feel so inclined. So far, imagination and mind appear to be identical.

2. Also, we generally distinguish our abilities by the diversity of the acts they enable us to perform. The ability to walk and the ability to talk are easily distinguished as soon as we know the clear-as-day difference between the acts of walking and talking. What, then, are the corresponding acts of the imagination and the mind? The act of imagination is imagining. The act of the mind might be called *minding*, but that is not the usual way of speaking. We usually say the mind *thinks*. Is the act of thinking different from imagining? We never use

the verbs *walk* and *talk* interchangeably, but we often use the verbs *think* and *imagine* interchangeably. When I ask, "Do you *think* it will rain today?" you might look up at the clouds and reply, "Yes, I *imagine* so." If I ask you to *think* of a pink elephant with purple spots, I am of course asking you to *imagine* one. Insofar as thinking and imagining seem to be the same act, the power to think and to imagine seem to be the same power.

3. The similarities between thinking and imagining do not end there. When we think, we form a product that we call a *thought* or else an *idea*. When we imagine, we also form a product, which we call an *image*. And in many cases we use the words *image*, *idea*, and *thought* interchangeably. My wife has all kinds of ideas or thoughts about how we might rearrange the furniture in our living room, but plainly these ideas of hers are in fact images, mental pictures in her mind of those possible arrangements.

If our man on the street is not entirely right to identify your mind with your imagination, he is at least right that they are not easy to tell apart.

Are your mind and your imagination entirely the same after all?

Winning the Lottery—Just Imagine

These reasons for taking *imagination* and *mind* as synonyms, while worth considering, are inconclusive.

Man-on-the-street's reason 1 proves that *imagination* and *mind* both name mental powers, but does not prove they must always name the same one.

Reasons 2 and 3 prove that the words *imagination* and *mind*, or *imagining* and *thinking*, sometimes get used interchangeably, but not that they always do. We sometimes use the words *see* and *imagine* interchangeably too, as in "Where do you see yourself five years from now?" We sometimes use the words *see* and *understand* interchangeably too, as in "I see what you mean." It hardly follows that everything called *seeing* is an act of understanding. (Were that true, an eye exam would be an intelligence test.)

Not only are these reasons inconclusive, but our man on the street, thoughtful and cooperative as he may be, is in fact mistaken. Not all your mental acts are acts of imagination. Although your imagination can sometimes be called by the name *intellect*, and you sometimes call the act of imagining by the name of *thinking*, you also possess a power of thinking, an intellect, that is completely other than your power to imagine. This is *intellect* in the strict sense.

How can we tell that you have an intellectual power that is distinct from your imagination? Your convictions about what is true or false are a good place to start. Thinking that something is so is not the same as merely imagining that it is so. You are free to imagine, at will, that you have just won the lottery, or that there is a serial killer somewhere in your house, but you are not free to think these things are true whenever you wish. In order to think they are true, you need a reason to think they are true. Your power of forming judgments about what is true and what is false is somehow distinct from your imagination.

Your reactions, too, will differ in each case. If you just imagine that you have won the lottery, you don't feel the need to start calling all your family and friends. If you really think you have won the lottery, you do. If you just imagine that there is an intruder in your house, you don't feel the need to reach for a golf club while dialing 911. If you really think there is an intruder in your house, you do.

This is an excellent start. Intellect and imagination are somehow distinct powers, even if we also use their names interchangeably at times. We are beginning to move beyond the common knowledge of these powers. Are there other differences between imagination and intellect proper?

Thirty-Billion-Sided Polygons

Yes. This is especially clear in the case of things that you can think about but cannot imagine. If some things are thinkable but not imaginable, then thinking and imagining cannot be the same, and the power of thinking must be different from the power of imagining.

> Imagine a square inscribed in a circle. (Not too hard.)
> Now imagine a regular octagon inscribed in there. (Tougher!)
> Now imagine a regular thirty-billion-sided polygon inscribed in the same circle.

This last request—if you are like me—is impossible to fulfill. The polygon itself is not impossible, but it is impossible for you to form an image of it that is distinct from the circle in which it is to be inscribed. Forming an image of a thirty-billion-sided polygon that is distinct from a circle goes well beyond the resolving power of your imagination.

Yet you readily understand that such a polygon is possible, and that it is distinct from the circle in which it is inscribed. The polygon has angles in it, the circle does not. You accurately understand the difference even though you cannot accurately picture it.

More than that, you actually know a bunch of things about the unimaginable polygon. For example, you know that the thirty-billion-sided regular polygon inside a circle contains less area than the circle itself but more area than a twenty-nine-billion-sided polygon inscribed within the same circle. The differences in the definitions of such things as circles, thirty-billion-sided polygons, and twenty-nine-billion-sided polygons make their differences perfectly accessible to your thinking, whereas your imagination is insensitive to these differences, since it cannot picture them.

You are to be congratulated. Apparently you are capable of another type of thinking besides image forming. You are endowed with an intellect that comes with unlimited resolving power.

"Checkable" Truths versus Conceptual Truths

Among the countless truths that you grasp, there is a little-noticed difference that we can observe and that will further improve our understanding of your intellect. One type of truth is impossible for you to know without checking into it—you must use your sense powers to examine the subject that the statement is about before you can see for yourself that it is true. That done, you will know the truth of the statement. Checking is both necessary and sufficient in such a case. We might style this kind of truth a "checkable" truth.

Here is an example of what I mean. Suppose I place a carton of unopened and undated milk in front of you, and ask you whether the milk has gone sour. You do not yet know, but can certainly find out. The best way to find out is absolutely not to run off and hide in a closet somewhere and think quietly to yourself about the meaning of the statement "That milk has gone sour."

Examine that statement all you like, turn it over in your mind a thousand times in the darkness of the closet, and you still will not be able to tell whether it is true. The answer does not lie in the statement itself, but in the milk carton. Obviously, you must open the carton and give the milk a whiff. From the comfort of your closet, you might *guess* that the milk has gone sour, and even guess correctly. But you cannot *know* that you are right. And as many times as you guess correctly about such a question, you will also guess incorrectly. You can't know the truth of the matter until you have checked into it with your external senses. Whatever the truth is about the milk, it is a checkable truth.

Or suppose someone says, "It's snowing outside!"; and instead of looking out the window, you once more withdraw to the broom closet. You are retreating from the one source of information that can tell you whether the statement is true or not. The statement "It's snowing outside!" is a checkable truth. Once you've checked it and seen that it is indeed snowing out, you know it is true, and until you check, you don't.

Not all checkable truths are about individual instances of things, such as "that milk". Others are about entire kinds of things, or all individual instances of some kind of thing. For example, "Every human being is in the Milky Way Galaxy." Supposing this statement is true, it needs checking if we are to be sure of it. There is no way to verify it simply from the meaning of the statement itself. (In fact, just from the meaning of the statement itself, we cannot even verify that any human being exists at all, let alone in the Milky Way.) Maybe there is no way for us to check on every individual human being in the universe, and so this truth would be "uncheckable" in the sense that we could never finish checking into it. But somehow checking every particular human being in existence would be the sufficient and only surefire way to certify its truth, even if we could form very strong probable arguments in its favor from a number of assumptions about space travel and the unlikelihood of other human beings having come into existence elsewhere in the universe.

Is it really necessary to speak of "checkable" truths, as though they were something special? Aren't all truths checkable—that is, impossible for us to know until we can check them, and fully known to us once we have checked them (when that is possible)? Isn't it impossible, in other words, to know that something is true about a bunch of things we have never personally checked? We can believe such things, take them on someone else's word, or make guesses about them, but surely we can never know something to be true about things we have never personally inspected. Isn't that right?

Actually, it isn't. Behold the marvelous power of your intellect: it enables you to know (and not merely guess) the truth about all kinds of things you have never specifically checked. Impossible-sounding, perhaps. True nonetheless. Consider the statement "Every bachelor is unmarried." I do not say that it is especially brilliant (we will come back to that in a minute). But is it true? Of course it is. And you know it. And you are not merely guessing. And you can know this is true from the seclusion of any broom closet in the world, without meeting every bachelor personally in order to shore up your conviction about this general statement. This is not a checkable truth, then. It is neither possible nor necessary to check its subject, "every bachelor", in order to become sure of its truth.

We might style this kind of truth a "conceptual" truth. You can tell it is true even with your eyes closed, or from inside a closet. To know such a truth we do depend on prior sense experience, of course, and on the present use of our memory and imagination, not just our intellect. Probably none of us would ever have thought up the idea of bachelorhood (or anything else) had we never experienced any sensory contact with the world. Nonetheless, once we have formed the concepts and brought them to mind, we can see the truth of the statement without having to check "every bachelor", and indeed it is impossible to check that by sensory inspection. In calling such a truth a "conceptual" one, I do not mean that we can come to know it independently of any sense experience ever, or that it is a truth about mere concepts. On the contrary, it is a truth about things—bachelors, to be specific—but its truth is something we can see without having to go consult all the individual instances, once we have formed certain concepts about them.

Some people object that "Every bachelor is unmarried" is not a truth worth naming and considering. It is trivial, and perhaps a mere redundancy or tautology. "Unmarried", after all, is part of what "bachelor" means, which is precisely why we can be sure the statement is true without having to check in with individual bachelors.

The same is true for "Every triangle has three sides", and "Every sentence is made of words", and "Every compound contains more than one element." Such truths appear to be of no worth, since they do not advance our understanding.

This accusation, however, is unjust. Such truths can and do advance our understanding in many instances. Statements attributing part (or all) of the definition of the subject to that subject (such as "Every bachelor is unmarried") are not empty and worthless. It is a service to make explicit some of the subject's defining elements that might otherwise lie implicit and unnoticed in our thought. For example, we all know, roughly, what we mean by a *square*. We all know one when we see one. But how many of us can formulate an exact definition of it? When, early in a new academic year, I ask the freshest of freshmen at school for a definition of *square*, many of them answer, "A four-sided figure all of whose sides are equal." It is true that every square has to be such a figure, but this formula is not yet a complete definition of *square*, since a rhombus, too, is a quadrilateral with four equal sides, yet a rhombus is not a square, because its angles are not right. If we say, "A square is a quadrilateral with four equal sides and four right angles," only then have we said exactly what a square is. This statement does no more than say what *square* means, and yet this is not pure redundancy, repeating what we already have explicitly in mind when we say *square*, since it is possible to have the defining elements of a square in mind only vaguely and confusedly when we say the word *square*—so vaguely, sometimes, that we, like newly minted freshmen, might struggle to say exactly what we mean and precisely how such a figure differs from others.

The charge against this kind of conceptual truth is therefore unjust. Such truths can advance or clarify our understanding. Nor is every conceptual truth the sort that attributes a definition to its subject. Conceptual truths come in other flavors, too. Consider this case: "Every square contains less area than the circle that passes through its four corners." If you know what a square is, and what a circle is, and what area is, you cannot fail to see the truth of this little statement. If in the privacy of my own home I have inscribed a square in a circle on my living room wall and have told you as much but refuse to invite you over to come see, you will know, even without being given any opportunity to inspect it, that my particular square, with which you are in no special way acquainted, has less area than the circle in which it is inscribed. You can know the truth of the statement above, in other words, without having to check all individual squares. This truth is therefore not a "checkable" one, but is instead of the conceptual variety. The predicate, moreover, does not tell us what *square* means, but instead describes a property that must belong to every square.

Here is another example: "The doubles of equal things are also equal." This, too, is verifiable without checking all individual cases. If some number of apples is equal to some number of oranges, then you know that *double* the number of apples is equal to *double* the number of oranges without ever needing to see the apples or oranges in question. And yet the equality mentioned in the predicate of this statement is not the equality mentioned in the subject. (The equality of the doubles is distinct from the equality of the things that get doubled.) Our predicate really adds something new over and above what the subject means. The statement is nonetheless self-evidently true.

Nor is every conceptual truth a self-evident thing. For example: "$10^2 + 11^2 + 12^2 = 13^2 + 14^2$". This statement is true of any instances of the numbers 10, 11, 12, 13, and 14, whether we are talking about numbers of apples, oranges, or porcupines. It is not exactly obvious or self-evident, however. If you are like me, you will have to do a little calculating to verify the equality. But you will only need to do it once. You won't need to go through it again just before bedtime to make sure it is still true, or try it again at the gas station to see whether it is true there as well. You won't be left wondering whether it is true on the dark side of the moon. You will know that it is true there. You will see not only that it is true, but that it is one of those truths that *has* to be true, always and everywhere. It is not like the statement "Wanda has a cold", which might be true right now, but can swap sides, going from true to false and back again as many times as Wanda gets sick and recovers. If you ever forget that the equation is true, you might need to redo the calculation, but in so doing you will only be reconvincing yourself that it had always been true. And you can do the calculation in your closet, if you like, without checking all possible individual instances of the numbers 10, 11, 12, 13, and 14.

Does the mathematical character of these examples prompt you to wonder whether conceptual truths are confined to mathematics?

Rest assured that conceptual truths exist outside mathematics as well. For example, "There is truth" is itself such a truth. (It could never be true that "there is no truth", since that statement itself would then be a truth.) Again, "Whatever knows the relationship between two things also knows each of those things in some way." We used that truth in the last chapter, and we can see it is true in general without checking all the particular instances of it. Here is an intelligible truth about physical action: "Nothing acts on itself without some distinction between what is acting and what is being acted on", as a person who is scratching himself must be distinguishable into the part doing the scratching and the part being scratched. And here is an intelligible truth about causes: "If something is inclined of itself to be or behave a certain way, but it is not being or behaving that way, then there is an outside cause influencing it."

Examples like these convince us that there are all kinds of conceptual truths out there after all, and that you come equipped with the ability to know them. You are therefore the owner of a very intriguing power: the power to know something with certainty about an infinity of things you have never seen. Every such truth that you know—and the number of these is beyond count—gives you insight into all possible instances, past, present, and future, of some kind of thing. Because you know that "seven is a prime number", for example, you know that the property of being "prime" belongs to any seven stones on Mars, or to any seven atoms in any apple on the other side of the world. Because you know that "the doubles of equals must be equal", you know that if I have two equal lengths in my possession, and I double each of them, then the double lengths also have to be equal, even though you have never inspected them personally. You know, moreover, that this would have to apply to all possible pairs of lines that are equal to each other, even those that do not yet exist.

Nor does the reach of your understanding stop there. This truth that "The doubles of equals must be equal"—does it apply only to equal *lines*? What about equal *numbers*? Oh, it applies to them, all right. To all possible pairs of equal numbers? Absolutely. And how many such pairs are there? An infinity. What about areas? Works for them, too. And volumes? Yes. And also for angles, speeds, weights, and on and on, and in each such category the principle applies to an infinity of instances. Now a further shift: Aren't the *triples* of equals also equal? Indeed they are. And quadruples? Of course. Does this ever stop? No. So you can understand infallibly an infinity of truths in an infinite number of categories without needing to examine a single individual case.

Quite the far-reaching power, your intellect—much more so than your imagination, which is stuck representing individual instances, and cannot issue a single proclamation about an infinity of things, much less know it to be true.

Once again, we see that you have an intellectual power that is not the same as your imagination. This distinctive ability of your intellect to grasp conceptual truths, however, raises a most natural question: Whence comes this strange power of yours to know, with perfect certainty and infallible accuracy, certain properties that belong to every particular square, or to every particular "thing that is acting on itself"? Where do you get your knowledge about cases you have never seen before? How do you do this?

The Secret Life of Universals

What is the secret behind your intellect's grasp of the infinite? How does it perceive truths that apply to an infinity of instances?

The secret lies in its power to grasp and isolate a certain kind of sameness in things. Earlier we saw certain *differences* your intellect picks up but your imagination misses, such as the difference between "circle" and "thirty-billion-sided regular polygon". But your intellect picks up on more than subtle differences in things. It can also grasp the pure *sameness* in things in a way that your imagination cannot.

You must be able to grasp something common to all possible triangles, for example, or else you could never be sure that "every triangle can have a circle drawn through its three points", or that "no triangle is a square." Any particular triangle you encounter in your sense experience will necessarily include the things common to all triangles, but it will also combine these commonalities with other things peculiar to its own individual case. Consider, for example, the triangle ABC right here on the next page. Whatever is common to all triangles must of course belong to it—it has three straight sides, three corners, and contains an area, for instance. But it also presents certain features found only in some triangles, such as its specific area and the particular ratio of its sides and its peculiar shade of gray. Besides these things, it also has other properties all its own, and which it shares with no other triangle in the universe, such as the place it occupies on this page.

Imagine for a moment that you could not form any idea of triangle ABC that isolated the features it held in common with all other triangles, but instead every notion you had of it, just like ABC itself, necessarily included its idiosyncrasies, such as its gray color and its unique location. Suppose you were similarly limited regarding all other triangles, and all other things. Then all your ideas would be of individual things in all their individuality, and so all your names would have to be proper nouns. If you could form verbs at all, they would be 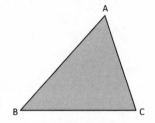 "proper verbs", each one expressing only a single individual action performed in a unique time and place in history, in all its individuality. You could not speak, in fact—or not in the usual sense of the word. Much less could you ever know the truth that "every triangle has three sides", or the more sophisticated truth that "every triangle can be circumscribed by a circle."

Of course you do know such things, and you can speak in common nouns and verbs. Therefore you form notions of things that are not bound up with their individual peculiarities. You can form notions of things that include only those features of theirs that they share in common with other similar individuals, notions that leave out the peculiarities of each individual. When you say *triangle*, for instance, you mean *three-sided plane figure*, which notion does not include *gray* (nor does it include *not gray*), and it does not include *here on this page* (nor does it exclude that). It remains strictly noncommittal about such peculiarities of this or that triangle. A notion like this, isolating the repeatable content common to an infinity of possible particular instances, is called a *universal idea*, or else just a *universal* for short.

Once you form a universal idea, say an idea of what a triangle is, you can then inspect this in your mind, and see certain things that must belong to it. The idea has a kind of life and comes with inherent laws of its own, and you can discover these after you have formed it in your mind in response to seeing particular instances and noting the commonality in them. Any universal idea can thus tell you certain things about itself. These are the conceptual truths about it. Other questions it will stubbornly refuse to answer. For example, if you inspect the universal idea of what a triangle is, you will find that any two sides taken together must be greater than the third side. But if you are wondering whether any triangle in the world is purple, your universal idea of what a triangle is maintains a strict silence on the question, since it is open to all colors, as well as to being colorless. For all the universal idea of a triangle can tell us, it might be that every triangle in the world is purple, or it might be that none is.

Your mind is full of universal ideas. It is thanks to them that you are sometimes able to know things about an infinity of particulars you have never checked. If you were destitute of all universal notions about triangles, you could not verify any statements about triangles except in the particular cases you had bothered to inspect. As it is, you are sure of many universal truths about triangles and about many other things, due to your native ability to form universal ideas of them.

What power in you is responsible for the formation of universal ideas? If the word *intellect* names your power to understand truths, and especially conceptual truths, then we must attribute the work of universal formation to your intellect, since universals are the foundation of your ability to grasp such truths.

Can we also attribute this act to your imagination? Can we, in other words, identify your universal-forming intellect with your image-forming imagination?

This question is effectively the same as asking whether a universal idea is an image. If a universal idea is an image, then your image-forming power, your imagination, will be the power by which you form universals. If instead a universal is not an image, then it will lie beyond the power of your imagination to form a universal.

Let's put the matter to the test. Consider your universal idea *animal*. By it, you grasp what is common and essential to all animals. So it is that *organism* is in the definition of *animal*, but *bony* is not (nor is *boneless*). Not all animals are bony. Not all animals are boneless. Only those things that are true of all animals can be in the idea of *animal*, which names what is common to all animals, and only that. Can you imagine this universal notion? Can you imagine what is common to all animals, and only what is common to them?

I confess that I cannot. This is not due to the poverty of my imagination in particular, but to the limitations of imagination in general. Try the experiment yourself. Imagine an animal. Does it have any bones? If so, then you have not imagined what is common to all animals, since not all animals have bones. Does it lack bones? If so, then you still have not imagined what is common to all animals, since not all animals lack bones. You cannot form an image of an animal without committing yourself one way or another. The image must be of something bony or else boneless, and again it must be either four-legged or not, have a tail and claws or not, and so on. It must also have some particular color and shape, and yet no color or shape is common to all animals.

If what you mean by *animal* is an image, then it should be possible to draw it. Draw a picture, if you can, that accurately portrays precisely what you mean by *animal*, nothing more or less. Does it have feathers? Then fish are excluded, even though your idea of *animal* must include them. Does it have fangs? So much for cows.

That settles it. You simply cannot form an image of what is common to all animals. You have no trouble, on the other hand, understanding what is common to all animals, since you understand, for example, that it is common to all animals to be alive, or to have the sense of touch, and a whole bunch of other predicates. These universal ideas of yours, unlike your images of animals, do not oblige you to include any features that are peculiar only to certain animals.

Your universal idea of *animal*, then, is not an image. It is therefore not a product of your imagination. Your power of forming universal ideas, your intellect, is another power entirely.

It is very tempting to try to force universals into being something relatively tame and imaginable, such as collections or sets of similar objects. I cannot imagine what is common to all triangles, but I can imagine a set of individual triangles. Can this imagined collection of assorted triangles be the same as my universal idea of what is common to all triangles? Not at all. If "what a triangle is" were the same as a big collection of triangles, then any single triangle would have to be a collection of triangles. "What a triangle is" means something found in each single triangle. So if "what a triangle is" were the same as a big collection of triangles, then the big collection of triangles would have to be found in each single triangle, which is ridiculous. The collection of triangles is not found in any single member of the collection. But "what a triangle is" *is* found in each single triangle, and is in fact a mere part of it. Being a triangle, for example, is part of the triangle ABC we encountered earlier—only a part, since there are other things about ABC besides being a triangle (since it is also gray and many other things).

If you are like me, you cannot imagine an infinite collection of things, but only finite numbers of things. To tell the truth, I doubt I can form a clear image of so many as a hundred things. If I were stuck with nothing but my imagined collections of things, if these were the only kinds of ideas I could form, I could never verify or wonder about anything concerning all possible triangles, or all possible instances of the number two, or all possible penguins. I cannot imagine the set of all possible triangles. So I cannot use such an image to check each one and see whether each is capable of being inscribed in a circle. That is not how I verify such a truth. Besides, I cannot even form the idea of "the set of all triangles" except by consulting my universal idea of what a triangle is.

Strange and unimaginable as universal ideas are, the truth demands that we not try to deny their existence and replace them with something more comfortable and manageable. They are a plain fact of human mental life. Your body forms countless chemical substances without requiring you to notice it, and you become aware of them only by paying special attention to the human body at work (mainly by means of an "outsider's view"). In similar fashion, your intellect forms universal ideas without requiring you to notice it, and so you become aware of them only by paying special attention to your mind (by means of your "insider's view"). Once we do pay such attention, however, our formation of universal ideas becomes a simple matter of fact. No doubt we form classes and define collections and sets in our minds too, and these mental (and sometimes imaginable) constructs are extremely useful. Only it is a mistake to suppose that these are the same as our universal ideas, or that they can do the work of them.

We have progressed well beyond common knowledge of your mental powers. That we possess imagination is common knowledge. That we possess intellect is common knowledge. That the two are distinct powers is, perhaps, a common suspicion, but we have now confirmed this, and with uncommon clarity seen in what the distinction consists. Your imagination deals only in images, which come with individual peculiarities every bit as much as the individuals being imagined, such as the triangle ABC in our earlier example. Your intellect deals instead in universals isolating features common to many individuals, and universals cannot possibly be images.

The difference between your intellect and your imagination not only helps us to understand you better in yourself, but also will help us understand the difference between you and other creatures that might be called intelligent in some sense of the word. It is to this question that we will turn next.

4

Paragon of Animals

Reason and speech bring men together and unite them in a kind of natural society. Nor in anything else are we further removed from the nature of wild beasts.

—Cicero, *On Duties*

Animal Lures Man

I was taking one of my walks near the outskirts of campus. The winding narrow path I followed was hemmed in by trees and bushes on either side. My next class was not for another hour, and I can always use a little morning silence and sunshine before applying myself to the talky indoor work that goes on in a classroom under fluorescent lights. From somewhere up ahead came the crackle of dry leaves underfoot. A student? No. When I looked up I saw a doe. She had seen me too and had frozen, staring straight at me, standing just off the path, less than ten yards away. I could see only her head and neck above the shrubs. I stopped, too, to avoid frightening her off. She did not run away. She only continued staring for some moments. Then she leapt backward once or twice into the woods, never taking her eyes from me. Odd. What was she doing? She hopped twice more, still looking at me. Did she want me to follow her? Was she a deer equivalent of Lassie, trying to tell me some poor child had fallen down a well and would I please come help?

I took a cautious step forward on the path toward her, and when she saw this she turned tail—she did not flee, exactly, but trotted casually out into the woods. I soon lost sight of her. Well, that was that, I thought.

Continuing on my way, I came to the spot where she had been standing, and I got a surprise. There beside the path was sitting a tiny fawn. It stood up unsteadily when it saw me approach. I am no expert, but from its tiny size, its disproportionately long and spindly legs, and its tottering stance, I guessed that it was no more than a day or two since it had been born. I stared at it in admiration. It stared back at me, too, although I could not imagine what went on its mind. After some little while I realized I should leave it for its mother to come back for, so I turned around and headed back toward campus.

I had progressed long enough on my return journey that thoughts of my upcoming class began to filter through my mind—what question should I ask my students about Aristotle's definition of nature? What would really get them going? Maybe I could ask them for the difference between a natural thing and an artificial one, and when they said, "Artificial things are man-made" (which they surely would say), I could ask them whether water synthesized in a lab is therefore artificial water. Oh, that should stir them up all right. Then I could follow up with—hold on. What was that? I stopped. Listened. Nothing. I resumed walking, but then—yes, there it was again: "pock pock pock." I turned around and saw the little fawn just a few paces behind, following me. Amazing. I kept on walking, thinking if only I could get all the way to class without the little one getting scared off, my students would think I was another Saint Francis. It was marvelous to see it struggling along on those improbable stilts it had for legs. When I walked, it followed. When I stopped, it stopped. I was the leader! We were nearly at the end of the paved path and the school buildings were rising into view when the doe returned to collect her fawn. She emerged from the woods between me and her offspring. She was so near I could almost have touched her had I reached out. She did not even look at me this time. I had proved to be no threat. She disappeared back into the woods at a slow and easy pace, her baby in tow.

Only later did I fully realize that the doe had been very clever. I had walked quietly enough along the paved path (no dry leaves crackled under my feet) that I had surprised her. She could not just run off, since her fawn could not follow at speed, and I might then make a meal of the defenseless creature for all she knew. So she tried to lure me away. She seemed to guess that I had seen only her at first, not yet her fawn, and so she kept my eyes locked on her as she sidled off into the woods. Had I been a dog or some other predator, I would have given chase. She would probably have outrun me, and she could then circle back for her fawn. Her behavior was very shrewd, wasn't it? And brave, too. She had put her own life in harm's way for the sake of the next generation.

This is just one of any number of my own run-ins with animal cunning. Probably you could supply more exciting ones of your own. Most homeowners have an amusing animal story or two. My backyard was invaded by gophers years ago, and I have had endless troubles with them. More recently, I was harassed by a raccoon that was wreaking havoc on my lawn in search of grubs, and absolutely nothing I used as bait could lure the wary bandit into my Havahart trap. Not eggs, marshmallows, sardines, cat food (I did catch a cat one evening), salmon, grape soda, or anything else besides the handful of grubs in my lawn could stimulate its interest. Apparently it was "trap smart", and my only hope was to get rid of every last grub in the lawn and convince the marauder that my yard was not a cafeteria.

My father-in-law went to war with the gray squirrels in his neighborhood. He wanted to feed the birds, not the squirrels, but the squirrels were always eating all the seed before any birds could arrive. He purchased one of those bird feeders on a pole with a plastic half dome mounted on it, concave side down, to make it impossible for them to climb the pole up to the feeder. No way up? No problem. They just crawled up a tree and out along a branch bringing them sufficiently near the feeder to leap *down* to it like paratroopers. I have seen videos of squirrels crawling along a clothesline, hanging upside down from it, in order to drop down onto the same type of "squirrel proof" feeder.

It is impossible to deny the intelligence, even the ingenuity, of certain animals. This fact can make it strangely difficult to state in no uncertain terms the difference between ourselves and other animals, which is the main business of the present chapter. Our general project is to learn what kind of being you are, to acquire a more defined understanding of you than is usual for most people. An essential part of that job is to distinguish you from all other things, especially those most similar to you.

Defining You

The basic job of a definition is to explain in a clear and summary way what a thing is. No mere definition expresses a thorough understanding of a thing, but it is a significant improvement over the vague, undefined conception of a thing that we have before trying to define it. One way to go about defining something is to identify the general category immediately above it, and then to name its differences from everything else in that category. Try to define *square*, for example. Clearly it is a kind of *shape*, or even more particularly it is a kind of *quadrilateral*. That's half the battle. But how does it differ from all the other quadrilaterals? By being *equilateral* and *right-angled*. Put it all together, now: a square is "a quadrilateral that is equilateral and right-angled". Beautiful. That is a definition of *square*. How do we know? Because it does the basic job of a definition. It says what is essential to being a square in a way that applies to all squares and only squares. This doesn't mean we now know everything there is to know about squares. But it is a significant step toward understanding squares to be able to set them apart from everything else (that is, to define them).

Can we do the same kind of thing with you? What general category should we place you in? You are a kind of—what? I hope you will not feel insulted when I suggest that you are in fact a kind of animal. It is a funny thing, but many of us do not feel slighted when we are described as *mammals*, but call us *animals* and our dander is up. When I call you an *animal* I do not mean to imply anything about your manners or your intelligence. I mean only that you are a living thing endowed with sensation. There is no other word for such a creature, really. So I must call you an animal.

The biologists, too, are willing to call you an *animal*, although what they have in mind by the word is something like "a eukaryotic multicellular heterotroph that lacks cell walls". There is no reference to sensation in that. The biological way of classifying living things is intended not so much to bring out the diversities in what "living" consists in for each of them, but to bring out their genealogical groupings as a result of their evolutionary history (and also to bring out basic differences in their body structures and cells). The biological way of classifying living things is therefore a scientific hypothesis, and not a codification of basic differences we all perceive among living things. I mention the biological use of the term *animal* only to leave it aside, and to prevent anyone from supposing that I am using the ordinary words *animal* and *plant* in the special sense that biologists have given them. I am using the words in their older and more ordinary sense. When I say *animal*, I mean a living thing naturally endowed with sensation. When I say *plant*, I mean a living thing naturally devoid of sensation. This is not a disagreement with the biologists, but a difference of vocabulary, and a difference of concern. In a similar way, an apple core to a botanist is a true *fruit*, since it is the seed-bearing structure of a plant, whereas to a gourmet chef it is not a *fruit*, but only an inedible part of one. The botanist and the chef are not embroiled in some sort of dispute. They only use the word *fruit* to mean different things, and to draw the different distinctions that their different kinds of expertise require them to talk about.

So you are an animal, if you do not mind my saying so. And you have no doubt heard that you are closely related to the other animals. Your DNA and mine, it is said, differs by less than 3 percent from that of chimpanzees (*Pan troglodytes*) and bonobos (*Pan paniscus*)—some say these species share 99 percent of our DNA, with gorillas not far behind at about 98 percent. Now it is certainly silliness, or even dishonesty, to conclude from this that you are much more like a bonobo than unlike one. I imagine that a day spent with you would not be 1 percent different, but immeasurably different, from one spent with a bonobo. In fact, I imagine that there would be a vast difference between spending a day with you and spending a day with certain other members of our species, but little difference between spending a day with one bonobo or any other. And even when it comes to your DNA, it is simpleminded to believe that a 1 percent difference can mean only a trivial and not a radical difference in the whole result. Consider, for example, this statement that contains 100 characters:

The bomb will detonate in ten seconds unless you cut the wires in the right order, so be sure to cut first the wire labeled P.

Changing just the final character produces a difference of 1 percent:

The bomb will detonate in ten seconds unless you cut the wires in the right order, so be sure to cut first the wire labeled R.

Is the difference trivial? Clearly not. The difference is radical. It is the 99 percent sameness of these two statements that is relatively trivial, whereas the 1 percent difference is the difference between life and death.

As a few tiny differences in letters and words can make all the difference in meaning, so a few tiny differences in DNA can make all the difference between health and disease, perhaps even between life and death, and so it is not too surprising that a relatively small number of differences in DNA can spell the difference between one form of life and another that is quite different. One might also wonder whether DNA is really the chief principle governing what will be made out of all the proteins it encodes, or is that ultimate product decided more by epigenetic factors? And if the latter, do these, too, differ by less than 1 percent in you and a bonobo?

While these particular questions of genetics and epigenetics are fascinating, they are not our concern. Let us grant in a general way, without assigning percentages, that you have much in common with other animals, and more with some than others. What sets you apart from them? Oh, lots of things. You and I and our kind exhibit many traits unique to us and found in none of the beasts. We are featherless bipeds, for one thing. In addition to our striking upright posture we can also boast about our opposable thumbs. We wear clothes. We smile and laugh. We manufacture and use cars and computers. But these things seem somehow secondary. They are not at the core of what we are, but only stem from our nature. What is the root of all our differences from the other animals?

Probably the most striking difference is that we talk. This striking difference seems to point to the root difference in us, since our talk is expressive of what we conceive in our minds, and it is our minds that give us our special edge over the animals. We contrive all our tools, clothing, housing, medicines, and weapons, as well as our means of transportation, by means of the insights of our reason. That is why the specifically human difference that philosophers add to the general category of *animal* is *rational*. Sometimes *rational* means "uses reason and uses it well", in which sense not all people, indeed perhaps alarmingly few, are rational. But the philosophers mean by *rational* that a thing is of such a nature as to possess an intellect capable of grasping universals—even if certain deficiencies in the brain prevent the intellect from understanding very well, or even at all. Every human being is the kind of thing that, when conditions are right, endeavors to grow two feet and could really use them, even if injuries or reproductive or developmental mishaps sometimes prevent the actual possession or use of two feet. Consequently, every human being without exception is *bipedal*. In the same way, every human being is naturally meant to have and use an intellect, even if certain eventualities prevent proper intellectual development in some, and so every human being is *rational*. If squares are "quadrilaterals that are equilateral and right-angled", we humans are "animals that are rational".

Here is the sticking point, though. What proof do we have that reason is our unique possession? Is it that we speak? Koko the gorilla and Kanzi the bonobo were able to learn some human sign language, or so some have said. And doesn't everyone know that parrots can talk? All kinds of birds chatter and apparently communicate to one another an abundance of relevant intelligence concerning the presence of enemies, the willingness to mate, and the like.

Or is tool making or problem solving the unique proof of reason? Well, even spiders weave structurally sophisticated webs for ensnaring their prey. How is this not reasoning, adapting means to ends, and tool making? As for problem solving, the mother deer, the sly gopher, the resourceful squirrel, and the cautious raccoon can solve problems like nobody's business.

All right, then, what about self-awareness? Could that be the sole proof of reason? That has its problems, too. Some higher animals, such as chimpanzees, seem able to recognize their own reflections in a mirror, given enough time. They even use a mirror somewhat as a teenager would, inspecting and preening themselves by means of it, making weird faces in it. Don't they therefore have a concept of themselves?

The undeniable and impressive intelligence of animals gives us pause, and makes us wonder whether the differences by which we set ourselves apart from them are in the end mere differences of degree. We are the *smartest* animals, much as the cheetahs are the *fastest* land animals. That is all.

But something is amiss in this magnanimous concession. Our claim to otherness in kind from the rest of the animals is not an expression of human snobbery. If we demote ourselves to clever apes, we have glossed over the gaping wide quantum leap from great-ape intelligence to human. Evolutionary biologist Theodosius Dobzhansky wrote that

> man's structural peculiarities only suffice to place him in a monotypic zoological family, with a single living species. His mental abilities are far more distinctive. If the zoological classification were based on psychological instead of mainly morphological traits, man would have to be considered a separate phylum or even kingdom.[1]

What animal has ever made a discovery comparable to Maxwell's proof of the electromagnetic nature of light? To the fundamental theorem of calculus? Even observations such as these miss the point. Many of our own kind, too, are incapable of understanding the truths of advanced physics and mathematics, and very few of us indeed are capable of discovering them by our own intelligence. The ability to understand these things sets physicists and mathematicians apart from the rest of us by a difference only of degree and only in some special subject—it is not what sets us apart from the animals.

Far more relevant to the human difference is the utter inability of even the brightest chimps to formulate (indeed to have) the most ordinary sentiments. Imagine a chimpanzee sitting at the dinner table, dressed like everyone else, displaying none of the telltale signs of apehood—no head scratching, leering, grimacing, pursing of the lips, or rocking from side to side. The creature is instead sitting quietly, pensively, politely. Savannah, a fourth grader seated across the table from our chimp, has just been invited by her mother to describe her day at school, and she obligingly reports that her teacher has been reading out loud to the class from the first *Harry Potter* book. "Cool!" says the chimp. "Last night I saw the movie for the first time, and I'm still not sure which is better, the movie or the book, you know? What do you think, Savannah? Hey, be awesome and pass the salt, yeah?" Even this modest display of intelligence, which any semiliterate English speaker could muster, would earn the chimp a permanent place in the annals of science and an appearance on every TV talk

---

[1] Theodosius Dobzhansky, "Chance and Creativity in Evolution", in *Studies in the Philosophy of Biology: Reduction and Related Problems*, ed. Francisco Jose Ayala and Theodosius Dobzhansky (Berkeley and Los Angeles: University of California Press, 1974), p. 333.

show in the world. But this meagre speech is infinitely beyond a Koko or a Kanzi. Why is that? Something radical seems to be missing.

In a pinch like this, where we feel there must be a sharp divide but we have difficulty putting our finger on it, we are inclined to go to experts for help. Certainly ethologists and linguists have noted important differences between human language and animal communication. The research of renowned linguist Noam Chomsky, for example, led him to conclude that we pick up speech by means of some innate, brain-based ability that is absent in all other animals, that there is accordingly a kind of "universal grammar" inherent in all human languages, and that animal communication does not embody the fundamental syntax that constitutes language in the strict sense.[2]

Or we might consult with Nobel Prize–winning ethologist Konrad Lorenz, who explains that the "language" of jackdaws is innate, not learned, since it is spoken even by jackdaws raised in isolation from other jackdaws. In response to the same stimuli, the isolated jackdaws make the very same sounds as their fellow jackdaws, whom they have never met. This proves further that jackdaw "words" are not "spoken" with any conscious intention of communicating anything to other jackdaws. These sounds are made as instinctive, automatic responses, not even rising to the level of interjections (never mind nouns and verbs). They are natural noise responses, akin to laughing or shrieking or weeping. But since other jackdaws also have inborn, automatic, and species-beneficial *reactions* to such sounds, the sounds work every bit as effectively as if the jackdaws were trying to say things to one another, like "Danger!" Observations like these led Lorenz to conclude that "animals do not possess a language in the true sense of the word."[3]

Special observations of human language development and of animal behavior are certainly necessary for answering many particular

---

[2] Chomsky once said, "It's about as likely that an ape will prove to have language ability as that there is an island somewhere with a species of flightless birds waiting for human beings to teach them to fly". *Time*, March 10, 1980, p. 57. For some of his work on the nature of human language, see *Aspects of the Theory of Syntax* (Cambridge, Mass., MIT Press, 1965), and "The Faculty of Language: What Is It, Who Has It, and How Did It Evolve?", *Science* 298 (2002): 1569–79.

[3] Konrad Lorenz, *King Solomon's Ring*, trans. Marjorie Kerr Wilson (Routledge: London and New York, 2006), p. 73.

questions. Is there a universal grammar for all human languages, and if so, what are its basic rules? How many different sounds do jackdaws make, and in response to what stimuli? How do they react when they hear those sounds, and why? But since all of us somehow perceive that animals cannot really talk, the general question of whether animals talk should be answerable also in the light of more general experience. We need the scientists to tell us the details of exactly how various species of animals communicate. Why they do not talk in the true sense of the word is something we should be able to discover for ourselves.

Imagine you are visiting the zoo and trying to make conversation with the giraffes (nothing deep, just small talk). How will the giraffes respond? Will they, like speakers of a foreign tongue, cock their heads to one side, squint at you a little, realize you are not speaking their language, then make some universal gesture as good as to say, "Sorry, friend, I don't understand those words of yours"? That would be the polite thing. But they will pay no attention to your small talk at all. If we assume giraffes have a true language, much as the people of Germany and China speak different languages of their own, then we will be forced to conclude that giraffes are a bunch of rude jerks who choose to ignore you rather than let you know that they would like to understand you but cannot.

That is of course absurd. The plain truth is that the giraffes do not possess a language of another kind, the way German is a language of another kind from Mandarin. They possess "language" in a completely different (and, yes, watered-down) sense of the word, even as the meaning of the word *language* is dramatically altered when we speak of "body language" (to say nothing of a "computer language").

What is it that the giraffes are missing? Why can't they learn English, even at a basic level? Why is even the much-touted use of sign language by the apes no proof that they are possessors of reason and speech?

The Human Difference

Capacity for true speech demands the power to grasp universals, something that is absent in animals. Every word we speak, with the sole exceptions of proper nouns such as *Paris*, *Led Zeppelin*, and

Walker Percy, are expressions of universal ideas. Your intellect's ability to grasp universals is what sets it apart from your other mental powers, such as imagination and memory. That ability is also what sets it apart from animal intelligence.

How can we tell whether animals can form universal ideas? We know that we ourselves can do so, thanks to our insider's view of ourselves—just what we don't have in the case of the other animals. No need to despair, however. Thanks to our insider's understanding of our own minds, we can deduce external consequences of possessing such a mind, and check for those in the other animals.

The reasoning goes like this. If a nonhuman animal could form even a single universal idea, then it could also form many of them and would express these of its own accord in easily recognizable signs. But we observe nothing of the sort in any nonhuman animal. Therefore no nonhuman animal can form even a single universal idea.

Let us follow the links in this chain of reasoning one at a time. Why would the ability to form one universal idea imply the ability to form many of them? Because if animals are truly capable of understanding anything at all, it is the particular things relevant to their lives. If a dog understands what anything is, it knows what *food* is, what *prey* is, what *a dog* is, what *a cat* is, what *an enemy* is, what *a mate* is, and so on. If it understands anything, it understands the things that matter in the life of a dog. It is of these things that it can be expected to have universal ideas. And there are many and diverse things that make up the life of a dog. So if a dog can form a universal understanding of something, it can form a universal understanding of a great many things.

Our hypothetical dog can form universal ideas not only of very particular things, such as *what a dog is*, but also of more general things, such as *what an animal is*. It is impossible to form a universal idea of *what a triangle is* without at least a hazy idea of *what a shape is*. Likewise it is impossible to form a universal idea of *what a dog is* without at least some notion of *what an animal is*. By this logic, our supposedly rational dog will also be capable of forming ideas of all the more universal categories that contain the particular ideas relevant to its canine life. It will form in its mind a great hierarchy of universal notions, some of which are more universal than others.

The same dog should also know, in particular, what a *signal* or *sign* is, since signs are a part of canine life. Dogs growl and bark and

whimper and yelp, and they bare their teeth and assume various significant postures, and respond to such signs as well. Now an animal
endowed with a mind brimming over with universal ideas, and fully
aware of what an expressive sign is, will perceive the advantage in
expressing its ideas to its fellows by means of signs, and will seek to
learn the ideas of its fellows by looking for outward indications of
them. Such an animal will not only communicate through signs, as
even insects do, but will use signs specifically to indicate universal
ideas. In other words, it will genuinely *speak*. Some people do not
have the ability to speak, although they retain the ability to understand, but this is because of something gone awry physiologically,
neurologically, or psychologically. Any fully equipped individual in
a species endowed with understanding of universal ideas will also
possess the power of speech even as we do. It might not use articulate
vocal sounds, if its physiology makes this impossible, and its vocabulary might be smaller than ours; but it will surely have many things
to say, and it will find some way to say them, whether by gestures or
some other unmistakable means.

If any of the animals we know about could form a single universal
idea, then at least the more intelligent of their kinds would be both
willing and able to converse with others of their kind and even with
us (just as we wish to talk to them) in true words signifying universals. Their ideas and statements might be rudimentary, as are those
of young children or people who suffer from mental shortcomings
of one kind or another. They would nonetheless have ideas. If animals had such rudimentary ideas to express, they would of their own
accord try to converse with us and express opinions. But they do
not. And it is not because they are snobs. Nor is it because they lack
intelligence in every sense of that word. It is because they have
no intelligence in the specific sense of a power to grasp universals.

That is what is missing. That is not the only difference, but it is
the most essential and root difference, between you and all other
animals. The absence of universal reason is also why animals never
ask universal questions—if great apes can be said to "ask" anything
at all, their questions are always about individuals or groups of them
(where someone or something is, for instance). You will never catch
one asking, even by hand signals, "Hey, wait a second; some numbers
are bigger than others, so what's the *biggest* number of all? Is it one

hundred?" Any creature capable of grasping what a number is (and not just individual bunches of bananas) will be capable of wondering about that. Small children ask that kind of question all the time. Apes don't. There's nothing in such questioning for them, and nothing in them for it.

Reason's Imitators

How, then, should we understand animal intelligence? What is it? Sometimes what we call intelligence in an animal is purely instinctive—an innate, self-beneficial, stimulus-specific response that the animal itself does not understand. A spider's web is in some sense ingenious, but its weaver does not understand any principles of engineering. It acts only in response to inborn promptings to "drop a thread here, now", and "drag another over there, this time a sticky one", and "connect it like this to that one". The prompts are of course felt impulses not expressed in words. By following such internal prompts, the spider is reciting the steps in an inborn program, going through the motions it feels it must go through without knowing why. That is why spiders never teach each other the art of web building. Nor do they need to learn it. They are more or less born with it. They might become more capable with practice, I don't know. But they don't go to school for it. And so all spiders of a particular type make their webs in more or less the same way. They don't gather in conventions to reconsider the efficiency of their particular design in view of last year's number of flies netted.

Some animal intelligence goes beyond pure instinct. Higher animals undoubtedly learn in some sense and form new mental associations. Parrots undeniably (and uncannily) associate human word sounds with things and events to which they are highly apropos. Even this, however, does not demonstrate understanding of the meaning of the words. A very small child who has no understanding of some obscene phrase, but who has seen the wonderful reaction it gets under certain circumstances, can readily serve up the obscenity at just the "right" moment. Similarly, the associations that animals are capable of making often astound us and appear like understanding, because we cannot perceive everything they perceive, and we ourselves do not possess their specific associative instincts, and because instead of those instincts we possess something else in their place, intellect, which naturally occurs to us first as the means of joining one thing with another. Thus our go-to explanation for animal behavior too easily becomes an imaginary version of our own intelligence projected onto the poor oblivious creatures. A classic example of this is "clever Hans", the horse whose owner, Wilhelm von Osten, honestly believed Hans could stomp his hoof in order to answer math problems. Hans was in reality reading the subtle clues in the body language of his owner or other people present at his performances. He could tell when people hoped he would stop stomping, and of course that would be whenever Hans reached the correct number of stomps in order to answer a question such as, what is two plus three? Neither von Osten nor Hans were trying to deceive anyone. But deceive people they did, von Osten himself included.

Animals can also discover a way out of a problem, then respond in the same way to similar situations in the future, as though they have learned and henceforth were applying a universal principle, such as "When in this kind of situation, if I do that sort of thing, I will get a banana." Problem-solving behavior by itself does not indicate such universal ideas in the animal mind. Just as instinctive promptings suffice for a spider to build its web, so do instinctive promptings suffice for a chimp to manipulate its surroundings in various ways until it gets a desired result. Subsequently, the pattern of behaviors that ended with the desired result gets stored in memory for future use. The pattern need not be (and indeed is not) remembered in the form of an abstract description of means to ends. It is enough if its past success reprograms the chimp's brain to behave in a way similar to the way it did when it succeeded. Even a human child (or adults operating in robot mode, not deliberately thinking about what they are doing) can place square pegs in square holes and round ones in round ones without invoking some universal idea of what *square* means, let alone invoking a definition of *square*. It is enough to have an image of a square in mind (that is, in the imagination), and to compare each peg to this particular mental image, which is not a definition of *square*. We ourselves make use of such mental paradigms all the time, and even externalize them in pictures. Nature guidebooks, or their online equivalents, provide drawings or photos of plants and animals to help us identify species. If the mushroom looks like this here on page twelve, then feel free to eat it—that'll be a truffle—but if it looks like the one there on page nineteen, then for heaven's sake don't eat it; that's a destroying angel.

There is something approaching the power of the universal in a typical instance that we carry around for reference, whether as a physical image or as a mental one, and whether of a thing or of some sequence or pattern. But neither a mental image nor a photograph is a true universal. It is only a particular instance of something, although a typical one to which we can usefully compare other instances. It is like a litmus test. Is this an acid? The litmus paper will tell you. But that does not mean the litmus paper is a universal idea of what an acid is, or that it knows anything at all. A well-made lock will open for an infinity of keys as long as they are all of the same shape. That does not mean the lock knows the shape common to all those keys. Similar response to similar stimuli does not prove a knowledge of the common feature that is the basis of the similarity.

A true universal idea differs from a typical instance in that it contains nothing except what is common to an infinity of different possible individuals, as we saw in the last chapter. No typical instance or example can do this. Any particular representation, say, of a triangle, must include certain incidentals, such as a color or texture or a definite ratio among the sides, and cannot present pure triangularity by itself. No particular instance can isolate pure triangularity from all things that are incidental to what a triangle is. But your mind can do this. You know in your own case that you form universal ideas, because you perceive within yourself (thanks to your insider's view) that you know what belongs to *triangle* as such, and what does not.

Other animals are incapable of speech and never express curiosity in the form of general questions. That is because they are irrational animals, devoid of reason in the sense in which it belongs to you. All their feats, amazing as they are, rely on other mental capacities for instinctive and learned association, none of them transcending the use of paradigmatic instances of things. Their mental templates may also be adjustable, refinable in light of experience, and this flexibility will make the behavior following from them appear even more as if it flowed from true and universal understanding. But nothing the animals do (or "say") requires anything beyond the grasp of particulars.

If we set out to find purely performance-based signs of our own kind of intelligence in the animals, we will surely find them in abundance. If we say to ourselves, "Whatever can give the correct response to a math question understands math," then we will find that Clever Hans understands math, and German, and a great many other things. If instead we devise careful tests to tell whether these performances are truly the outcome of a universal grasp of things, or are instead the products of sense, memory, instinct, and learned associations of particulars, and if we persevere, then the animals will eventually expose their ignorance of the universal ideas supposedly in play. When the face of the card held up to Clever Hans reads "2 + 3", and the back of it reads "10", Hans stomps his hoof ten times. Why? Not because he can read the back of the card, but because his trainer can, and his trainer thinks this is the correct answer to whatever the card says on the front (which he has not checked). And Hans, though by no means a mathematician, is adept at reading the expectations of his trainer.

We can now summarize the character of the chief difference between human and nonhuman intelligence. Animals form no universal and abstract ideas, but only particular representations of things and well-organized associations of them. Some of these may be adjustable in light of further experience, and may be applicable to many similar circumstances, and may therefore simulate universal understanding quite convincingly—provided we do not devise any special test to tell the difference. We, on the other hand, genuinely grasp what things are. We grasp not just this shape, but "what a shape is", for example, and we can combine such ideas to form universal truths in our minds. Animals give us many reasons to call them *intelligent* in some sense of the word, especially when they solve new problems by means of learned associations. But they never force us to attribute to them an understanding of timeless and universal truths. They invariably force us not to.

Your intellect therefore differs from animal intelligence as the infinite from the finite. An animal knows at most a finite number of individual instances of shapes, whereas you know certain things to be true about all possible shapes, which are infinite in number. This is the power of the universal at work.

This is a difference of kind, not of degree, between human beings and other animals.

You're Superior (and That's OK)

Those of us fortunate enough to live under democratic regimes tend to cringe when we hear the word *superior*. It conjures up in our minds images of Nazis or white supremacists. Since talk of superior races is groundless and leads to nasty injustices, some of us wonder whether we should also banish all talk of superior species and scold it out of existence by giving it an ugly name like *speciesism*.

Does it sound strange to say that our political customs can thus color the way we view the world of nature? If so, you might try putting this idea to the test on a state university campus. Conduct a survey and see how many students and professors readily accept (or at least are not hostile or entirely close-minded to) the proposition that "human beings are superior beings compared with other animals." I have conducted no such survey myself and can only guess what kind of data you would gather. My experience as a teacher means my guess would at least be a somewhat educated one. My suspicion is that you would encounter fierce resistance to the proposition— largely instinctive resistance, not well thought out, sometimes based on references to Darwin. Often the resistance would arise from a deeply felt conviction that it is somehow wrong for human beings to pretend to be superior, or else from a misguided belief that "humans are superior to animals" would logically entail that we have no obligations toward animals and can do whatever we want to them. At any rate, if you do conduct such an experiment, and find instead that the majority of college students accept the proposition without hesitation, please drop me a line and tell me all about it.

People's distrust of the notion that they are beings superior to other animals usually results from misapplication of the principle of equality outside its proper sphere. It is of course a mistake to ask which nickel in a roll is worth the most. They are all of equal value just by being nickels. It does not follow that all coins are of equal worth. That is just what is going on in the case of species. All human beings are of one nature, and it is in virtue of the human nature we all share in common with one another that we are also all radically equal in natural dignity. The poor souls on one side of the tracks should never be subordinated to those on the other, as though they existed for the sole purpose of making life more convenient for them. The basis for such equality disappears when we stray outside the human race and introduce another species into the picture—for example, ticks or fleas. These creatures have sensations and desires, so they are like us in some very general way. General similarity is a far cry from equality, however. There is a great inequality between the human and the tick. It is odious and wrong to look for that same kind of inequality between one human being and another. But there is nothing wrong with acknowledging it between the human and the tick. If you decide to kill a tick because it is inconveniencing you or your dog, you're OK in my book. If you are willing to run over a kid on a bike because you're in a hurry, I'd rather not make your acquaintance.

Our superiority to the animals means we need not accord them voting rights, the chance to run for office, or equal employment opportunities. It does not in any way imply that it is OK to extinguish our cigarettes on them. We have a duty to care for the other creatures of this world. This is partly because we depend on them for food and shelter and medicine and energy and the like, but there is more to it than that. We must also avoid cruelty and strive to live in a healthy symbiosis with other creatures, to preserve all species in existence, and in general to leave the whole world as beautiful and complete as when we found it, so far as possible. Although we do not exactly owe nature worship, it is nonetheless a fitting object of respect (even a kind of reverence), embodying an order superior to any of our own design, prior to us in time and independent of our existence. It is a masterwork deserving of careful study, imitation, and admiration. It is not merely a commodity to be processed, bottled, and sold.

The inequality between us and other living things does not mean we should accept animal cruelty or unsustainable logging practices. But there is something else about believing in the supposed equality of animals and man that sounds a hollow note. It is phony. I don't just mean that its proponents tend to speak up only for cute and cuddly animals. (Some of them are more consistent and protest the boiling of water, since it kills microbes.) I mean that the whole view masquerades as humility when really it smacks more of arrogance. If we ourselves are all radically equal in the dignity of our shared human nature, and rightly expect that this equality will be reflected in our political institutions and other human associations, well and good. But this is a human fact founded on human nature specifically and will not warrant any attempt to force every other nature into that mold. It is anthropomorphic and unjustifiably anthropocentric, not wise and bighearted of us, to pretend that all natures and natural associations must conform to the same standards that suit human nature and human associations. If we do not consult nature first, but instead come to it with the demand that it shall present us with none but natures equal in dignity to each other and to our own, then in a weird way we are really seeking to dominate it, to tell it what it shall be, to construct it or reconstruct it in the way we think it should be, rather than let it tell us what it really is in itself. This is to negate the very way in which nature ought to be superior to us and to measure us—namely, as a reality in its own right, an order preexisting any political one we might attempt to impose on it, and which deserves to be understood and respected for what it is and not merely for what we want it to be.

Out of respect for nature, then, let us set aside our political principles, so rightly applied to ourselves, and hear what nature itself has to say about the relations among natural beings. Let us not forget, either, that we number among natural beings ourselves, not just among political ones.

You Are a Microcosm

After acknowledging an essential difference between human beings and other animals, and breaking free of any political prejudice against the idea that human beings are superior beings compared with them, it can still be difficult for us to see exactly how to understand human superiority. Sure, we humans can talk and reason better than other animals can. But then we stacked the deck in our favor by picking something we are better at, didn't we? When it comes to speed and agility, other animals win the superiority contest. Moral comparison might be more neutral, fairer to all the species. But are we really the moral superiors in the animal kingdom? There are no saints among the beasts, but neither are there any Hitlers or Stalins.

So by what standard is it right to say that we are the best of the animals, and that human life is superior to any nonrational life? Why is it right to call the nonrational *sub*rational?

In order to answer that question we need to distinguish between what is better simply speaking and what is better only in some particular respect. Whenever we compare a number of things, we must employ some basis of comparison. If we choose as a basis of comparison something that is not essential to the things being compared, something that does not fall into their definitions, then we will not really be comparing the things absolutely speaking, but only in respect of something we chose to focus on. For example, *swimming* is not in the definition of *animal*. We are nonetheless free to compare two animals with regard to how well they swim. The shark is better at swimming than the horse. Does it follow that the shark is a better animal than the horse? Clearly not. Why not? Because *swimming* is not what makes an animal an animal. So far as this comparison goes, all we can say is that the shark is a better swimmer than the horse, not that it is a better animal. The shark is better in this particular respect that we have arbitrarily chosen to consider. It is not for that reason simply "better" than the horse.

On the other hand, when we compare two things by looking to what defines them or makes them what they are, and find that one of them is superior in that regard, then it is better not just in some particular respect that we have chosen to look at, but in an unqualified sense. This gardener, say, is better-looking than that one, and smells better, too. That makes this gardener better than the other one in certain respects, but not simply speaking, since *good-looking* and *nice-smelling* do not fall into the definition of *gardener*. A better-looking gardener is not necessarily a better gardener. On the other hand, someone who is better at laying out, tending, and cultivating a garden *is* a better gardener, and not just a better gardener in some particular respect.

Human beings are superior to the other animals in many particular respects, of course. We are better at writing novels and launching rockets. Such things do not enter into the definition of *animal*, nor into the definition of *a being*.[4] Those particular points of comparison

---

[4] By "a being", in this context, I do not mean "a sentient, intelligent being" in particular, as in "a being from outer space". I simply mean any single thing that has its own existence, whether a human being, or any other animal, or a plant, or a stone. I would use the word *thing* except that people sometimes object to calling a human being or an animal a *thing*, since *thing* seems to imply a nonliving thing.

alone would not justify the statement, then, that human beings are superior animals or superior beings, but only that we are superior novelists and rocket scientists. But human beings are also more complete beings than the other animals, and are capable of more complete and all-encompassing sense experience, and are more alive. For those reasons, we are superior to the other animals not just in some respect, but simply and absolutely.

Which is a more complete and all-inclusive being, you or an eagle? One way to rephrase this is to ask, which gets more out of which? Does the eagle get more out of you, or you out of it? To what extent can human beings become part of the life of eagles, and to what extent can eagles become part of the life of human beings? Eagles cannot find much room in their lives for us. They can't really take us in. They don't grasp or appreciate our anatomy and physiology and reproduction, for example, but we know all sorts of things about theirs. We even get the being of the eagle more than it gets itself, one might say. The eagle has no notion of its own look of fierce nobility that we have honored on coins, flags, and state emblems since at least the time of the Romans. We understand why eagles behave the way they do, and the origins of their behavior, whereas they perform their actions out of instinct, not understanding what they are doing or why. The bald eagle is unaware of its own former status as an endangered species. It could never understand that or even care about it. And now that human effort has enabled it to thrive again in the United States, it can feel no gratitude. By means of our knowledge, we take in all kinds of animals and plants which, for all the eagle knows or cares, might as well not exist. As ornithologist and Nobel Prize–winner Nikolaas Tinbergen put it, "Though all animals share one world, all may be said to live in different worlds, since each perceives best only that part of the environment essential to its success."[5] Your world is incomparably larger than that of an eagle. The human mind is in a way all beings, or is capable of becoming them all by grasping their forms—hence the old saying that "man is a microcosm", the universe writ small. No other animal can compete with the unlimited capacity of the human mind to take in other beings.

[5] Nikolaas Tinbergen, *Animal Behavior* (New York: Time-Life, 1965), p. 45.

Man emerges as the clear winner again when compared with other animals as an animal, as a being endowed with sensation and capacity for experiencing the world. This is the pride and joy of being an animal. Any animal that languishes in an irreversible vegetative state, as unaware of anything as any pile of dirt would be, has ceased living its life, so far as it is concerned. The question of which is the better animal, man or beast, therefore amounts to asking which one has a richer share in sense experience of the world.

We cannot spot the movement of a field mouse from a quarter mile off, but we can supplement our vision with instruments that can see farther and better than any eagle ever will. And we rational animals, propelled by our own efforts and motivated by our own curiosity, have summited Everest, explored the depths of the sea, plumbed cave systems, traversed jungles and deserts, mapped the whole earth, and pushed our way out into space. What nonrational animal would or could do all these things? What animal has devised tools and vehicles and recording devices purely for expanding the range of its experience? What creature other than man cares to peer for hours into a microscope or telescope when given the chance? We cannot fit a microbe into the mind of a dolphin, nor will we ever catch a chimp wondering what that smudge in the night sky might be that men call Andromeda. The animals other than man do have some share in sense experience. Some of them even appear to rejoice in it. Compared with man, however, the domain of any animal's experience is caught within a narrow compass.

The distinction between man and beast, and the superiority of human nature to subhuman, asserts itself also in the form of human freedom. Animals are like slaves to their impulses. When an animal resists one impulse, it is only in obedience to a stronger one. Incapable of grasping universal principles, their decisions are all in some way made for them by the natural pecking order among their instincts. In contrast to this, a human being, as you know from your own experience, can resist even powerful impulses and emotions, and choose instead to act in accord with some understood principle, to do the right thing simply because it is understood (even if not *felt*) to be the right thing. We do not always succeed. But the ability to shape our moral selves is a uniquely human privilege. And it is founded on our rational nature. We are not simply driven by instincts, but can learn to choose or pursue something because we have understood something about it.

Are we therefore morally superior to the beasts? Yes and no. Irrational animals are not capable of morals, good or bad. We are therefore capable of greater moral goodness than the animals, but also capable of greater wickedness. Men can fall beneath the beasts by their choices. But that only proves the superiority of human nature. The bigger they are, the harder they fall. The nobler the creature, the more deplorable its corruption and the more necessary its redemption.

Our capacity for understanding also opens up for us a wider view of goods and evils than our mere senses and sense desires permit. We therefore have more goods to choose from and evils to avoid than animals do—animals don't care about scientific theories, nor do they dread scientific mistakes. And even those goods we share with animals are more richly and perfectly our goods, since we understand them and see them more truly for what they are worth in the whole scheme of good things. Thanks to this circumspect vision of all goods, made possible by human intellect, we humans are the most fully informed, and therefore the most self-determining, the freest of all the animals.

We are also the most responsible for how we turn out.

The Universe in Four-Part Harmony

We can say analogous things about the distinction between animals and plants, and the superiority of the former to the latter. A plant does not take much of the world into itself. It is not much richer a being than a rock, which is no being but itself and which receives the influence of other beings only as new modifications of itself, not as indicators to it of an "outside". Even the humbler animals, such as worms and sea anemones, living in worlds perhaps not much larger than what their bodies can touch at any given moment, still manage to get outside themselves, to present inwardly to themselves, in the form of sensation, other beings, in some degree perceived as "other" and not as "self".

Ascending to visual animals, especially those with highly developed eyes and living on land, the world as reproduced within these creatures grows very large indeed, abounding in sharp details and sometimes alive with color. If the paramecium has sensation at all, it nevertheless has no awareness of the stars, perhaps none of the sky.

A dog or horse can see the sun and the moon and include them in some way in its interior repertoire of "other beings", even if it cannot wonder what they are. These higher animals gesture toward and intimate the microcosm of the human mind.

Plants entirely lack interior representations of the world and do not even rise to the level of knowing themselves. They live altogether without the benefit of that special type of self-expansion available to creatures that know. Just as the intelligence of animals mimics and foreshadows the human mind, however, so too does the life of plants mimic and approach the knowledge of animals. Venus flytraps are responsive to flies, and sunflowers to the sun—their reactive movements resemble those of animals in some remote way. That they nonetheless do not proceed from interior awareness is clear not only because of their outward dissimilarity to ourselves, but because even in ourselves, digestion, growth, healing from wounds, and other plantlike functions of life go on unconsciously, however marvelously and beneficially they respond to specific stimuli. Just as our bodies seem to "know" what they're doing, so do plants "know". That is, they produce good results such as we might try to produce by our knowledge, only they do not really have any knowledge.

We can now sum up the universe, so to speak, in its four major categories of beings. Of all the things out there, some of them are just things, having no life at all. These are the sticks and stones of the world, or the stars and sands, nature's furniture and materials. Others are things with life, but with no sensation. These we may call plants, growing things that take in other beings quite literally and then put them to work maintaining themselves. Next come things with life and sensation, able to "take things in" by way of knowledge, but still without intellect: the animals. Last and rarest are the things possessed of life, sensation, and intellect, such as ourselves and whatever other rational beings might dwell near other suns.

Each step up retains the positive features in the previous steps, and then adds something of its own. To mere things, the plants add life. To mere life, animals add sensation. To mere sensation, you and I add understanding of timeless truths and universals. Each added difference represents an advance in being, a broadening out of its possessor's existence, enabling it to embrace more things in itself.

5

Beyond the Brain

If the intellect were a part of the body ... it would not understand
universals but only particulars.

— Thomas Aquinas, *Summa Contra Gentiles*

A Head Examination

"What's your name?" This ostensibly simple question serves different
purposes in different contexts. Sometimes it demonstrates someone's
polite interest in us. Other times it means we are in trouble. Still
other times, it is a test. And so it was on this occasion.

"What's your name?"

I mulled this question over in my mind, thinking, "Oh, come
on now, I *know* this one," and, after ten seconds of concentration, I
remembered! One point for me.

"OK, what year is it?" my examiner went on.

What year? Ah, yes, years came in *numbers*, didn't they? So he was
looking for a number, then. A four-digit number. The rhythm of a
possible answer came to my mind: "BUM-Bum-BUMpity-Bum."
Hmm. What kind of number sounded like that? "Nineteen seventy-
five!" I exclaimed, "No, wait. I know that's wrong, it just has the
right kind of, hold on ..." It came back to me that I had been born
in 1969 and was now in college, so that would make the present year
1969 plus twenty or so, around 1989—yes! That was the answer:
"Nineteen eighty-nine." Another point for me.

"Good. Who's the president?"

Sheesh, these were getting tough. The first president that came
to me was Washington, and then Lincoln soon after, followed by
Nixon, Ford, Carter—then a total blank, an empty space where I

knew something should be, where something presidential in fact was, but somehow I had no access to it. There had been more presidents since Carter, and I knew them. But who were they? And why were they harder to remember than the presidents before them? In the end I was stumped by this one, but I figured that two out of three correct responses was not too shabby. After some more questions and some tests and a couple of hours of observation, the doctor sent me back to school with the diagnosis of a mild concussion and an order to rest for a few days.

It was my friends who had brought me to the hospital. Having noted my uncharacteristic absence from classes, they had looked in on me in my dormitory and found me in bed, disoriented, woozy, and saying rather novel things. Twenty-four hours before, while I was walking along a sidewalk in town on an errand, a certain clumsy move on my part had introduced my head to a fire hydrant. No blood. No lump. A touch of embarrassment. Thinking I was fine, I reported to my work-study job as usual when I arrived back on campus. An hour later, a severe headache and nausea came over me, and my supervisor dismissed me. Next thing I knew, I was in the hospital taking an exam for which I felt inadequately prepared.

I never doubted that my thinking depended somehow on my brain. For one thing, I had been told this all my life by nearly everyone who claimed to know. But there is nothing like a blow to the head to solidify the conviction.

Later in life, another kind of experience came along to confirm the existence of a connection between my brain and my thinking: migraines, truckloads of them. A sudden increase in the frequency, intensity, and duration of my migraines in the fall of 2010 led me to do a fair amount of research into them. There was hardly a migraine symptom that neglected to pay me regular visits—nausea, visual auras, blurred and dimmed vision, photophobia and "hyperacusis" (an unpleasantly heightened sense of hearing), and of course thrills and waves of pain in the eyes and head. All were now familiar friends. Many migraine sufferers find their capacity for speech and thought strangely affected. I am one such person. When I am under a full-blown attack, I can hear the words other people are saying to me and in some sense recognize their meaning, but I cannot retain them or form any abiding sense of what they have said. Much less can I come up with anything to say in reply. In the classroom, this condition has occasionally caused my students to wonder at my long silences, or to laugh at my odd verbal mix-ups when a slight migraine still permits a stumbling speech.

What I am now describing is not entirely a problem with my mouth, although it is true that even a mild migraine turns my mouth to mush and slurs my speech. Motor problems aside, there is also a cognitive disconnect. When one of my migraines is in full swing, I experience some measure of passive aphasia conjoined to a nearly total active aphasia, a disconcerting inability to access my mental treasury of words. My wife, Amy, will ask me a simple question: "Have you seen my keys?" I hear each of her words and with effort I realize what they mean, and even grasp the sense of her question for a fleeting moment. Then I stare back at her stupidly, mutely, devoid of ideas, a totally passive blank. I can produce no verbal response, not even within my mind. Soon even what she said is gone from my memory, leaving behind only the lingering sense that she spoke to me and now awaits my reply—then I feel like a schoolboy startled from daydreaming by a teacher's unregistered geography question. Friends and family learned to recognize when I was in such a state, and not to take it personally when I seemed unwilling to speak. I was not unwilling. I was unable.

Until we experience such strange mental paralysis ourselves, many of us are liable to believe our words flow within our minds unstoppably, independently of any intermediate physiology. It simply isn't the case. A migraine is not purely or even primarily a spiritual event. At least in part, it is something going on inside the cranium. That physical causes underlie it, however ill-understood these might remain, is clear because not all migraine triggers have a psychological ingredient. Many triggers are purely physical or chemical causes, such as a rise or fall in atmospheric pressure, or a change in one's caffeine intake.

In these and other ways, ordinary experience points to some kind of dependence of our consciousness on our bodies, and specifically on our brains. This fact bears on the pressing question concerning our immortality. It even appears to settle it. If it is true that all our acts of consciousness depend on our bodies in one way or another, and our bodies are entirely mortal, then is not our consciousness, too, entirely mortal?

Human understanding is our brightest hope for something immortal in us. Many of our sensations and emotions we share with the animals, and they can be affected or even induced or suppressed by drugs. There might be certain kinds of love in us that are purely spiritual, independent of our chemical constitution, arising solely from our comprehension of something good or beautiful. This brings us back to seeing and knowing, however. If all our knowing is a purely physical activity in us, then so will be any love that arises from our knowledge of the goodness of things. Knowing is causally prior to loving and desiring. We cannot love or desire anything without first having some kind of awareness of things, however dim.

The whole question therefore comes down to your acts of knowing. If all your acts of knowing take place in your body, then your consciousness is bound to your body and will die with it. If instead some of your acts of knowing do not take place in your body, then your consciousness is in some degree independent of the existence of your body. Among your knowing powers, your intellect is the one most likely to be nonmaterial. It alone can contemplate immortality and dwell on eternal truths. If it cannot survive death, probably nothing in you can; nothing recognizably yourself will remain after the dissolution of your body.

For that reason, I will in this chapter focus on the question whether your intellect is a part of your body.

Counting Flamingos

At first the evidence seems to favor the view that your intellect is a power of your body, and of your brain in particular. Modern brain-imaging techniques enable technicians to see which parts of your brain "light up" whenever you perform certain activities. Local changes in blood flow and oxygenation in the brain are detectable by means of an fMRI (functional MRI) scanner. Such changes, as it happens, also occur in response to neural activity. The more neural activity, the more oxygen-rich blood is needed to support it. Therefore the high-resolution moving pictures of differences and changes in blood flow are effectively moving pictures of neural activity. Different patterns of activity erupt in different regions of your brain when you see, hear, remember, imagine, speak, and yes, even when you reason or think about universal truths. Why would definite regions of your brain become more active when you think about certain things unless it were precisely in those parts of your brain that you were doing your thinking?

We don't need fancy brain-imaging machines and techniques to tell us that we depend on our brains in order to think. Alteration or damage to the brain from injury, birth defects, disease, drugs, or even just lack of sleep will adversely affect our ability to understand things. A knock on the head can make it impossible to think about the Pythagorean theorem. General anesthesia can make it impossible to think about anything at all.

So why not reason like this?

If your thinking depends on the functioning of your brain,
then your brain is the organ by which you think.
But your thinking *does* depend on the functioning of your brain.
Therefore, your brain is the organ by which you think.

A hasty assumption lurks behind this reasoning. Compare it with the following:

If your seeing depends on the functioning of the light bulb,
then the light bulb is the organ by which you see.
But your seeing *does* depend on the functioning of the light bulb.
Therefore, the light bulb is the organ by which you see.

Since this conclusion is absurd, there is something wrong with this light bulb argument. But what? Clearly the if-then premise is false. Even if your act of seeing depends on the functioning of the light bulb (if you are in a room without windows, for example), that doesn't mean the light bulb is the organ by which you perform the act of seeing. The performing organ is only one kind of thing your act of seeing depends on. Seeing also depends on the presentation of a visible object. That is how the light bulb comes in. It makes things visible, exposing them to sight. It does not actually do any seeing.

The if-then premise in the argument about your brain is subject to the same analysis, and the same distinction applies. Your act of thinking depends on your brain, as we have seen. But what kind of dependence is that? Is your brain the organ that is performing your act of thinking? Or is it instead presenting you with objects to think about?

Suppose you have permitted us to observe your brain activity. You climb into an imaging machine and make yourself comfortable. A computer monitor mounted inside the machine occupies your field of view. By means of a speaker in the machine, your observers ask you to count the number of flamingos you see among all the different animals in the animated video that is about to play. As the video commences and you begin to count, your observers note a marked increase of activity in a certain region of your brain. Can they conclude that this is the part of your brain in which your act of counting takes place? Not without further evidence. It could be the part of your brain in which seeing takes place—or the part of the brain in which flamingo recognition takes place. You cannot count flamingos without flamingos to count. Your act of seeing and recognizing flamingos continuously supplies your power to count with objects to count. Maybe counting takes place in a part of your brain too, and not just seeing, recognizing, and remembering the things you are counting. Be that as it may, the fact that your act of counting continuously depends on simultaneous activity going on in some part of your brain does not prove that your act of counting takes place in that part of your brain. That part of your brain might instead be the organ performing other cognitive acts that supply your power to count with objects to count.

That is the logical loophole in the argument above about your brain. The if-then premise assumes that the only way your thinking could depend on your brain is if your brain is the organ in which thinking gets done. That is untrue. Your thinking is different from your imagining, but it depends on your imagining. Whenever you think, you use your visual or tactile or auditory imagination, maybe all of them at once. If you think in English, for example, you are expressing your ideas to yourself in imagined English words, imagined sounds. Those imagined sounds are not the same as your thoughts, since you could express the very same thoughts by different imagined sounds, different words in another language. Those words in your imagination nonetheless focus and express your thinking. The more intense your thinking, the more intense will be your simultaneous imagining in aid of your thinking. The dependence of your thinking on your brain therefore does not establish that your brain is the organ by which you think. It could also be that your brain is merely the organ by which you perform the other cognitive acts (sensing and imagining) that supply your intellect with things to think about and that focus its attention with verbal symbols.

For this reason, the simultaneity of brain activity with your thinking, and the dependence of your thinking on simultaneous brain activity, cannot prove that your intellect resides somewhere in your brain. Your intellect depends on your brain at least in one way other than as a power does on its organ. Other cognitive powers in you, such as sense and imagination, must provide your intellect with objects among which to find patterns and out of which to form universal ideas. Your sense powers are another story. They also depend on your brain for all the kinds of reasons earlier adduced (they are affected by drugs, illness, fatigue, etc.). But in their case we can be certain that they depend on your brain as the organ performing their acts of sensation. They cannot depend on it to supply them with objects to sense, since they do not get their objects from other knowing powers somewhere in your brain, but enter into direct contact with them in physical reality. Vision acquires its objects when visible things act on the eyes. Consequently, vision's dependence on the brain can only be of the performing-organ type, not the object-supply type. Your imagination is similar enough to your senses (so similar that when you are dreaming, you believe you are actually seeing and hearing) that it, too, must reside in a part of your brain.

Since your brain comprises the organs of sense and imagination, your intellect will depend on your brain at least because it depends on these powers to give it things to think about. Whether it also depends on your brain as a power on its organ remains an open question. And there is good reason to consider it on its own terms, rather than assume that it, too, must have an organ simply because your other knowing powers do. Your intellect stands worlds apart from your senses and imagination by its power to grasp the universal.

Rules of Residence in the Brain

Universal ideas are what is special about your intellect. It alone knows them. Nothing else in you can form them. So our whole question now boils down to this: Can your universal ideas be in your brain?

One way to find out is to take a closer look at your senses and imagination. Do they exhibit any decisive symptoms of being in your body? If so, we can look for those same symptoms in the case of your intellect, and if we find them, we may conclude that your intellect is a power of your brain after all. If not, that will be a powerful sign that your intellect is a nonmaterial power.

A power that belongs to a body part performs different parts of its work in different parts of the body part. The gripping power of your hand works partly in each finger, partly in the thumb, partly in the palm. If a knowing power belongs to a body part, then it will follow this rule. It will do part of its work over here, another part over there, in different parts of some body part. Consequently, the chief symptom of a cognitive power belonging to a body part is that its work will also be distributed in space. It will form cognitive representations that are divisible into spatially distinct parts.

My meaning will become plainer with the following considerations. Whenever we know or perceive things, we produce internal representations of them. We usually do this so effortlessly that it sometimes takes a little reflection to realize that our seeing a tree, for example, involves constructing a visual likeness of it within ourselves. In the classroom I have sometimes encountered students who doubt this, who think they simply see things "out there" without forming within themselves any visual representation of them. I ask them to go cross-eyed a little. Now they see two of everything. Why is that? Is it because the number of things in the room has suddenly doubled? If not, then the two appearances of each thing must be due to something going on within my cross-eyed students, not in the objects around them. Or I ask them to press (gently) near their eyes with their fingers. When they do, the whole room appears to them to jiggle. Unless this gentle pressing with their fingers really caused the whole room to jiggle, it must be instead that they are jiggling something else that resembles the room. This is the visual likeness they are producing in themselves when they see, and by means of which they see.

These representations of things that your knowing powers form can tell us a lot about the powers themselves. In particular, when the representations exhibit spatial relationships to each other, that is because they exist in something made up of spatially distinct parts.

In other words, sensory representations are spatially distinct because they exist in different parts of a sense organ.

For example, the visual representations of things that you produce in yourself always form a kind of "field". They are spread out in a kind of space. The grass occupies this lower portion of your visual field, then a tree stands above the grass, and the blue sky comes in at the top. Things are above and below each other, to the left and right of each other, in your field of vision. No doubt this spatial arrangement in your vision corresponds in some way to the spatial arrangement of things in reality outside you. Your visual field is nonetheless a work of your vision, something it made within itself, in more or less faithful imitation of those exterior realities. The spatial extension (the spreading out this way and that way) of your visual field is a necessary consequence of its existing in some portion of your brain, since your brain is itself a thing extended in space, having a shape and size. Since a movie screen has diverse parts and is spread out in space, any image cast on it will also have diverse parts and be spread out in space. Your brain is like the movie screen, so that any representations it forms must have parts in different regions of space.

Touch also forms spatially related representations of things. This is especially clear in the case of your tactile sense of the shape and position of your body. Your feeling of the upper part of your body is a different feeling from that of the lower part of your body, and those two feelings are also spatially distinct. Where one feeling stops, the other begins. If you trace your finger along your arm, even with your eyes shut, your tactile impressions of the different positions of your finger are different, and they exist in a spatial order that somehow corresponds to the order of parts in your arm.

The most obvious relationships among your auditory impressions are temporal ones. Your hearing of this note in the song comes after hearing the prior one, but before hearing the next one. Nevertheless, spatial impressions also exist among your auditory impressions, even if they are not as striking. At the very least, your hearing of things in your left ear has a distinct "from the left" quality, and your hearing of things in your right ear is "from the right", the basic assumption behind stereo.

Your imagination exhibits the same symptom of being something spread out in a part of your body (presumably your brain). In your visual imagination, as much as in your vision itself, the image of the tree stands above that of the grass and beneath that of the sky. Or imagine a square. Now, holding on to that square in your mind, imagine also a circle at the same time. Do the two have any spatial relationships to one another? Yes, necessarily so. Either the square and the circle are outside each other, or one contains the other, or they overlap, for example. And if they are outside each other, then they are either on a level with each other, or one is higher up than the other. And the square is either equal to the circle in area, or else it is larger or smaller. Since your imagination takes up room in your body, residing in some region of your brain, its representations of things must be distributed in the different portions of that region, and so those representations will bear spatial relationships to one another.

Sense powers and imagination are powers of your brain, and they act like it. Each of these cognitive powers forms representations that are divisible into parts bearing spatial relationships to one another. That is the telltale sign that these powers exist in some organ of your body, and form their representations of things in it.

Does your intellect also exhibit this symptom of being in some part of your body? Do the representations of things that it forms bear spatial relationships to one another? The representations it forms of things are its universal ideas of them. Think, for example, of what a square is. Now, holding on to that universal idea, think also of what a circle is. Do these two things you are thinking of bear any spatial relationships to one another? Is "what a square is" above or below or to the left of "what a circle is"? A ridiculous question. These things have no "where" to them, and bear to one another no spatial relationships at all. Does "what a square is" contain more area than "what a circle is", or are they equal in area, or is "what a circle is" the bigger of the two? An equally fatuous question. The universal idea of a circle has no size, just as the definition expressing it mentions no particular size. Consequently the universal idea of a circle and that of a square can have no relationships of size.

Not even your ideas of spatial relationships have spatial relationships to each other. Are your ideas of *parallel* and *perpendicular* parallel to one another? Or perpendicular? Or askew? All nonsense. Or what about the universal truth that "every triangle can be circumscribed by a circle"? Where is that in relation to the truth that "whatever contains a breadbox also contains what is in the bread-box"? Do these two truths about spatial relationships overlap some-how, or is one of them to the left of the other? Does one sit on top of the other or contain the other? Meaningless questions. These truths do not present themselves to your mind as things that have spatial relationships of any kind. They are quite unlike a circle and a square in your imagination.

The one symptom common to all your other cognitive powers, declaring them to be distributed throughout certain parts of your body (or your brain), is noticeably missing in the case of your intel-lect. The representations it forms are not spatially distinguished from or related to one another.

Your intellect does not behave like a power that exists in an organ of your body. And that's because it isn't one.

Bare Naked Circularity

Universals seem to be rather picky about where they exist. They do not exist in any old place, but exist only in your mind. Why is that? What prevents "what a circle is" from existing in a universal way on a sheet of paper, for example?

Consider the circle on this page (call it C). Since C is a circle, of course "what a circle is" must also belong to C (or else it wouldn't be a circle). Circle C is not purely "what a circle is", though. It is a whole bunch of other things besides. It is, for example, white, located on this sheet of paper, and smaller than a bicycle tire. None of those things can be part of what a circle is, since none of them is common to all circles. So our friend C is not just "what a circle is", bare naked circularity. It is that plus a lot of other things that do not pertain to its circularity.

Circle C is just one failed attempt to get pure, universal circularity onto a sheet of paper. Can we do better? Can we get pure circularity drawn on a sheet of paper somehow? The moment we grasp what that would mean, we see that it is impossible. The mere act of putting "what a circle is" on this sheet of paper is enough to individualize it, giving us not pure circularity, but "this circle, right here", together with a host of incidental features none of which belongs to "what a circle is" as such.

Why is this? What is it about a piece of paper that foils our every attempt to get "what a circle is" onto it without turning it into "this particular circle, different from all others"? Why can't a piece of paper receive "what a circle is" by itself, universally, without insisting on showing us individual circles?

The problem is not something unique to paper. The same holds true for a chalkboard, a computer monitor, or human vision or imagination. All of these things alike can host individual circles, but can never receive just "what a circle is" by itself apart from individual circles. They are all incapable of supporting pure universals like that. What common feature in these things prevents them from accepting "what a circle is" without individualizing it? What forces them to make individual circles instead?

Dimensions. Each of these things—the paper, the chalkboard, human vision and imagination—has dimensions. Each has length, width, and depth. Each of these things receives "what a circle is" by admitting this shape into its own dimensions. A sheet of paper has a surface, and that surface has the two dimensions of length and breadth. Its way of receiving "what a circle is" lies in the possibility of putting circularity here or there on its surface. But whenever we do that, we are necessarily making an individual circle.

Consider the two individual circles depicted below. They are the same shape and size. So why are they not just the very same circle? What makes them two distinct objects?

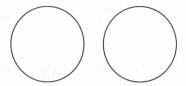

There might be many differences between them, but the fundamental difference is that each is printed on a different bit of the surface of this page. If it weren't for that difference, there would be only one circle. If we cut the two circles out, they would still be two different circles, and this would still be due to the difference in the bits of paper that had received the same circular form.

"What a circle is" can become distinct individual circles only in this way. Individual circles are born when some material with dimensions repeatedly receives circularity, like identical cookies stamped out of a sheet of cookie dough. Conversely, circularity cannot enter into a material thing (a thing having dimensions) without forming an individual circle. We can sum the matter up in a little formula: "What a circle is" + "this quantitative stuff that can receive it" = "this circle". This is nothing special about circularity. The same goes for other definable things about which we can form universal ideas, but which exist outside our minds only in particular individuals. For example, "What a dog is" + "this quantitative stuff that can receive it" = "this dog". We won't get an individual dog until we get "what a dog is" to exist in materials that have dimensions, and we can't put "what a dog is" into such materials without also getting an individual dog out of the deal.

Precisely what makes a definable, repeatable, communicable kind of thing—a nature or essence such as circularity or "what a dog is"—into a particular individual is the placing of it into a receptive material that has dimensions and spatial properties. Things with specific dimensions and spatial properties are necessarily individual things, and they consequently individualize any nature they receive, whether it be circularity or the canine nature. This means that anything having dimensions and spatial properties will be utterly incapable of receiving a general nature while leaving it general. Therefore, nothing with spatial characteristics (such as your senses or imagination) can preserve universality in the kinds of things it receives and represents.

On the other hand, your intellect is perfectly capable of representing things in a universal manner. That is its specialty. When your mind forms its universal idea of "what a circle is", circularity does not become an individual circle. Instead, it stays universal. It remains purely "what a circle is" without any extraneous additions. Your idea of what a circle is does not include anything that would force it to become this or that circle.

Your intellect is itself an individual thing, of course. It is yours, and not mine. And your idea of what circles are is your idea and not mine, and maybe you had that idea in your mind before I ever did. But even though your idea of circularity is your own individual idea and no one else's, it is still universal as far as circles are concerned. It is an individual *idea*, but not an individual *circle*.

Putting together these observations, we can now reason to one of the most beautiful conclusions of philosophy. Here are the steps:

Anything having dimensions must individualize what it receives.
The human intellect does not individualize what it receives.
Therefore the human intellect is not a thing that has dimensions.

Your intellect can receive "what a circle is" without turning it into an individual circle. Nothing that has dimensions can do that. Your intellect, therefore, is not a thing that has dimensions. That means it is neither an organ in your body, nor a power distributed through the parts of some organ of your body. It is a nonbodily, nonmaterial power. Unlike all your other knowing powers, your intellect is not a property of your brain at all.

Why We Need Brains

And now a lovely corollary falls into our hands: you are something much more than a machine. Our bodies in many ways resemble machines, or rather our machines embody many principles that nature (including human nature) has employed before us. Consequently, we more easily discover the likenesses between ourselves and our machines than the differences.

One general difference is that we know things. However much our sensory equipment might resemble a computer program, and even operate on similar principles to some extent, the sensory simulations of the world that we produce in our brains differ fundamentally from the images on a computer monitor. The digital file may bear an analogy to certain sounds and images, and by running the right program a computer can reproduce those images on a monitor and the sounds in a speaker. But the movie is no more seen or heard (or enjoyed) by the computer than it is seen by a movie screen on which it is projected, or heard by the air that vibrates with the sound of it. A mere computing machine does not take its input or its output to be "representations of things", but as far as it is concerned (if it can be said to be "concerned") all the things it processes are just its own things, its own internal goings-on, not somehow likenesses of other things. A chess program does not say to itself, "Aha! these incoming signals go with a specific chess move that my opponent is making against me." It merely redistributes electrons in accord with the pathways and rules built into it, just as the wiring in your house does not take the currents running through it to be "about" something else, and the plumbing in your walls does not take the water coursing through it to be "of" something. Regarding input as somehow "about something else" is irrelevant to the functioning of a computer program. And there is no reason to attribute such an attitude to a computer, except to amuse ourselves.[1]

Our senses are different. When you see a house, you are not devoid of awareness as the wiring in your house is, or as a computer program is. Nor do you experience the appearance of the house as something existing purely within yourself, or as a bunch of electric input corresponding to nothing. Instead, you experience the shape of a thing foreign to yourself, other than yourself—it is not just "a shape", but it is the shape *of that house*. That is the great glory of seeing, and the whole point of it. That other things somehow in this way get to reexist in you is precisely the miracle of knowing. There are those who doubt that things outside their minds ever correspond in any way to the images and thoughts they form of them, but we will not here lose time over these poor (and uncommon) people.

Your sense powers already raise you up above the machines. These powers bring other things into your inner world and leave them recognizable to you as other things, not mere "input" to be run through an unconsciously performed process whose output is of interest only to someone else.

Still, your sense powers reside in certain organs of your body, and they produce their sensory representations by employing certain properties of matter. Thanks to imaging techniques such as fMRI, it

---

[1] I suppose one day we might have difficulty telling certain programs apart from people, at the rate things are going. But that makes no difference to the unbridgeable difference between a person and a computer (or a simulation of a person). A polygon inscribed in a circle can be given so many sides that it is impossible to tell it apart from the circle itself—but this ability of the polygon to simulate a curve, and our inability to tell the difference, does not change the fact that "straight" and "curved" are categorically other, and not reducible to each other.

is possible to map the image of something you see to the neurons at the back of your brain. However oddly distorted and immersed in utter darkness that "image" on the brain may be, it is your visual representation to yourself of the visible object. It is also the product of the electrical and chemical activity of your neurons, and it has shape, size, and location.

Universals are another story entirely. There can be no mapping of these on the brain. They do not exist in your brain at all, any more than on a sheet of paper. Certain symbols of universal things, such as your visual images of printed words on a page or imagined words in your mind, can occupy space in your brain. But the universals themselves that these symbols signify must be free of particular spatial relationships to other things, something impossible to avoid in a brain. Electrical circuitry can do many things, but it cannot form anything free of spatial limitations and individualizing conditions. It is in principle powerless to form a universal idea of anything. You have many things in common with the machines. You nonetheless differ from them categorically and permanently, in kind and not in degree.

The nonmaterial nature of your mind emphasizes your difference from the other animals in the world. Your intelligence differs from that of the animal as the universal from the particular, since no animal can form a universal thought. But the universal differs from the particular as the infinite does from the finite, since every universal enables its possessor to know things about an infinity of individuals. We can now further conclude that your intellect differs from the mind of an animal as the nonmaterial from the material. This is no mere difference of degree. You are much more than "a perfectly good animal", and to call you the best of the animals is a gross understatement. There is something in you that goes entirely beyond what it means to be an animal.

Although your intellect is not your brain or even in your brain, it nevertheless depends on it. A knock on the head affects thinking, even (or especially) thinking about universal truths.

But in what way? There were two possibilities. Your intellect depends on your brain either (1) as the organ in which it exists *and* as the organ of other cognitive powers supplying it with its materials for thinking or (2) *only* as the organ of other cognitive powers supplying it with its materials for thinking.

The first of these alternatives is impossible. Your intellect is not a power in your brain or in any bodily organ. It is incorporeal. Accordingly, it does not depend on your brain or on any part of your body as a power depends on an organ to host it. Instead, your intellect is to your brain as your sense of sight is to visible objects. Without visible objects, your sense of sight can exist, but it will have nothing to do. Without your brain, your intellect can exist, but it will have nothing to do. Your intellect depends on your brain because your brain is the organ of *other* cognitive powers supplying your intellect with its objects—with the raw materials out of which to extract universal content while leaving aside the peculiarities of the individual things represented in sense or imagination.

The dependence is quite real, and quite strong. When your sensory activity languishes, your intellectual activity suffers correspondingly. When all your sensing and imagining are shut down, as in a dreamless sleep, all your thinking about universals ceases as well. In relation to your powers of sense and imagination, your intellect is like a judge who relies entirely on witnesses not because they will pass judgment or hand down rulings, but because they alone can supply the matter to which laws may be applied and about which decisions may be rendered. Prevent witnesses from entering the court, and all rulings cease. That is not because witnesses are the ones who hand down rulings. Prevent sensation, imagination, and brain activity, and all your understanding of universal truths must stop. That is not because your senses, imagination, and brain are the things that understand universals.

Your senses depend on your brain only for their power, not to supply them with their objects, which they contact directly. Your imagination depends on your brain both for its own power and for other powers that supply it with its objects (you cannot normally imagine qualities without having sensed them first in some way). Your intellect, on the other hand, depends on your brain only for its objects, not for its power. There is an interesting symmetry among your powers.

You are shaping up to be something truly astonishing. And more than a little strange. You have a body, but we now see that this is not the whole story about you. You have a nonbodily, nonmaterial side to you as well. Our investigation into your nature remains incomplete. Having partly unraveled the tangled question about your mind's relationship to your brain, we are confronted with a new question: What kind of being are you, to have both a body, but also an incorporeal mind?

6

A Life-and-Death Question

The source of intellectual activity is also the form of the human body.

—Thomas Aquinas, *Summa Theologiae*

Night School

The summer of 1991 was a memorable one for me. In previous summers I had earned dribs and drabs of college tuition money in my New Hampshire hometown while cleaning the halls and desks of my old high school—not the most pleasant or most profitable job. But I had little choice since the school I was attending let out later than most. Other college kids had snapped up the better-paying jobs by the time my summer break began. When 1991 rolled around, the year before my senior year, I'd had enough of scraping gum off the undersides of desks and decided to try my luck elsewhere. Having grown up in small-town New England, I was fascinated by big cities. And I knew some people in Chicago. So I planned to spend my summer there, hoping to earn more money in a more exciting way, and also to experience some new things.

And I did. A lawyer friend let me live rent-free in his walk-up attic, and with his assistance I found a cushy job working as a typist for an insurance company in downtown Chicago. I was assigned to the "field office planning" department, which had advertised an opening. I must have been hired to fill a superfluous position in order to spend the surplus in the department's budget (so that it would not be decreased in the next quarter). Once a week or so, someone would sheepishly ask me to type a half-page letter, and when I brought it back five minutes later he would invariably be amazed and profusely grateful. That was pretty much all I had to do. The rest of the time I spent reading. I read all of *War and Peace* while sitting at my desk, occasionally looking out on the sweeping view of the city through my window, waiting for the little typing jobs that practically never came. During lunch breaks, which sometimes stretched to two hours, I would take long walks through the architectural gallery that is downtown Chicago. Each day my rambling would take me to a different skyscraper, where I would walk in to explore its atrium and compare it with all the other ostentatious lobbies I had seen. I got to know the downtown area pretty well in this way.

There were scarier and less glamorous parts of Chicago, too, and I also got a taste of these. Through some personal connections I got a chance to spend a night at a firehouse and go for ride-alongs. I arrived at the station around dinner time. Over plates of spaghetti, all the firefighters were eager to explain to me that I was a sheltered and spoiled college boy, with no real experience and no adequate appreciation of how good I had it in life—about which things, time would teach me, they were exactly right. My time with them would be like "night school" for me, they said. They began to provide me with their own brand of education by telling me horror stories about the things they had seen in the line of duty. Just a week before, they had been called to a railway accident in which a man's arm had been severed. A week before that, they had assisted in fighting a chemical fire so hot it had melted the windshield on their ladder truck.

As the evening progressed, some of the crew settled down in front of the TV. Others turned in early, hoping to get as much sleep as possible before the inevitable interruptions began. I was lying half-asleep on a cot when the first call came in around eleven o'clock. It was exciting to gear up and ride out in the cab of an enormous truck, and to run red lights with impunity, our sirens blaring and horns honking. But the reason for the call was not very exciting. A trash chute on the outside of a building had caught fire. That was the only call for the firefighters that night.

The paramedics, on the other hand, responded to a dozen calls or more, and I rode along with them. One of these calls, sometime around one in the morning, brought us to a sixteen-story high-rise, one of several that formed a district of low-income, government-subsidized housing. To prevent me from attracting too much attention to myself, the paramedics made me wear a coat just like theirs.

They gave me some brief instructions before we entered the building: don't say anything, don't touch anything or anyone, stay right next to them. Done and done. The first surprise came the moment we walked through the front doors. There were no lights on anywhere. All the light I could see was that of the paramedics' flashlights. We got into an elevator with one other person, presumably a resident, whom the paramedics engaged in a brief exchange of semiverbal greetings. The air was heavy with the odor of urine. In the dim and spastic circles thrown by the flashlights, it seemed to me that the walls of the elevator were swelling or pulsating somehow. Then I understood what I was seeing: black cascades of cockroaches pouring out from cracks in the walls of the elevator car. Our stop was somewhere around the twelfth floor. There was no light in the hall except what we brought with us, and no doors hanging in the entrances of any of the apartments, only hanging bed sheets and towels. I stuck close to my guides as we held aside a towel and entered the residence that had placed the call. In the moving beams of light I caught glimpses of motionless figures lying here and there on the floor—no furniture to speak of; some stained mattresses; plenty of garbage. To this day I do not much understand that world into which I had stepped, but it was an eye-opener. Why were people living this way? What had gone wrong? Was there any way to fix it? I wondered what my life would have been like, what I would have turned out to be, had I been born and raised in such a place. The paramedics tended to a person suspected of overdosing (the reason for our call), but found he was responsive and in no imminent danger. We were soon back outside in the night air, to my immense relief.

On another ride, we arrived at a scene crowded with police cars and picked up a man with a gunshot wound. We were accompanied by a police escort to the hospital where I was stunned to see the police had handcuffed our patient to the rail of his hospital bed.

But of all the calls that night, the one that stood out most to me brought us to the house of a woman whose elderly father had lost consciousness after a heart attack. We arrived. I stood at the curb by the ambulance (or "bus") and waited, as I had been told to do. Moments later, out came the two paramedics with the old man on a gurney, attended by his distraught daughter. As the paramedics were busy lifting him on board the bus, the daughter, weeping, tugged my coat sleeve (I was still wearing a paramedic's coat) and begged me to tell her whether her father was going to die or not—she was a Catholic, she said, and needed to know. I nervously told her the simple truth that I did not know, and suddenly felt guilty for being such a useless presence in her tragic moment. Why was I there? As some sort of voyeur, satisfying my curiosity without lifting a finger to help anyone? It was partly for this reason that I did not go back for any more "education" after that night.

I was to ride in back with the patient and one of the paramedics. The other slammed the rear doors shut and got behind the wheel. One of the rear windows formed a frame around the old man's daughter. She stood grieving in the street in front of her house, her figure shrinking into the distance as we rode off to the hospital. The paramedic beside me was looking at his charge and shaking his head. He gave me a stethoscope to put on and made me listen to the patient's heart. I had listened to hearts in stethoscopes a few times before, but had never heard anything like what I heard that time. It was all wrong. Erratic. No discernible rhythm. "When a heart sounds like that," he said, "it means in a couple of minutes it won't ever make a sound again."

He was right. Before we arrived at the hospital, the man's shallow breathing had stopped entirely. A handful of minutes later I stood in a well-lit room that smelled of fresh coffee, staring at the man's bare feet sticking out from under a blanket that covered his face. The paramedics were flirting with a pretty nurse while filling out paper work. It struck me as an indignity for his bare feet to be left sticking out like that. It also felt wrong that I should know he was dead before his daughter did—I, who did not even know his name.

That was the first time in my life I saw a human being die. I was struck by the slightness of difference between the motionless, unconscious, breathing man, and the motionless, unconscious, unbreathing body—but also by the vastness of the difference. The difference between breathing and not breathing is slight to the eyes and ears, but shocking to our perception of the natures of things, to our awareness of what is in our presence. The change took place in the blink of an eye. The decline in health had perhaps lasted for years. But the actual end of this man was a sharp nick in time, dividing *human being* from *corpse*.

What was it that had departed from this man's body? What was it that produced this radical change by its presence and absence? Why was there a human being one moment, and then just a body the next? What had gone?

The Root of All Your Powers

The questions above are the next ones that we must now ask about ourselves, about you, if we are to answer the great question about the mortal and the immortal in you. Our discovery of the nonbodily nature of your intellect brought us much closer to an answer to that great question. But it also prompted this new one: Your intellect is not a power of your body. What, then, is your intellect's point of connection to your body? If it has none, you are split in two. And if that is true, it seems you would be like one of the walking dead, a ghost haunting a corpse as it might haunt a house. You and your body would not be one thing, but one thing inhabiting another thing quite distinct from itself. That just isn't you. You are a single being constituted somehow of your body on the one hand and your intellectual nature on the other. Until we understand better how these two things go together in you, we will not be able to understand what death is, or whether anything of you can survive it.

So let's make a fresh start in our investigation by asking, what is it that makes your body to be alive and to be you? By *being alive* and *being you* I mean "being able to do the things you do", such as walk and talk and think and cough and yawn and stretch and see and hear and eat and drink and grow and breathe and any other of your doings and undergoings. What is it in your body that endows you with all the powers for performing such activities, and which departs at death?

As soon as we ask that question, we see that we have not yet asked it well enough. We are looking for something hard to discover, and not known to most people. Our question, however, does not yet drive us toward such a thing, but requires only the most mundane of answers. What is it in your body that enables you to see? Your eyes, of course. To walk? Why, your legs. To breathe? Your lungs. And so on. Each one of your living acts (with the exception of understanding) is made possible by various organs and organ systems of your body.

Well, whoop-de-doo! A fifth grader knows that. Not to worry. A minor adjustment will separate our question from the fifth-grade variety. We need only add the word *primary*. What is the *primary* principle of life and of living activity in your body?

Here is what I mean. We do not find in you a random assortment of mutually independent powers. Instead, we can discern among your powers a clear order of dependence. And that order points to something primary in you that is responsible for all those powers of yours.

This is easier to see if we round up all your powers in a small number of major categories. We have spent a lot of time talking about your intellectual acts, and these are special, since they do not take place in your body at all. For that reason, your intellect belongs in a special category of its own (together with any other nonmaterial powers you might possess). We have also talked about another category of powers in you, your sense powers. These are in your body. They include your external senses such as sight and touch, but also some number of internal senses such as your imagination, your memory, another that we have called your "universal sense", and perhaps others. We never did take a thorough inventory of these. You also possess powers of desiring that follow on and somehow use sense perception. There is your ability to feel hunger or thirst, for example, but also your power of feeling anger or fear or any other emotion. You also have the power to move your body in response to your desires and feelings—to reach, grab, walk, turn your head and make facial expressions, and so on. You possess still another major group of powers that we have hardly talked about at all, the furthest from your intellectual powers. I mean your powers of taking nourishment, growing, healing from injuries, fighting off pathogens, and the like. These are your vegetative powers.

And that seems to be it. Every power you possess is either an intellectual power, a motor power, a desiring power, a sense power, or a vegetative power. Congratulations! You are the proud owner of five major categories of powers. These kinds of powers are not randomly associated in you. There is a definite order among them. Your most basic and necessary powers are your vegetative ones, and these were at work in you first. Next you developed your sense powers by growing your organs of sense while still in the womb. Your ability to desire things came together with your ability to feel pleasure and pain, but your sense powers enjoy a certain priority over your desiring powers nonetheless, since you can't love or hate things, desire them or wish to avoid them, without first being aware of them in some way. You began to use and develop your motor powers later still. If you ever learned to control your hand movements and to walk, you did so long after and with dependence on sensing and wanting things (you can't reach for a doughnut if you are without any sense or desire). Finally, your intellectual powers came into full use. Barring any special condition or injury, you reached the age of reason after learning to walk and run, and to this day you continue to develop your understanding of things although you have thoroughly mastered your ordinary motor skills. Your intellect requires long sense experience of things in order to encounter its objects and develop fully, so you must be able to use your motor powers in order to acquire food and other necessities and also to experience the world interactively before your mind can flourish (or, if you cannot get what you need for yourself, someone else who is able to get around must help you).

So your powers develop and come into use in a definite order, the later ones depending on the earlier and more basic ones. The order, going from those most dependent on others to those most basic and least dependent on others, is this:

1. Intellectual powers
2. Motor powers
3. Desiring powers
4. Sense powers
5. Vegetative powers

The way we find some of these powers in other kinds of creatures confirms this order. Just as your vegetative functions can continue even when you are totally unconscious, so we can find living things that nourish themselves and grow and self-repair but which are without sensation, such as a cactus. Whatever creature does have sensation, at least the sense of touch, will be able to experience pleasures and pains and therefore desires too, however primitively, but the desiring will follow upon the sensing, and so the power of sense is still more basic. And just as you cannot walk without sensation and desire, but you can desire things without being able to walk, so too we find some animals with desires but with little power of self-motion, and no ability to move from one location to another, as in the case of a barnacle or a coral polyp or some other form of sessile life. Finally, we can find all four of the lower categories of powers in certain living things that possess no intellectual life, as in a starfish. The order in the list above is from the rarest to the most common of powers among living things, and also from the most dependent to the most fundamental and independent.

Your powers naturally develop in a certain order. This one-way order in your powers is like an arrow pointing back to some first principle in you, some fundamental root of all your powers. What is this common root? What is the primary and most basic thing in you that gives rise to all your special powers in their natural order? That is our question.

The difference between life and death already tells us something important about this primary source of all your human powers: it must be something existing *in your body* somehow. After all, it produces many powers that are in your body, such as your power to sense, to move around, to desire, to take food, and to heal from wounds. Moreover, the primary cause of your living activities is the principal thing making your body to be alive and to be you instead of just a corpse. And that special difference is something in your body, since your being alive is also (at least in part) in your body.

So now we have our question: What is the primary thing in your body that makes it to be alive, to be you, and to have all these various powers? That is what we want to know.

Rather than take random shots in the dark, we should adopt a method in order to approach this difficult question. Let's begin with the kind of answer that most readily suggests itself to people, the most natural guess based on the kinds of evidence available to all people in all times and places. This first guess almost certainly will not get us to the truth right away. Most likely it will be a rather primitive answer. Why bother with it, then? Because at least it should be easy enough to discover. And then we will have something definite to work from. By finding fault with our first guess, definite ideas will suggest themselves to us about how to improve on it. If we follow this way of refining our guesses as the facts about you will require, we should be following a more or less definite path to the truth, and once we arrive there we will no longer have to guess.

But what is the most natural guess? What do we most readily propose as the primary reason your body is alive and you? What does the most generally available evidence suggest?

First Guess: *Your Breath*

Now don't laugh. We expected the first answer to our question to be wrong and even in some way primitive, and breath is just such an answer. Nonetheless, it is also the answer that first suggests itself in our ordinary, prephilosophical, prescientific experience, and we may hope it will prove a useful starting point.

If you see someone on his deathbed, alive one moment, gone the next, what is the most obvious thing that departed from his body? Breath. He breathed his last. And then there is the classic test for life. Hold a mirror to the person's face. If it fogs up, that is a sign of life. Also, barring an especially violent death, a person's fresh corpse looks very much like the person, in most ways. All the same parts are there, and in the same arrangements. Only the subtle and basic movement of breathing is gone. No visible substance has departed. Very well, then, what departed at death must be an invisible substance—like air. At first blush, it seems the difference between a living body and a dead one is that the living one has breath in it. Air is the animating principle!

So it is that many peoples of the past believed (and maybe some of the present still believe) that the life principle in our bodies is some airy substance, "the breath of life". Even some early philosophers (before Socrates) believed that air or wind was the animating principle in a living body. They were encouraged when they saw that air can, apparently, move around by itself in the form of a breeze. It even "animates" the curtains when the window is left open. The Latin words *anima* and *spiritus* first meant "breath" or "breeze", as did the Greek word ψῡχή (*psuché*, from which we derive our word *psychology*), all of which words came later to mean "the breath of life" or just "life" or even "soul" or "spirit".

Whatever elements of truth this ancient opinion might contain, it is certainly more wrong than right. Air is not alive, for one thing. It does not really move itself around. Other causes, such as the sun, cause air to move and produce wind.

We are searching for the thing that, when it is present in a body, makes it to be alive. Air cannot be the answer. If air were the precise thing that, when present in something, made it to be alive, then everything with air in it would be alive, including an inflated red party balloon. Anything could be "animated". In reality, only special types of things—bodies with organs and organ systems—can be alive, and the idea that air is the animating principle does not account for this rather obvious and important fact. Besides, a dead body has clearly lost the ability to breathe, the ability to *use* air even if air is breathed back into it by someone else. And air is not the first principle causing someone to be able to use air. Consequently, air is not the first principle of life.

Just as we hoped, however, we are not coming away from this first guess empty-handed. We do not yet have our answer, but we see quite clearly that air-breathing equipment, and vital organs in general, are closer to the truth than "air" is. Let's make this our second guess.

Second Guess: *Your Vital Organs*

All our organs are principles by which we carry out living activities. But not all of them are "vital"—that is, things without which we cannot live at all. We can live without eyes, hands, legs, tongues, spleens, and many other organs, even if life without such parts is a struggle. We cannot live long at all without livers. We cannot live long without kidneys (or substitutes for kidneys, such as dialysis machines). We can have and use hearts without having hands, but we cannot long keep and use our hands without having hearts (whether natural or artificial). As do our powers, so too do our organs exist in an order of dependence pointing back to something primary. And our primary organs are our vital ones.

Might this be our answer? Could it be that the primary cause of life and of living powers in your body is some primary vital organ or organ system in you? Your brain, perhaps, or else your heart and lungs and circulatory system?

No doubt your vital organs are closer to what we are looking for than air is. Vital organs are unique to living things, and explain why some of them, such as ourselves, need air to live, and are able to use it. We have advanced a little toward the truth.

And yet your vital organs cannot be the fundamental principle that we seek. Vital organs and organ systems are not the primary principle of life in you. Your vital organs themselves, after all, have life in them (your life, in fact). And they perform living activities, too, which they can also lose the power to perform. So there must be something special in them, something that they can lose, which elusive something is the cause of their ability to live and to function. Just as we asked, "What is the difference between a living body and a corpse?", we can also ask, "What is the difference between a living, functioning, vital organ, and a similar-looking, nonfunctioning part of a corpse?"

Everyone knows that at least some vital organs can be transplanted. Their shelf life between donor and recipient is rather short, however. If the time of expiration goes by before a successful transplant, the organ is no longer viable. It is dead. What happened to the poor organ? How is it different now from the way it was when it was still "viable"?

We might be tempted to think that your liver and other vital organs are alive and possess their special powers because they include a special life-giving material in their makeup, a primary vital ingredient. When this special vitalizing stuff is in them, they live and do their thing. When it dissipates or runs out, your vital organs die, and you die. This idea is similar to the first idea that air is the stuff of life, although this new idea makes your life stuff more a part of you, a special ingredient or element in you, whether your blood or something subtler.

But this is not the truth, either. Your liver produces some specifically human substances, but these in turn are invariably made of nonspecial substances, substances found in nonliving things as well as in you. Your body contains no special ultimate ingredients, no life-specific elements that cannot also be found in inanimate bodies. Living things and their parts are ultimately made of the very same chemical elements as nonliving things are. Not all the elements on the periodic table enter into your constitution, but all the ones in your constitution are found on the periodic table and also occur in dead or inanimate things. If we segregated all the atoms in a foolish volunteer and placed them in bottles according to type, we would end up with bottles of elements just like those in a chemical supply warehouse. If we dumped them all into a large kettle and stirred them around, we might get a nasty mess, but we would not get back our foolish volunteer, nor any of his organs, not even dead ones.

Why not? What is missing, if we have all the necessary ingredients? Here we must take a moment to consider a general question, since the answer to it will equip us for settling the question about your vital organs in particular. The general question begins with a simple observation: if we have all the ingredients for some particular kind of thing, we do not necessarily have that thing. Why not? What is missing?

A recipe involves more than just a list of ingredients. What makes a Martini, for example? Gin and dry vermouth. But does that mean any glass containing gin and dry vermouth is a Martini? A gallon of gin and a drop of vermouth is not a Martini. The right ratio makes all the difference.

In general, if a specific thing is made of ingredients, materials, or components that are capable of being lots of different things, there must be something besides the ingredients themselves that is the reason why they become this specific thing rather than that. In the case of a Martini, the specifying something-or-other is a particular ratio. But it is not always a ratio. Consider these two sentences:

Gordon cheated on Tessa.
Tessa cheated on Gordon.

They say quite different things. And yet they contain exactly the same words the same number of times each. In this case, the decisive difference is not the ratios in which the words occur, but the order of the words.

In still other cases, it is neither a ratio nor a specific order that makes certain components into this rather than that. Picture a pile of bricks and a mound of wet mortar. That's just a mess. But the very same materials in the very same ratios can also be a brick wall. What's the difference? Not order, exactly. The bricks that make up a brick wall don't have to be used in some special order, like words in a sentence. But they do have to be placed in some special arrangement.

Sometimes a simple shape is what causes a material to be this rather than that. The same mass of bronze can be either a statue of Abe

Lincoln, or instead a statue of Zeus, or else a thousand little bronze tennis trophies. The difference is all in the shape or shapes into which we cast the bronze.

All these examples happen to be artificial things, but the same sort of pattern exists in nature. Not just Martinis and other mixed drinks, but chemical compounds, too, are specified in part by the ratios in their ingredients. The difference between CO and CO_2 is not a difference in the types of elements they contain, but in the ratios in which those same elements occur. And the difference is not trivial— the difference between CO_2 and CO in your living room could spell the difference between life and death.

Quite diverse things can play the role of a specifying feature that causes certain materials to be this rather than that. This diversity makes it difficult to settle on a single name by which to call them all, and yet it is desirable to find one, since they all play similar roles in the things they constitute. When the same materials can be many things, sometimes what makes them into one thing rather than another is a ratio, other times it is an order, other times a shape, other times something else. What common name shall we use to speak about such things?

The philosophers call them *forms*. And so do you, actually. At least, I do not imagine you would shy away from saying that a different word order *forms* a different sentence out of the same words. What *forms* a pile of bricks and mortar into a brick wall is their arrangement in courses. The shape of Zeus *forms* a lump of bronze into a statue of Zeus. The word *form* seems to mean first of all a shape or arrangement of parts, and then it broadens out to mean anything at all that we add to materials or ingredients in order to make them (*form* them) into some specific thing.

Not every such specifying feature is a shape. A ratio is not a shape, for example. So why do we use the word *form*, a word that first of all means shape, to name all these diverse kinds of specifying features in things? One reason is that shape is the thing that most obviously and commonly makes materials into specific artificial things. The very same mass of steel can become a fork, a spoon, a knife, a picture frame, or a thousand other things with different names and definitions. What is it in the steel that is responsible for its being one of these rather than any of the others? Primarily its shape.

Another reason why the word *form* stands out as a good name for what specifies things is that we recognize and name different natural things most of all by their distinctive shapes. If I hold up a card with a swatch of brown color on it and ask you to identify the specific animal the color is associated with, you would struggle. If instead I hold up a card with the outline of a horse on it, you recognize the specific type of animal instantly.

So whenever something added to certain materials, ingredients, or components makes them be one specific thing rather than any of the other things they are capable of becoming, we may call the specifying addition the *form* of the thing.

The forms we have considered so far are rather inert, such as the form of a brick wall. Not all forms are like that. Consider the formation of a surgeon, for example. What must be added to a person with the potential to become a surgeon, someone who is "surgeon material", in order to produce an actual surgeon rather than any of the other things this person might potentially be? Surgical training. Surgical training and experience forms someone into a surgeon. Surgical knowledge and skill is not something inert, but active and dynamic, enabling its possessor to perform surgery. That is something very different again from a shape or ratio.

And a form does not always have to be something added to a single thing. It might instead be added to many things, organizing them into some kind of cooperative group. What, for example, forms a bunch of individual soldiers into an army? A chain of command, or something of the sort.

We now have available to us a new piece of conceptual equipment to help us speak about and understand the world, and you in particular. A *form* is whatever exists in something with many different potentials and makes it to be one specific thing rather than any of the other things it has the potential to be, whether that be an army or a brick wall or a statue of Zeus.

With this idea in mind, let us now return to the question of your vital organs. They need an explanation for their life and functionality as much as you do. Just like you, they are made entirely of ingredients that are able to be other things, and so there must be some reason why those ingredients are functioning vital organs rather than anything else they are able to be. What is the ultimate reason your heart is alive and beating instead of dead and still? Its ultimate materials cannot be the answer, since those same materials can be dead and still. There must therefore be something about your heart other than its materials that is the reason it is alive—something added to those materials and causing them to be a living heart rather than a dead one. And we have agreed to call such a cause a *form*.

Your vital organs are not the primary cause of your being alive, then, for the simple reason that there is also a cause of their being alive—namely, their form (whatever that may turn out to be). This answer to our question about the difference between life and death in the human body is the truth. It is no mere guess. There must be something in your body that is the primary reason it is living and human rather than not, and the kinds of materials in you are not the answer. Then it is some difference in those materials. It is some kind of form, a specifically human form.

True and certain as this is, it is not quite satisfactory. It is a very general answer. Forms come in many varieties, as we have seen. What sort of form is it that makes your molecules into cells, and your cells into your vital organs, and your organs into you? Is it a shape? A ratio? Something else?

One answer immediately suggests itself. What makes an organ a real and viable organ? Why, *organization* of course. *Organization* means all the special ratios, local distributions, spatial arrangements, and interactive relationships that we find among certain types of molecules constituting a cell, or among certain types of cells constituting a tissue, or among tissues constituting an organ, or among organs constituting an organ system. At the top of this ladder of organization we arrive at the complete organism—you, for instance.

Vital organs cannot be the primary principle of life in a living thing. Their very organization is a prior principle of their own life and their own power to sustain life in a complete living thing. That leads us right to our next guess.

Third Guess: *The Organization of Your Body*

Slowly but surely we are closing in on the identity of the cause in your constitution that is primarily responsible for your body being alive. Each guess at its identity invites criticism, which in turn suggests a better guess. Our present guess, the organization of your body, is so good that it is hard to see that it is not right. We know that the primary cause of life in you is a form of your materials, and we are guessing that it is more specifically some sort of organization, some series of levels of ordered interaction and arrangement ranging from macroscopic to microscopic. If such organization is altogether absent, or if any single indispensable link in such a chain is missing, death results.

This answer is anything but primitive. It has a lot going for it. Life comes and goes with a certain prerequisite organization and cooperation in the parts of a living body. All living activities improve or worsen with the organization within the body, and within and among its cells. Organization is prior to organs. It is the specifying feature causing certain materials to be organs in the first place. Organization is also unique to living things in nature, if an *organ* means a part by which something takes action for itself for improving or maintaining its condition. Organization seems to be the key to life. When the minimal working order is present, so is life, and when it is not, life departs.

This even sounds like ironclad proof, and a significant number of people today are satisfied with the idea that what first makes your materials to be you is just their organization.

Nonetheless, this answer, too, falls short of the truth. Neither the macroscopic nor the microscopic organization in your body can be the primary cause responsible for your body being alive and being you. Your present macroscopic order won't do, since you once existed without it. Early in life, while you were developing in utero, you were able to live without the organization of your brain, and of your heart and lungs and circulatory system. If you doubt that the embryonic form of you was truly you, it remains that it was a living being capable of producing all your parts by its own living activities. It is most natural to say that it was you, only in unfinished form, since it seemed entirely preoccupied with the business of shaping itself into the finished you. Be that as it may, the embryonic version of you was certainly alive. It grew, developed, and took nourishment. The first root of life in this being could not have been the organization of a heart or brain, since it had neither and later would produce both.

Any level of your body's organization above a single cell was brought into being by the living activity of cells. Such higher-level organization does not seem to be a first principle of life in you, then, since it came forth from a prior life endowed with a less complex level of organization. Higher-level organization, in other words, is more an effect of life than a first cause of it.

The secondary nature of large-scale organization might make us turn to small-scale organization as the first principle of life instead. The smallest unit of life seems to be the cell. Could some basic, minimal, organizational structure within a cell be the first cause of life? Could the structure of DNA, perhaps, be the first principle that constitutes a living thing? Some have said so.

And yet this answer is also tangled up with insuperable difficulties. The sequence of nitrogenous bases along a strand of your DNA simply cannot be the primary and essential form that makes your materials to be you. A thing's form is what makes that thing to exist and be present as soon as that form is there, just as there is a statue of Zeus the moment the form of Zeus is in the bronze. And when the bronze stops being a statue of Zeus, the form of such a statue cannot continue to exist in it. But a human body can still have all its DNA even after it is dead and cold. So the structure of DNA is not the fundamental thing that, when it is in the body, makes it to be alive. The structure of your DNA is the form of your DNA, a mere part of you. It is not the form of you.

Another problem is that repeated instances of any type of form means repeated instances of the thing it forms. As often as we find the complete form of a thing, so many instances of that thing do we get. Put the complete form of a melody into certain notes some number of times, and so many times do we hear the same song repeated. However many times we put the shape of a statue into the materials for such a statue, so many instances of that statue do we get. If your DNA were the form of you, then there would be as many instances of you as there are complete instances of your DNA. But your own DNA sequence exists in you in trillions of complete copies. So there are trillions of instances of you, on this view. Each skin cell you slough off would be a human being, and you in particular. But a skin cell, even if it can live for some time apart from you, is not a human being. After isolation from you, any viable part has its own life and therefore its own distinct form, however brief and incomplete such a life may be.

Nor is that the last problem. Any level of organization or sequencing, whether macroscopic or microscopic, might explain your organs in some way, but cannot possibly explain the life of your mind, which does not exist in any of your organs. You did not grow your intellect. Its power in no way derives from any bodily configuration, big or small, simple or complex. There is no way to get your cerebral organization or your DNA or anything like these things to be the source of your intellect, which does not exist in your body, and which is not divisible into spatially distinct parts. What we are seeking, however, is the root cause in you of your life and your powers, including your intellect. Your DNA is not a viable candidate.

The organization of your body (at all its different levels) is very fundamental to your life and many of your powers. But neither it nor any other discoveries of modern biology fits the description of the cause we are after. This is not because of anything wrong with modern biology. It is not because science has gone somehow astray. The reason modern biology cannot supply an adequate answer to our question is simply because it does not really ask it. Biology looks for the ultimate chemical and physical causes of things, but not simply for the ultimate causes of them. And it tends to look for the causes of living activities observable from the outside, not for the causes of living activities observable only from within, such as your activity of understanding universal truths. That sort of phenomenon of human life, real, undeniable, and generally experienced though it may be, does not come up much in books about biology. Once we ask about the cause of it, we are on the road to seeing that understanding universal truth is not an activity that takes place in the brain, or in any organ of the body. Your body's organization, fundamental as it is, cannot be the first and most fundamental cause of life in you.

There is something deeper still.

Fourth Guess: *A Ghost in a Machine*

Since philosophers not only attend to the outsider's view of a human being, but also pay particular attention to the insider's view, it should come as no surprise that some philosophers were and are quite attuned to the nonmateriality of the human intellect. Some of these, such as Plato and Descartes, aware of the impossibility of basing human intellectual powers on the body, looked in a very different direction (from the one we have been pursuing) for the primary principle of life in you. They concluded that the basic root of your powers and activities is a purely spiritual substance, your spirit, which has its own existence completely distinct from the existence of your body. This spirit of yours, they thought, existed in your body something like a pilot in a ship, or we might say a driver in a car, or a cyclist on a bike, or perhaps Tony Stark in his Iron Man suit. Tony Stark has his own existence, and his suit has its own existence, distinct from his. So too (says this way of thinking) is your spirit one thing, and your body a completely different thing, each one with its own existence.

This idea that the True You is a pure spirit, and that your body is just something that you are using, has certain advantages to recommend it. It preserves the truth about your intellect being nonmaterial, for one. For another, it fits well with the experience we sometimes have of being at war with our own bodies.

On the other hand, this idea also commits new sins of its own. True, the more materialistic guesses we have so far surveyed cannot account for your incorporeal intellect. But the Cartesian view we are now considering cannot account for your bodily senses. Your sense powers must belong to your body, not just to a purely spiritual you, since within themselves they form certain representations, such as your field of vision, that are divisible into spatially distinct parts. That is the telltale sign that your sense powers reside in body parts. Besides, other critters besides human beings have senses—not just cats and dogs, but even ticks and worms and all kinds of lowlifes, so to speak. So unless we want to say that these creatures also have purely incorporeal spirits haunting their bodies, we will have to admit that sensation is something that bodies do. And if your body performs your acts of sensing, then your body must be you, and not just some tool you are using or suit you are wearing.

We cannot segregate Spiritual You from Bodily You in so simple a way. Descartes tried to wiggle out of this problem by denying that animals had any sensation at all. He thought of them as senseless machines without feelings or desires or awareness of any kind. That idea runs against experience, not with it. It is the symptom of an attempt to save a drowning theory. Whatever we say is the primary cause of life in you, the facts force us to say it is something that is in your body more intimately than Tony Stark is in his suit. The suit is not a part of Tony Stark, and has its own existence distinct from his. Your body is a part of you and has no existence distinct from yours so long as you live in it.

Sifting Out the Truth

After so many failed attempts to find the primary cause of life in your body, we might be tempted to give up. We might even begin to question whether there is such a cause. But to doubt the cause is to doubt the effect. And there can be no doubt that a profound difference separates a person from a corpse. There must, then, be a root cause of this difference, some primary animating principle.

And we are in a position to say something, now, about what that cause is. Our wrong, but gradually improving, ideas have not been total failures. Each improvement said something right, with which we could find no fault. Thanks to our educated guesswork and to the corrections that our facts about you forced us to make, here is what we can say with certainty about the animating principle in you:

1. It has to be *something of your body*, since it is the ultimate root of your sense powers, and these reside in your body. Whether it is a part of your body, or an organization of your body, or something else of your body, it is not just a free-floating spirit, but somehow together with your body it makes one being, you.
2. It has to be *no part of your body*, since any part of your body is able to be alive and to lose its life just as your whole body is. The life of any part of your body requires an explanation just as the life of your whole body does.
3. It has to be *some kind of form of your body*, and cannot be the materials of your body, since all the ultimate materials of your body are found even in nonliving things, and none are special to you, except insofar as they become formed in some you-specific way.

4. The root of all your powers *cannot be an organization*, since it is the root of your intellectual power, which is nonmaterial and does not reside in any organ of your body.

5. And yet it has to be *analogous to something in other living things*, even those without intellect, since the animating principle in them is also what makes their materials to be alive and is the cause of their vegetative and sensitive activities, which are generically similar to yours and mine.

Weaving together these givens into one idea of the life-giving cause in you, what do we get? The facts force us to say something like this: the primary cause of life in you is *a form of your body that is more basic than its organization*.

This puzzling description of the life-giving cause in your body is essentially correct. But it will not be satisfactory until we can specify what kind of form it is that makes your body to be alive.

We need to learn more about the form of your body if we are to put together your incorporeal mind with your all-too-corporeal, stubbed-your-toe-again body.

7

Black Birds and Blackbirds

In each thing that has many parts and in which the totality is not like a mere heap, but the whole is something besides the parts, there is a cause.

—Aristotle, *Metaphysics*

Exciting Combinations

The two chemists stood side by side, stroking their chins and gazing into the Erlenmeyer flask. They were close now, they knew, to the proper formula. Very close. Two parts calcium oxychloride to three parts chromium oxide was undoubtedly correct, but what about the cobalt chloride? What of the cupric sulfate? Sodium ferrocyanide was certainly called for, but how much? They had precious little of it, having exhausted the bulk of their supply in prior experiments. No matter. If the chemistry set was nearly depleted, they still had plenty of Aqua Velva, which, by its foul odor, promised to be toxic in the extreme. Half a bottle of it went into the flask, followed by a tablespoon each of apple cider vinegar and rubbing alcohol. Three capfuls of blue dandruff shampoo (for viscosity) provided the finishing touch.

The first chemist instructed the second, his assistant, to insert a rubber stopper in the flask and give the whole business a vigorous shake. This done, they held the flask up to the light, and behold!— roiling clouds of various colors rose up in the mixture and sank again, beads and bubbles contended with one another to reach the surface first, and a sea-green froth overtopped it all. In short, it was ready. Quick, no time to waste! To the backyard, now, where the enemy had raised up proud fortresses and cities, laying waste to the lawn. Out came the stopper and down went the entire potion into the largest of the ant metropolises. Success! Almost instantly, black rivers of panic-stricken ants erupted from the adjacent holes by the hundreds, many covered in toxic goop and already in the throes of death.

So went one of my more frivolous (and unsupervised) chemical experiments. Others were somewhat more instructive, but compensated for this by being also more dangerous. There was, for example, my attempt to make gunpowder, and my discovery that muriatic acid could burn holes in the concrete around the house. The supervised procedures, those involving not a fellow fifth grader but my father, were least dangerous and most instructive. Under his direction, I learned how to fill test tubes with hydrogen and oxygen by electrolysis of water, and how to distinguish those gases by how they affected a lit match.

My chemical curiosity began as a magic-show fascination for frothings, minor explosions, subliming substances, and color-changing liquids, but eventually transformed into something deeper. I remember thinking the world was gratifyingly full of surprises, a magical enough place all right, but it was odd and frustrating that one had to work so hard and save up so much money to get the really interesting substances, the ones that did things. Why couldn't those exciting things be found out in the woods behind the house? Most of the world seemed to be made of fairly inactive, dull stuff, like water and dirt. Mix them up and what did you get? Plain old mud. No explosions, no surprise color changes, not so much as a fizz or a pop. Why was that? What was this difference between active substances and seemingly inert ones?

Then again, even boring old water was actually constituted, somehow, of two exciting invisible substances—oxygen, which, when a flame was introduced into it, caused it to burn suddenly with much greater intensity, and hydrogen, which produced a satisfyingly loud *pop!* when a lit match was brought near. Why did these two exciting and invisible substances, when combined in the right manner, produce the far less active, perfectly visible, and tangible thing we call water? How could water be made of things so different from itself? How could something so new come out of those things? And why didn't every combination of substances produce something radically new? When I stirred sugar into water, the sugar disappeared, but I could still taste it. Probably this was only a mixture of sugar and water, both still present but too finely combined to be discerned by the naked eye. But table salt did not seem to be just a mixture of sodium (a highly reactive shiny metal) and chlorine (a green, toxic gas). What made the difference between a mixture of two things that remained two things, and two things combined into one entirely new thing? These early chemical researches of mine were my first attempt to grapple with the general question how a single new thing can come to be from many previously existing ones—and how we can tell whether that has happened.

We must now ask a similar question about you. Our overarching question is, what are you? So far, we know that you have both a material body and a nonmaterial mind, and that these two diverse parts of you somehow come together to constitute a single you. We know, furthermore, that your body and mind depend on a common cause, your animating principle, which is the essential form of your body. We must get to know this unifying ingredient in your nature a little better.

But how? What question should we ask about it next? Since the primary source of your life and living powers is a form of some kind, and we wish to learn more about what sort of form it is, we might get somewhere by comparing it to and contrasting it with other more familiar forms.

Consider the form of a car. As a whole, that form makes all the car parts to be a whole car, and the parts of that form make each part to be a car part. What the form of a car does not do, however, is make each material substance in the car to be what it is. Suppose the engine block is made of cast iron. Then the way it is formed by the auto manufacturer makes the iron to be an engine block, but does not make it to be iron. It was iron already. It remains iron when it is in the car, and continues to be the same chunk of iron even after the car is crushed in the junkyard. The form of a car, in other words, does not cause everything in the car to be what it is. Its influence goes down only so far and then stops. It makes the whole car to be a car and makes the iron, glass, plastic, copper, and rubber to be various parts of the car, but does not make them to be iron, glass, plastic, copper, and rubber.

Is your form like that? Certainly it causes all the you-specific organization in your materials. But does it stop there? Do your basic materials continue to have their own forms in you—the forms of various chemical compounds and elements, for example—so that your form is like a superstructure imposed on a number of other substances?

That is our present question.

The Most Fundamental Difference Possible

In order to approach our question, we first need to draw an extremely fundamental distinction. The distinction I have in mind is not only fundamental, but is in fact the most fundamental distinction possible among things.

That in itself invites us to wonder. We are aware of many differences among things in the world. There are toxic and nontoxic things. There are alcoholic and nonalcoholic things. Some things have nuts in them, some don't. There's black and white, original and fat-free, tall and short, living and nonliving, straight and curved, and on and on. Among differences, though, we see that some are more basic than others. The difference between black and white, for instance, is a difference among colors, but there is also a more general and basic difference between colors and flavors.

What is the most general and basic difference among things? One way to find out would be to list as many things as we can, with as much variety among them as we can think of, and then ask ourselves what is the most basic and general difference among them all. This is just what I do in the classroom when I want my students to discover the most fundamental difference in things. I stand at the blackboard and ask them to help me write up a list of *beings*, as different from each other as they can imagine. Actually, I just say *things*, both to avoid jargon and to prevent my students from thinking I am looking for anything specific, such as intelligent beings—but I warn them that by *thing* I don't mean *thing* as opposed to *person*, but just anything at all that can be called something and is not absolutely nothing. Once that is understood, the list of *things* my students come up with usually looks something like this:

A desk
A chair
A book
A person
A dog
A stone
A star
A paperclip
A tree

Sometimes students try to outdo each other with zany or hyperspe-
cific suggestions such as a hyena or a pot roast, but that makes no
difference to the distinction we are about to draw. We may add them
to the list above, if we like.

After obtaining a sufficient student-generated list of things like the
one above, I next produce a separate list of my own right beside it,
which will typically look something like this:

A smile
A cough
A quick jump to the left
An uneasy feeling that things aren't going so well
Being in prison
A greenish shade of blue
A sharp edge
Having scuba-diving equipment on
Being kicked
The act of sewing a button onto a shirt

When I finish writing on the board, I turn around and ask the students
what the difference is between their things and my things. Usually,
the first answer I get is that the students listed concrete things, but I
listed abstract ones, or, equivalently, they listed real things whereas
I listed ideas. So I ask them whether the edge of a knife is just an idea
and is not something real—whether a knife cuts you not because
of something real about it, but because of an idea we have of it.
This bothers them. They do not wish to say that. Then I ask them
whether getting kicked is an abstract idea, and not a concrete thing.

They reject this, too. What about being in prison? Is that just a state of mind, or is it somehow a reality? No one wishes to say it is just a state of mind. They are certain now that the second list is in fact just as concrete as the first, that it is indeed a list of things after all, and not a list of ideas.

Now they are really puzzled. What *is* the difference between the two lists? Obviously there is some important difference between them, but what is it? It is harder to say than it had at first appeared.

On most occasions, one or two students will eventually put their finger on it. The first list, they say, is listing things, pure and simple, while the second list is listing *things of other things*, features or properties of other things. And that is indeed the difference I am hoping they will see.

The word *properties* is often reserved for essential properties of a thing, such as the chemical properties of some element on the periodic table. Sodium is more reactive than helium is, for example, and carbon forms more compounds than gold does. It is not the essence of sodium that it is "more reactive than helium". That is not its very definition and constitution. But that attribute belongs to it because of its constitution, because of what it is, because of its essence, and so it is an "essential" property. That is a *property* in a fairly strict sense of the word.

But there are also many nonessential features of a thing—your location, for example, or your mood. These don't belong to you just because of what you are, but for other reasons. I will call these nonessential attributes *properties* as well. Philosophers tend to call nonessential properties like these *accidents*, from the Latin *accidere*, meaning "to befall". Such incidental properties—how you are sitting just now, the fact that you are laughing, how tan you are—are the things that befall, happen to, or get added onto a thing by causes beyond the bare essence of that thing. In modern English, however, *accidents* are things that a dog does to a carpet or that happen behind the wheel. Neither of those is what we need to pin a name to right now. So I will stick to *properties*, while acknowledging the important difference between essential properties and nonessential ones.

Prior to the properties of things are the things they belong to, the owners of properties. Neither "being ready to go scuba diving" nor "being in prison" can just be a thing all by itself. Such things exist only as properties of a more fundamental thing. They are merely certain ways that some other being (a diver, an inmate) is being. If we trace properties back to their primary owners, to the things that are not properties of any more fundamental things, we come to the real things in the world, the first-class things, the owners-of-properties.

The technical term used in philosophy to name such a first-class being, an owner of properties as opposed to a property, is *substance*. In chemistry, a *substance* usually means a kind of nonliving matter with a definite chemical composition throughout. When that is what the word means, table salt is a substance, but a horse is not (the horse, instead, is made up of many substances—that is, of many diverse chemical compositions). In philosophy, where the word is used in quite a different sense, *substance* means any single entity that has properties and is not itself a property of some more fundamental thing. Salt might be a substance in this sense, but a horse might be, too— which is part of what we want to discuss in this chapter.

Both senses of *substance* are valid and useful, of course. The philosophical meaning is older than the chemical one, however, and makes sense of the parts of the word. The English word *substance* is from the Latin *substantia*, which in turn comes from the Latin verb that means "to stand under" or "to support". The *substance* of a thing means what stands under its outward appearances and behaviors, what underlies the properties we perceive.

This distinction between substances and their properties is not a grammatical one. It is tempting to think: "Ah, I see, this is the difference between nouns and adjectives." That would be a mistake. Nouns name things as if they were substances, and adjectives signify things as if they were properties. We must not ignore the "as if" part. Sometimes nouns do indeed name substances (as in *water*), and sometimes adjectives do indeed signify their properties (as in *wet*). But not always! Suppose from a sheet of pure gold I stamped out a triangle and brought it to class for show-and-tell. What do you suppose my students would call it? "A golden triangle," of course. That is also what I would call it. It is only natural to speak that way. And yet there is some fiction in the parts of that speech. *Triangle*, the noun, talks about the triangle as if it were a first-class thing, an owner-of-properties, whereas *golden*, the adjective, talks about the gold as if it were a property of the triangle—which is exactly backward. The gold is the actual substance in this case, and the triangular shape is a property of it (and a nonessential one, at that). We could also, in somewhat forced language, call the golden triangle "triangular gold". That is less natural in terms of English usage, but it is truer to the reality of the thing. The adjective *triangular* would signify the shape, which is a property, and the substantive noun *gold* would name the substance to which that property belonged.

The distinction between a substance and a property is accordingly not a convention of language. No matter what language you speak, or what parts of speech you employ to talk about it, a piece of gold is not a property of its shape. The shape is a property of the piece of gold. There is a real difference between a substance and a property, and a real priority of the one to the other.

Despite how novel this vocabulary is to most people, the basic distinction between substances and their properties is not the innovation of philosophers. They have only noticed it more consciously than most people do, and applied names to it. This difference is nothing new to you, in other words, even if your attention has never before been drawn to it explicitly. If you found my list of things as odd as my students do, that is because you were already aware that such things are not called *things* in the full-fledged sense of the word. You were already aware, in other words, of the most basic distinction among things—that some things are first-class things, owners-of-properties, whereas others are just the properties of those.

It is also clear, without the need for any clever reasoning but simply as a matter of ordinary experience, that there *are* things that exist as properties, such as those on my list. They really exist, but they exist only as modifications of other things and do not hang around existing by themselves. They are not the primary beings in the world. The substances are the primary beings.

The same goes for the existence of substances. That there are such things is evident through immediate experience, and stands in need of no proof. My students bear witness to this by listing nothing but substances (or things they presume to be substances) when I ask them for a list of things. It is not possible for there to be nothing in reality except properties of other things—there have to be things that own those properties, and that are not themselves properties of anything else. However we slice it, substances are inescapable.

Are You a Substance?

With this most fundamental distinction ready to hand, we may now ask how we ought to classify you. Are you a substance? Or are you instead a property of a substance (or substances)?

Depending on where we begin our thought about you, we seem to be led to opposite answers. Starting from your own ordinary and practical experience of being you, it is very obvious that you are a substance. You are a single being in your own right, a first-class entity, a property owner, and not some property of another thing or things. When you do or say anything, it is precisely you who act and speak, not something else whose property you are that is acting and speaking. When you fall down the stairs, it is really you who fall down the stairs, and not your shape or your color except insofar as these properties of yours tag along for the ride. It is you who do things and have things done to you, not something else whose property you are. So you are a substance. That is how you perceive yourself, and how others perceive you, too.

But what about all the little substances in you? You are made up of countless atoms and molecules, for example. And these seem to remain themselves while they are in you. Were a new water molecule to enter into your constitution, we could in principle track it through all its comings and goings in you. It would interact with other molecules and do all kinds of interesting things within you that it could not do outside you (it might, for example, assist in any number of your vital functions, and thus lend a hand in the hard work of helping you to stay you). Upon becoming one of your constituents, it would not vanish or go up in a puff of smoke or simply melt away into you like a drop of rain in the ocean. It would remain a water molecule, and hence a substance in its own right, wouldn't it?

If you now exhale this water molecule, we will find that its structure and properties are much the same as they were before it became a part of you. In fact, it is precisely because the water molecule insists on keeping its basic properties when it exists within you that it is useful to you at all. The water molecule taken from you seems to be like a marble removed from a marble collection—a thing that used to be part of a group but is no longer, and which remains the same individual thing that it was all along.

We observe the same phenomenon in somewhat larger parts of you, too. Most of your cells are large enough to discern by means of an ordinary microscope. They are nicely distinguished by their membranes. Different kinds of cells in you are in different places and possess distinctive properties, such as different appearances and functions. For that reason, they seem to maintain their own individuality within you. When we remove some skin cells from you and place them in a culture dish, for a time they continue to live and function much as they did before. But if we are to judge from their appearances and most of their observable properties, outside you they remain what they were within you, skin cells, just as marbles are still marbles both in and out of the box.

The same goes for much larger parts of you. If you choose to donate a kidney, it is still a kidney when it is removed from your body. It still looks like a kidney and behaves like one. It is still alive and viable for some time, too.

All of these pieces of evidence about you seem to point away from your being a substance and toward the idea that you are instead a collection of substances. If this is the truth, then we will be able to say something about your form—it does not cause anything to be a substance, but merely unifies many already-existing substances. Your body is a sophisticated chemical factory, and it synthesizes many compounds not otherwise found in nature. But once these are made, they can also be removed from you and still retain some of their basic shape and functionality, provided they are kept in a suitable environment. Even these seem to be the substances that they are independently of your form, once they have come into existence.

So we can take substances out of you and they remain what they are, and we can put various substances into your constitution and they remain themselves, or so it would appear. Coming at you from facts such as these, it appears that you are not a single substance, but an enormous number of substances instead. And if that is true, your form would have to be some kind of property belonging to those substances, some kind of interactive arrangement among them, like a chain of command in an army.

What a conundrum! If we start from your everyday experience, which includes your insider's view of yourself, then the answer would appear quite obvious. Of course you are a single individual being, and hence your body, which is a part of you, is also one thing. You are not a committee of beings, or a colony. That is not how you perceive yourself from within. If instead we try to answer the question in light of an outsider's view of you, especially one that is enhanced by scientific instruments of observation, we seem to arrive at the opposite answer.

Two Types of Combination

To solve this riddle about you we must acknowledge the difference between two ways of combining different things into one. One way is to unite many individuals into one collective. The other way is to unite many individuals into one individual.

Imagine a number of marbles in a shoebox. We speak of it as "one" marble collection. This is a collective unity. The whole collection is not an individual thing the way each marble is. A single marble, while within the shoebox, is still distinct from its fellows. If we take it out of the shoebox, it retains the same existence and individuality it had when mingled with the rest of the collection—it is not a new marble, or a new being. It is just the same old thing in a new place, that's all. If we put it back in the box, it remains the same individual marble that it was, although it now acquires new relationships to the other marbles and has resumed its place in the collective whole.

Suppose now that we melt all the marbles down and recast them as a single giant marble. That's another story. Now they have formed another kind of unity quite different from that of a mere collection. The individual marbles are no longer distinct individual marbles at all. They have lost their distinct shapes and sizes that accorded each of them its status as an individual marble. They are no longer individual marbles, but only different parts of one giant individual marble. And that new individual is not a collection of marbles.

When many individual things come together in such a way that each one retains its individuality in the new whole, then we have a collective whole, not a true individual. The members of such a whole might very well take on new properties as parts of the whole and behave differently within it. Newly enrolled students at a university, or new recruits in the army, will soon find themselves changing in certain ways, conforming or adjusting to their new circumstances. Still, a student body or an army is not an individual being, but a number of individuals united by a common location, a common purpose, and by other unities of order and relation. They are, in other words, collective wholes.

In extreme cases, a collective whole can become eerily similar to an individual. A cult, for example, is a number of individuals who have made over their individuality, as far as they can, to the cult leader, who will do their thinking and choosing for them from now on. But the members must still do their own eating and breathing, even if in some sense they will not do their own thinking. Since they are still many distinct bodies and not one, they remain distinct individual beings, although they have divested themselves of certain things that are appropriate to their individuality.

When we melt marbles down into one marble, the original marbles disappear so completely that they do not really exist at all anymore. It is therefore not true to say that the new marble is made up of many marbles, as though we could discern the original marbles within it somehow. Does this always happen when things surrender their individuality to a new individual?

Not always. There is another way that many individual things can combine into one individual without completely erasing the differences between the individuals that entered into its constitution. An easy way to illustrate this possibility is with combinations of words. We can combine many words into a single phrase or sentence. The sentence "The black bird alighted on the wire" is not an individual word, but an ordered collection of words. So too the adjective-noun phrase *black bird* is a collection of words, not an individual word. We can also combine those same two words in another way, not into a phrase, but into a compound word, *blackbird*. Is this also a little collection of words? Do the words *black* and *bird* persist in this combination and continue to be two distinct words?

Not in the least. If *blackbird* were two words, then it would mean the same thing as the phrase *black bird*, only said more smoothly. But *blackbird* does not mean the same thing as *black bird*. (Otherwise every bird that was black would be a blackbird, which is false—just ask the raven—and again, every blackbird would be a bird that was black, which is also false—just ask the albino blackbird.) *Blackbird* is not

two words at all. It is a single new word in which the component
words have lost their status as distinct words. A compound word is
not a collection of previously existing words, but a transformation
of previously existing words into a single, new word with its own
distinct meaning.

I Feel Like a Unit

The foregoing distinction between the two types of combinations of
things brings our question about you into sharper focus, but still does
not get us all the way out of the maze. Do the parts of you combine
into a collective, or into an individual? That there are two possibilities does not tell us which one applies to you. We must bring the facts
about you to bear on the question. To accomplish this in a thorough
manner, we must consult both halves of the experience of you.

Turning first to the outsider's experience of you, the relevant facts
it brings to light are that

   1. you are made of many parts,
   2. which are distinguishable by their own diverse qualities and in
      some cases by their own boundaries,
   3. and these same kinds of qualities and boundaries often can exist
      in them before they enter into you, or continue to exist in
      them after they part ways with you, or both.

What is the force of these facts? To which view of you do they tend?
To the view that you are a collection of substances, or to the view
that you are an individual?

They militate quite forcefully, even decisively, against the idea that
you are like an ocean composed of drops of water that melt away and
become indiscernible in the whole. If you are an individual, you are
not a homogeneous one like that, as even a cursory glance at you
makes plain.

But if we ask whether you are like an ordered collection of words,
black bird, or instead more like a compound word, *blackbird*, the external facts do not compel us in either direction. You might be a closely
associated collection of substances, or you might instead be a single

individual substance made of many diverse parts that lose their status as individual substances while they exist in you. The outsider's view alone cannot tell us one way or the other. Or rather, if it goes one way, it leans toward the view that you are an individual. There is an outwardly observable difference between *black bird* and *blackbird*, after all—namely, the space (or pause) between *black* and *bird* in the one case, and its absence in the other. Your cells are not like separate cells in a petri dish with a distance between them, and your molecules bond and interact with one another in various ways. Also, all your parts grew and developed out of one original cell. They came into being as parts of something already in existence, which supports the interpretation that they are not individuals themselves, but parts of one. Still, this might not make it entirely impossible to think of your body as a collective. After consulting with the outsider's view alone, we are still left to wonder.

So what does your insider's view have to add? By means of it, you perceive yourself as though you were a single individual being. Everyone has that kind of self-perception. Even Richard Dawkins, believer as he is in his theory that you are a colony of genes, and that you are nothing more than their clever way of reproducing themselves, says of himself that "subjectively, I feel like a unit, not a colony."[1]

Let us take a closer look at why that is. Why do you perceive yourself to be an individual? What is it in your experience that gives this impression?

It is especially in your acts of perceiving, imagining, remembering, understanding, and, generally, knowing that you perceive that you are an individual being. Your vegetative acts do not reveal this to you as much, or not by themselves. You assimilate food. You heal from wounds. You grow. Your cells act in wonderful concert in doing all these things. But the members of a choir or a basketball team also act in wonderful concert. For all your vegetative acts can tell us, you might be a unified collective as a choir or team or army is, rather than a true individual.

Your self-perception consists not so much in your awareness of your vegetative functions, then, but in perceiving your own acts

---

[1] Richard Dawkins, *The Selfish Gene* (Oxford, N.Y.: Oxford University Press, 1989), pp. 46–47.

of knowing and desiring. It is an ongoing fact of your continuous experience that there is a single you performing all these acts of knowing that go on within yourself, even if you perform many of them in diverse parts of your body. It is one and the same you, for example, who sees out of both eyes. Your eyes are not beings in their own right, each one doing its own seeing. The acts of seeing that take place in your two separate eyes (or, if we prefer, in separate parts of your brain) are not the separate acts of separate seers, but the one unified act of a single seer, you, in your separate parts.

Why not say instead that your acts of knowing are the joint effort of many substances in you that are your parts? After all, one action can be the net result of many cooperating causes. If, for example, each of the many parts of a wall gets painted by someone, then the one wall is painted as a whole, even if no one person painted all the parts. Or if each part of a thing gets lifted, then the whole as a unit is lifted, even if there is no one person or thing that lifted all the parts. Why not say the same about your acts of knowing? If one part of you knows one part of something, and another part of you knows another, won't a complete knowledge result, such as a whole field of vision from the many parts of it?

This explanation does not agree with how you experience your field of vision. Your act of seeing is not the aggregate of millions of distinct acts of seeing performed by different cells in you, each one a seer in its own right and doing just a little bit of the job. Were that the case, no one would see the whole picture, just as no one person painted the whole wall in the former example. But you do see the whole picture, all the things in your field of vision. So your seeing is not the work of many little seers each seeing different things, but of one seer, you, who is seeing all the different things at once in and by means of each of those parts of you. That is why you attribute your acts of seeing to yourself and not to your parts. You saw a movie last night—your eyes or neurons did not also see the movie, as though they had their own visual experiences and enjoyments apart from yours.

Your immediate experience thus makes it clear that there is one seer, you, who sees all that you see. Other types of knowing bring the point home again in a different way. Take depth perception. If you and I sit next to one another on a park bench, each one of us covering one of our eyes, then neither of us enjoys depth perception, not even the two of us taken together. Why not? Because seeing with depth perception is one act of seeing at once in two eyes, not two different acts of seeing, one in each eye, going on at the same time and in proximity to each other. Two different seers perform two acts of seeing, not one. Consequently, they cannot perform the one act of seeing called depth perception.

Knowing comparisons and contrasts is another example of something that cannot be accomplished by a team effort. If the two parts of a table get lifted by two different lifters, and no one lifter lifts both parts, the one table gets lifted nonetheless. But if the two sides of a comparison get known by two different knowers, and no one knower knows both sides, the one comparison never gets known. Imagine you and I are sitting side by side aboard a train, and a man is sitting right across from us. His briefcase is standing upright on the floor between his feet. From where I am sitting I can see his left shoe but not his right. From where you are sitting you can see his right shoe but not his left. Can either of us see whether his shoes match? Clearly not. If I text you a description of his left shoe (and you trust my description), then you will be able to tell whether his shoes match by putting my reported act of seeing together with your experienced act of seeing. In other words, you realize that his shoes don't match only once you know both shoes, one by seeing and the other by my report. Whenever one comparison is known, it is necessary that a single knower know both sides of it at once. So if you know any comparison of two things, and yet you know the two things by two different parts of yourself, those two parts of you are not different knowers, but two parts of a single knower, a single substance, you.

We could multiply examples of this sort of thing. If you smell the wine but do not taste it, and I taste it but do not smell it, neither one of us will become aware that it strangely does not taste the way it smells (which happens sometimes). Or if you know that "Wilma is taller than Craig", and I know that "Craig is taller than Yolanda, but neither one of us knows both statements together, then neither of us will be able to draw the conclusion that "Wilma is taller than Yolanda." There is no such thing as collective wisdom in that way.

Your immediate and continuous awareness that you can compare and contrast the many things that you know by your senses, imagination, and your intellect makes it plain that you are a single knower who owns all these powers and all the parts of your body to which some of those powers belong. It is not despite the diversity in your acts of knowing, but partly because of that diversity, that you perceive yourself to be a single being in your many parts. The diversity of your parts and powers is not at odds with your being one being, one substance, but is just one way in which your substantial unity reveals itself.

In these and other ways, your insider's view reveals that the perceptive parts of you constitute a single entity doing many things, not many entities each doing its own thing. But the perceptive parts of your body—certain parts of your brain, most likely—developed in conjunction with all the other parts of your body and came about by the same kinds of processes. So it stands to reason that the whole business called your body is really one being, one owner of properties, one substance.

Where there are only two alternative understandings of something, and one of them agrees with all the facts and the other only with some, the one agreeing with all the facts must be the truth. The outsider's view of you alone does not absolutely force us to think of you either as a collective or as an individual. Although it leans toward the view that you are an individual, it permits the view that you are a collective. The idea that you are a collective, however, agrees only with some of the facts about you, and clashes with the data available to you through your insider's view of yourself. So it is not the truth. Instead, you are a single individual substance. *Black* and *bird* are not many words in *blackbird*, but are only many parts of one word that retains many of the properties of the words that enter into it. Your parts are not many beings in you, but are only many parts of one being, you, who retain many of the properties of the substances that entered into you.

The internal experience of your body's unity does have its limits. It reaches only so far. You rightly say, "I see," and you interiorly experience this act in yourself. You rightly say, "My skin cells divide," too, but you are not similarly aware of this act within yourself, but witness it, if at all, through the same kind of exterior observations of you that others might make. Some of the actions going on in your parts are quite evident to your insider's view, while others are more obscure, and others entirely opaque. The higher the activity in you, and the more human-specific, the more perceptible it will be in your internal experience, whereas the more basic the activity and the more common to other animals or even plants, the more imperceptible it will be. Reasoning, for example, is something you can readily reflect on in yourself and deliberately perform. You can distinguish and write down the steps in your own reasonings. On the other hand, how your immune system functions, by what elementary processes and in what sequence, does not expose itself much (if at all) to your inner reflection. We get to know such things mainly or exclusively by outside observation.

This limitation to what your inward gaze can reveal to you about yourself leaves open the possibility that many things inside your body are not parts of you at all. Bacteria, both friendly and unfriendly, are a case in point. I do not experience the actions of the bacteria in me as my actions. Although I cannot on that basis alone preclude the possibility that they are parts of me, neither does my internal experience of myself oblige me to acknowledge them as parts of me. Perhaps they are guests—or enemies. Probably we produce many substances that are not really parts of ourselves. The spider produces silk. We produce stomach acid, saliva, sweat, milk, and tears. Many things are clearly parts of you. Others are clearly not. Others still are not so clear one way or the other, or not on the basis of your insider's view alone.

So we must not push your insight into your unity too far and try to make it answer questions it is not capable of addressing.

Meet Your Substantial Form

At last we can answer our opening question. Your body's form, the one that makes it to be alive and to be you, differs radically from the form of a car. The form of a car causes all its parts to be a car, and the parts of that form cause each part to be a car part. But the form of a car does not cause the basic materials in the car to be the substances that they are—steel, plastic, glass, and so on. The influence of the car's artificial form stops at these, and each of these has its own natural form by which it is this substance rather than some other kind. The form of the car, in other words, is not a *substantial* form. It does not cause its materials to be a certain substance, but only causes preexisting substances to be arranged in certain ways. It is like the form of an army, which consists in a chain of command and military training, and causes many soldiers to be one army, and causes each member of it to be a soldier, but which does not cause its members to be human beings. The form of the army presupposes the human beings, and then adds something further to them. It does not form substances, but begins with substances ready-made, and then forms some kind of organized collective out of them.

Your form, on the other hand, makes your parts and materials to be a single substance, you. Were that not so, then each little part of you would keep its own individual and substantial being while existing in you, and you would be demoted to a collection of substances—a thing that the foregoing reflections showed you are not. Your form goes deeper into you than a car does into the materials for a car. Your form gives being and substance to your very parts. Outside you, your organs or cells or molecules can exist as substances in their own right. Upon entry (or reentry) into your constitution, such parts give up their own existence as substances and exist now only as parts of you, having that existence through your form. As the *black-* part of *blackbird* exists no longer as the word *black*, but only as the *black-* part of *blackbird*, so a carbon atom in your substance exists no longer as its own individual substance, but only as a carbon part of you.

So your form is substantial. Your essential form, the thing in your body that makes it to be alive and to be you, is not a property like a shape or arrangement, since it constitutes a substance, an owner of properties and behaviors. It does not form an already-existing substance into a modified substance, as a shape forms gold into a golden statue, in which there is no new substance but only a new modification of an old one. Nor does your form organize an already-existing number of substances into a collective, as the form of an army does. Instead, your form is responsible for a new substance in the world, you, and it gives substantial existence to you as a whole and to all your parts as well, so long as they are you.

An enormous difference separates you from any machine such as a car. We already saw that you possess a nonmaterial intellect. Certainly that sets you apart from the machines. But that is something perhaps unique to your kind. Something far more general about you, something true about other animals as well, also sets you apart from the machines. A dog or cat might not have a nonmaterial mind, but surely it can see out of both eyes and hear and smell. A creature like that is also a single substance performing these many and diverse acts in its diverse body parts. By extension, a plant is also an individual substance with a substantial form of its own, since its body exhibits an organic unity similar to that of an animal body, and since it comes into existence by processes generically similar to the generation and development of an animal. Perhaps even a chemical compound is not a collective of elements, but a single new substance that is more like a compound word than a phrase.

On the one hand, we have brought to the surface a profound difference between you and all our artifacts. On the other, we have discovered a deep kinship between you and all other natural beings.

8

What Growth Says about You

Among the properties of a thing, its quantity is the one nearest to its substance, and its shape is nearest to the form of its substance.

—Thomas Aquinas, *Commentary on Aristotle's* Physics

That First Bicycle

Do you remember your first bicycle? Mine was spectacular. Fire-engine red with a sparkly white banana seat. It was a gift from my parents for my ninth birthday. I was shrimpy, even for a nine-year-old, and had some difficulty reaching the pedals. My solution was to push down hard enough on the upper pedal so that, when it sank out of reach, the lower one would swing up under my other foot. The action felt more like stomping than continuous pedaling, but it sufficed to propel me forward with the precise velocity that a steady wobble demands. The whole trick was getting started. With my bike beside me, I would run along a curb (giving me a slight height advantage), and then hop on when I had gotten up to speed.

My wheels turned the world into a bigger place for me. They took me to places I had never been before except while sitting in the backseat of a car, from which vantage point the outside world stood beyond hearing and smell, flying past me largely unnoticed and unreal. That was more like watching the world on TV than experiencing it. Thanks to my bike, these same places now took on an unaccustomed solidity, freshness, and tang. I discovered I could actually exist in them, and not just watch them flash by in succession as so many blurred scenes in a movie with muted sound.

One such newly accessible place was "Big Belmont", as all children in the neighborhood called the long, steep hill not far from my parents' house. On one particular sunny morning, precariously perched atop my shiny, bright-red annihilator of distance, I scorned the steepness of Big Belmont and rode down at maximum stomp. I ran into a patch of sand (a common road hazard in New Hampshire, where sand is used in abundance in the winter to offer cars more traction in the snow) and hurtled over the handlebars. Thanks to my catlike reflexes and quick thinking, however, I managed to absorb most of the energy of my fall with my nose, which even now looks a touch crooked to me when I shave in the morning.

I had many adventures with this new companion of mine, most of them injury-free (all of them helmet-free!), and saw my circle of experience widen out to unhoped-for dimensions. My parents gave me permission to ride to school with a neighbor kid named Jim, who knew how to get to our elementary school by a path through the woods. Until then I had always ridden on a big yellow bus that took nearly half an hour to pick up all the other kids at the numerous stops before dropping us off at school. As a consequence of the circuitous, stop-and-go bus ride, I had imagined the school to be five or even ten miles from home. I was amazed when the shortcut through the woods proved the school was less than a half mile from my house as the crow flies.

Unless you have had a similar bicycle at a similar age and in a similar four-season climate, you can hardly imagine how forlorn I was to bring my beautiful red machine down into the basement for its first winter. I was now immobilized, and the bleakest days of the claustrophobic school year were upon me. I paid regular visits to my poor lonely bike, assuring myself that it was clean, dry, and its tires firm and ready. The cold dark months wore slowly on. The snowfalls eventually relented somewhat. The feeble sun began to grow brighter once more. At long last, patches of damp earth began to peek out from beneath the melting snow. All were symbols of freedom soon to be regained. On the first afternoon when the temperature dared to climb north of about forty degrees, out came my bike into the light of day, for a ride in the slush.

Oh, the joy of it! And what was this? Over and above the pure elation of restoring my freedom, nature had added another gift—I no longer had any difficulty reaching the pedals. I had grown.

Growth is a strange and wonderful thing. It is not like the expansion of a heated metal, or of water when it freezes, which are mere rarefactions of materials that were already there. Growth requires the intake of new materials into the one who is growing.

Nor is growth like the inflation of a balloon. The added air is foreign to the balloon itself, pumped in, and not in any way transformed by it, but only forcibly contained. True growth involves the previously smaller thing assimilating new matter into its own constitution.

Nor again is the growth of a dog or horse like the growth of a checkout line at the grocery store, or like the growth of a city or army or bureaucracy, nor even like the growth of a forest or ecosystem. In all these other cases we have something like accretion or aggregation, an increase in the number of things constituting some ordered whole, which is in plain truth a multitude of beings, a collective, not actually a single individual. When we speak of the *size* of such a whole—the *size* of the army—we have stretched that term a little bit beyond its initial sense. *Size* first denotes the magnitude of a single, continuous thing. Only by extension from this idea does it come to mean the "size" of a group. Growth, in the strictest and fullest sense of the word, means a single individual's increase of size resulting from its own selective intake, separation, recombination, and part-specific allocation of new materials that it assimilates into its own nature. A crystal does not grow at all in this sense, nor does a fire. A crystal or stalagmite does not draw molecules into itself from its environs, and then chop them up, categorize the bits and pieces, and bus them off to parts of itself where they are needed and where they get reassembled in new and useful ways. But you do that. And that is a wonderful distinction belonging to you and other living beings, and such a distinction ought not to be glossed over or lumped in with other things called *growth* in a much shallower sense of that word.

What about the form that makes you alive? Did it also grow, together with your body? Does it have a size and a shape, as your body does? Is it made up of different parts, so that the top half of your form is in the top half of your body, and its left and right halves reside in your body's left and right sides?

We will not understand the nature of your form very well until we answer this question about it.

Parts or No Parts?

Most familiar forms are in some way made up of distinct parts. The form of the Statue of Liberty, for example, has parts. The shape of Lady Liberty's face is one part of her form, and the shape of her right hand is another, and these distinct parts of her shape are in different portions of the copper she is made of. Something similar is true of the structure of a house or of a sentence. The form of the foundation is not also the form of the roof. The structure of the independent clause is not also the structure of the main clause. This hardly seems avoidable. A form that exists in certain materials must fall into distinct parts corresponding to the parts of those materials, must it not? Your form exists in your body, giving life and power to all its parts. On this showing, your form would seem to be a divisible thing, one part of it in one part of your body, another in another.

Then again, your intellect has no parts, no shape and size, which is why it can grasp universals and why its ideas even of spatial objects bear no spatial relationships to one another. This spells trouble for the idea that the form of your body is made up of parts. How could a form that has distinct parts produce an intellectual power that has none?

Whichever thing we say about your form—that it has parts, or that it doesn't—we will have some explaining to do.

To solve this problem, the most fundamental distinction among things comes in handy once more. Among things, some are truly and simply Things with a capital *T*, we might say: the owners of properties and doers of deeds. These are the substances of the world, including you. Other things are second-class things, the things that belong to the substances—namely, their properties. In which of these basic categories does your three-dimensional size fall? Your body has size. It has a certain quantity and various dimensions of length, width, and depth, and because of this it is divisible into parts. This is surely something very basic about you, and all other bodily things, too, since it is common to all things in the natural world. Is this geometrical aspect of you the same thing as your substance? Or is it instead a property belonging to you?

Restricting ourselves for a moment to the outsider's view of things, it is difficult if not impossible to refute the idea that the dimensions of a body simply are the very substance of it. The properties of a baseball seem to exist in its spherical dimensions, for example. Whiteness and the motion over home plate belong to the sphere, not the other way around. The sphere is not a property of its color, nor a property of its motion over home plate. The spherical volume seems to be the owner of properties, and it is certainly much more basic, more substantial, than its color or movement. So why not say that the spherical volume of the baseball is its very substance? And why not say, for more or less the same reasons, that your three-dimensional quantity is your substance, is what you are?

Because you grew. One and the same you has worn many different sizes and shapes over time. (That it was the same you throughout is clearest by your insider's view of yourself, just as I know it was the same me who once struggled to reach the pedals and who later reached them with ease.) Since many sizes and shapes have come and gone while the one and only you endured through those changes, therefore you are not the same thing as your size. Your body is you, or at least a part of you, and it remains you, the same being, under many different sizes and shapes. So your body is not the same thing as its size or shape, but is instead something more substantial than these, in which these can come and go.

When I say this sort of thing in the classroom, students will sometimes object that the human body might still be the same as its three-dimensional quantity, just as long as we say it is a quantity that can change size. They do not at first realize that "a quantity that can change size" is an absurd idea. A quantified thing, an owner of a quantity, such as you, can change size. But a quantity itself is a size, and so it cannot change size. To illustrate the point, I hold up a clean sheet of paper in front of my students, then crumple it up, or else I make a paper airplane out of it. Then I ask, "What changed?" Invariably they say, "The shape." Certainly that is correct in some way. They mean that *shape* names the general category of which we have different instances at the beginning and end of the change. But then I ask, "What changed *from one shape to another*? What used to be one shape, but now is a different shape?" Now it is impossible to answer, "The shape". There is no shape that went from being one shape to being another shape. There is no shape that used to be a flat rectangle and is now an airplane shape. No shape can endure throughout that change. What goes from being one shape to being another shape is not a shape. Likewise, what goes from being one color to another is not a color. And what goes from having one size to having another is not a size. But you, a substance, went from having one size to having another. So you are not a size, and your substance is not the same thing as your physical occupation of space.

Thanks to your growth, we know that your dimensions are not precisely you, hence are not a substance, but are just a property of yours. Being a property is the way that quantitative dimensions exist. And once a property, always a property, you might say. If the act of jumping up and down cannot exist in you except as a property of you, then wherever we find such an act, it is a property of something and is not a substance. The bouncing of a boulder down a mountain cannot be a substance any more than your bouncing on a trampoline can, even if this is more obvious to you in your own case and you come to realize it about the boulder as a consequence. Likewise, dimensions can never be a substance, but are always a mere property of a thing. Even a boulder is really something more fundamental than its dimensions, although it cannot grow.

All of this implies that your human form has no parts. Why? Because the forms in you that do have parts, such as your shape or organization, are *less* fundamental than your physical dimensions. Organization is a property of the things organized by it. Shapes, arrangements, and organizations all presuppose dimensional objects to shape, arrange, and organize. If your form had parts, dimensions, then it would be like one of these kinds of forms, and consequently it would be less fundamental, less substantial, than your dimensions. Since instead it is the cause of your very substance (as we saw in the last chapter), it is *more* fundamental than your dimensions, which is only a property of your substance. Consequently, your form has no parts.

Even if you had never grown, we could still see that the form that makes you to be the substance that you are cannot have any parts. If it did, it would be something like the form of a house, some sort of shape or arrangement. Such a form does not constitute a substance, since it must shape a substance or arrange a number of substances already in existence, to which it subsequently belongs as a property. Your form, on the other hand, is the cause of a substance, you. Therefore it is not the property of a substance, and therefore it is not the kind of form that can have parts.

We should not overlook the general nature of this reasoning. It is not based on something unique to you, or even to living things in general. The form of a substance is something prior to it, constitutive of it, whereas a property of a substance is something consequent upon it. Therefore no form of a substance can be a property of it. Just as you and your form are in truth something more fundamental than your size, shape, and organization, so the substantial forms of all substances, even nonliving ones, are more fundamental than these divisible forms. If a water molecule is in fact an individual substance, for example, and not a mere cluster of smaller substances, then the substantial form causing its components to be a water molecule also has no parts, since that form is more basic than physical dimensions, not consequent upon them. The structure of the molecule is divisible somewhat in the way a shape of a statue is, or the way the organization of your body is. But that spatial structure is still just a property of the water molecule, as your shape and organization are properties of you. Fundamental and necessary properties, yes, but properties all the same, and not substantial forms.

The unifying power of your form also testifies to its indivisibility. The material parts of your body are able to be (and once were) other things besides you. This is how we discovered your form in the first place, as the thing in your materials primarily responsible for their being one substance, you, rather than any of the countless other substances they might be instead. Suppose, now, that your form also has parts, as your body does. One part of your form is in your left foot, another part in your right hand, and of the part in your right hand there is again one part in your thumb, another in your index finger, and so on. This would mean your form is physically divisible, just as your body is. Consequently, it would be capable of being cut up into other things than the one form it is at present, and so there would have to be a cause of its being this one form it is right now rather than other things, even as the parts of your body require a cause to unify them into a single substance. We cannot say that it is your body that unifies your form, since it is your form that unifies your body and makes all its parts to be the single being known as you. Can you smell the infinite regress approaching? If it has parts, then your form must be divisible and hence must have its own unifying form. Well, does *that* unifying form have parts, too? We must either admit an infinity of forms in you, or else stop at one that has no parts. In the interest of avoiding an absurd infinity of forms in you, we should just admit that your form has no parts and be done.

Whole in Every Part

That your form has no parts fits well with its being the cause of your intellect, which also has no parts. Less clear is how your form can exist in all the parts of your body if it has no parts itself. It must exist in every part of your body. Were your form not in your head, for example, then your head would not be alive or a part of you. But it is alive and part of you. So your form must be in your head—and in your heart, and in your liver, and in every part of you. How in the world can a thing with no parts exist in all those different parts of you?

There is only one way. If your form exists in every part of you, but has no parts of its own, then it must exist whole and entire in every part of you.

Like Einstein's mind-bending thought of warped space-time, the idea (not original with me) that something could exist whole and entire in each part of something seems at first a big pill to swallow. The kinds of forms that first come to mind do not have this remarkable attribute of being found whole in every part of the things that they form. The whole form of a car is not found in every part of the car. The shape, structure, and order in the whole car is not also found, whole and entire, in the glove compartment. The whole form of a house is not found just in the basement. The whole form of the word *syllable* is not found in its third syllable. The whole shape of your face does not exist in each part of it, as though there were two eyes, a nose, and a mouth, in every single cell of your face. Although your DNA might in some subtle and incomplete way contain the whole structure of your face in principle, even then it remains absurd to say that the whole shape of your face is in every part of your DNA, or in every atom of it. So how can the whole form of you be found whole and entire in every part of you?

Certainly your shape and organization are not found whole in every part of you. Neither are the powers that rely upon your organization found whole in every part of your body. Your sense of sight, for example, does not exist in your hand. But we are not discussing your powers and organization at the moment, since they are properties.

The most fundamental form in you is your substantial form, and this is not a property of your substance, but a constitutive principle of it. It is the human nature in you, the "what you are" of you, in your materials. A form like that, a "what it is", can at least in some cases exist whole and entire in the different parts of the thing it forms. Straightness, for example, exists whole and entire in every part of a straight line. If a tiny part of a straight line did not have straightness in it, whole and entire, then that little piece would not be straight, and consequently neither would the whole line be straight.

You are a more complicated case, since a straight line is made of straight lines, but a human being is not made of human beings. The form of straightness does not require, and in fact requires the absence of, any contour differences in the parts of a line in order to make it be a straight one. The human form is not like that. It demands a certain diversity in the materials that it forms in order to abide there, as the form of a word demands certain letters and not others. It is perhaps more similar to the form of a circle, or circularity, if we are to find something both relatively simple yet still somewhat comparable to your human form. Circular curvature exists whole and entire in every arc of a circle, or else the arcs would not be circular ones. If only part of "what circular curvature is" existed in some particular arc, then it would not have circular curvature. The parts of a circle are nonetheless not circles; a circular line is not made up of lots of little circles. A 30-degree arc is not a circle, nor is a 180-degree arc, and furthermore these two parts are unlike each other. The 180-degree arc is not just a blowup of the 30-degree one. Circular curvature, though present in every one of these parts, yields a circle not in each of them, but only in the first complete assembly of all kinds of arcs, which we find in an arc of 360 degrees. The human form, too, though it is whole in every part of the human body, requires a complement of diverse parts if it is to be thus present in them, and it yields a whole human being in the whole diversity of the body, and only a special part of a human being in each part.

Inconstructible You

As strange and unimaginable a thing as your form is turning out to be, it is not a contradiction for such a thing to exist whole in every part of your body, and the facts about you do not permit any other understanding. This strange truth also solves the difficulties we ran into earlier, and explains why they were so difficult to begin with (something whole in every part of you is not an idea that naturally suggests itself to us). For example, only if we say that your form is whole in every part of you can we preserve the fact that it causes every part of you to be alive and to be you, but also the fact that it is the root cause of your intellect, which has no parts. On the one hand, since it is whole in every part of your body, it can be the form of both the whole of your body and of every part. On the other, what is whole in every part of you does not itself have parts, and so it can be the root cause of a nonmaterial power such as your intellect.

My students sometimes wonder why the problem goes only one way. If a thing without parts can cause something with parts (as your form causes your body to be you), why can't this happen also in reverse? Why can't something that has parts cause something else that has none? Why, for example, can't your body, or its organization, be the cause of your intellect?

The answer lies in a rule about causes: a cause must be qualitatively more intense, more unified, more undivided than its effect, or at least not less. This is clear in many familiar cases. The toasting of your bread can cause the temperature in the whole room to climb by some fraction of a degree. We cannot turn this around and, merely by raising the temperature of the room by some fraction of a degree (say by filling it with people), toast your bread. The toaster produces intense heat, which can increase the diffused heat in the room. But the diffused heat cannot produce a concentrated effect, intense heat. This basic rule about causes puts more concentrated causes at an advantage. They can produce things that are more spread out than themselves, more diffuse, but the more diffuse things cannot produce them.

While your substantial form is not divisible into parts, it is not like a geometric point, either, which exists only in one spot and nowhere else. Your form is in every part of your body. Nor again is your form like a shape or structure. Such a thing may extend throughout your whole body, but only because one part of it exists in one part of you, another in another, and the whole of it exists in no one of your parts. Your form is an altogether different sort of thing. It has at once the advantage of a thing with dimensions, because it exists in many different parts of you, but also the advantage of an indivisible thing, because it is present whole and entire wherever it is. If it were a thing with physical dimensions, it could not possibly do this. But it is something prior to physical dimensions altogether, and in a different category, the category of substance. Your form exists more intensely and completely, and in a less dissipated way, than your body does, which is why it can cause your body. This entails no violation of the rule about causes.

Your body, on the other hand, is spread out in space. So it is not whole in every part of itself, but is instead a diffused thing, spread apart from itself, one part here and another one there. Your intellect is not spread out that way, but is a more intense thing than that. It is not divorced from itself with one part here and another there, since it has no parts. Nor does it have some specific location, as a geometric point has. For a body to produce an intellect would therefore violate the rule about causes. It would be like the room temperature toasting the bread.

The nonquantitative nature of your form enables us to answer another question about you and other living things. Is it possible to construct a living thing out of nonliving ones, like a Lego model? For the sake of argument, and consciously ignoring any impossibilities that the idea might actually involve, imagine a gifted and well-funded scientist has contrived a machine that could shove all the molecules required for one luna moth into exactly the right spatial arrangements, pretty nearly all at once and with the right conditions of temperature, pressure, and the like. Would we get a luna moth?

Suppose we did. Would the scientist then be right to take credit for having built a luna moth in the same way that I might take credit for building something out of Lego bricks? Would this be the ultimate proof that a living thing is just a machine after all?

Not at all. The actual form of a luna, the nature of such a creature, is not an arrangement or shape or any sort of quantitative form we humans and our machines can imagine and then impose on matter. The luna may not have a nonmaterial intellect as you have, but its outwardly observable appearances and behaviors indicate that it at least has sensations of various kinds, and a sensing being is an individual being, a single natural substance, not a collective. Its form is therefore substantial, generically like yours, although specifically different. Such a form is not an arrangement, not a shape, not an organization, and has no parts, being instead whole in every part of the animal's body. That sets the luna far apart from our machines, our houses, our forks and spoons and Lego creations, since the forms of all such things are nothing else than shapes and structures and the like. These things we make are not new substances, just newly arranged and disposed substances.

We cannot imagine, let alone design, a substantial form, a cause that has no parts. We can only come to understand it, little by little, as the first cause within a natural substance of its being and of its various properties. When we bring the right ingredients together in the right way, in the right arrangement and circumstances, some new natural thing might indeed come into existence, substantial form and all. Only we neither directly create such a form itself nor are we the reason that such a form naturally follows when we introduce certain conditions into matter. We can design a house with just about any sprawling shape we imagine, and then we can make it be. Such a form we truly design and originate. But when we synthesize water in a lab, we merely provide certain elements with the opportunity to come together in a natural form we did not invent, but only discovered: the form of water. These days, we can predict the possibility of many compounds, predict their properties, and then actually produce them, as in the world of drug design. Even so, we are only discovering nature's preset possibilities, not freely inventing an idea and then making nature obey, as we do when we finger-paint. We cannot bring together any elements we please in ratios of our choosing and thus form a compound. There is no such thing as a compound formed of one atom of argon, seventy two atoms of aluminum, and five hundred atoms of helium. We do not bond atoms the way we nail one piece of wood to another, or cement one brick to another, in structures to which they have no particular inherent inclination. When we bring bricks together into one house, we are creators. When we bring hydrogen and oxygen together into one water molecule, we are more like matchmakers.

The same goes for our hypothetical luna moth. Were we able, one day, to synthesize separately all the molecules of a luna moth, and then to bring them together somehow so as to make an almost-from-scratch moth, that would be a wonderful and strange triumph for us. We would still be wrong if we took the main credit for it.

Your Form Has a Name

As various artificial forms in wood produce various wooden artifacts, so do various substantial forms in nature's materials produce various natural beings—the elements, their compounds, plants, animals, and of course you yourself. Of all substantial forms, yours, the human one, has the most striking effects. It forms a being endowed with all five kinds of powers of life, and one of these, the intellectual power, is nonmaterial. It deserves a special name, this form of yours.

The best name for it is not far to seek, and surely has suggested itself to your mind throughout these investigations, or at least when you first caught sight of the title of this book. Its name is *soul*. That is the special name for the substantial form of a living being, or at least of a human being. Your soul is the thing in your body primarily responsible for it being alive, endowing you with your specifically human versions of the powers of growing, healing, taking nourishment, sensing, imagining, desiring, and movement. Your power of understanding, too, is rooted in your soul, although that power does not exist in any part of your body.

Though the word *soul* is the best name for the form of you, I have made little use of the word up to this point. Part of the reason is that the word typically means something incorporeal, nonmaterial, or at least something other than our physical organization. Prior to considerations such as those of the last few chapters, it is not obvious that any such principle exists in us. Now that this is clear, I will not shy away from its name.

Have we "proved the existence of the soul"? I would not put it that way. We started by observing that there is a profound difference between a living person and a corpse, and that there must be some primary cause of this within the person's body. By reasoning from other facts about you, we deduced a number of surprising things about this cause. We did not reason to its existence, since that was obvious from the start—as obvious, in fact, as the existence of a difference between life and death. We reasoned not to its existence, but to its identity as some kind of form, and a substantial form in particular. If you discover a murdered body, you need no proof that there is a murderer, just a way to prove that the murderer is, for example, the butler. Likewise, when you note the difference between life and death, you need no proof that there is a cause of this, just a way to identify the nature of that cause and some of its distinctive attributes. That is all we have done.

Soul sometimes refers specifically to our emotional part ("soulful eyes" are expressive of feeling). Other times it refers to a certain type of music. Outside of meanings such as these, and apart from religious contexts, the word *soul* has long idled in general disuse. Words left too long on the shelf often acquire a weird feel and a number of odd connotations, and I want to emphasize that I do not intend any of these. Does Casper the Ghost come to mind? Banish him. A soul is not a white, ghostly little body haunting your physical body, as though you had two bodies, a tangible one and a thin, airy one. A soul is not a body at all, but the form of one.

Could we call this same principle a *spirit*? Perhaps. That word seems to imply something not yet in evidence, however. "Body and soul" is a more common pairing of words than "body and spirit", and if there are any beings that are purely nonmaterial and never existed in bodies at all, people would tend to refer to these as spirits rather than as souls. The word *spirit*, in other words, implies even more than *soul* does that such a thing can exist outside a body.

The word *soul* itself might also suggest something immortal and capable of surviving the destruction of the body. That is another reason I have held off using the term. Is the form of your body able to exist without your body? Even now, that is not entirely clear. How can there be "a form of your body" when your body no longer exists and is no longer you? When we melt down a bronze statue, does its former shape fly off to some ideal realm of other divested shapes of things, to enjoy there a separate existence emancipated from the statue it used to form? A form seems to be just that, a form of a thing, and when there is nothing formed by it anymore, the form itself has nothing to do, and nothing to be.

But how apt is this troubling illustration? A shape of bronze is a mere property of the bronze. The bronze supports the shape, and the shape does not cause the bronze to be, but only to be a statue. Your form is radically different from such a thing as that. It does not derive its being from your body, but is the reason your body has being as such a kind of body. It is a substantial form.

Is your form substantial enough, though, to keep existing even after the destruction of the thing it forms? If your soul is nothing but a form of matter, if the sum total of its being is to be in certain materials and to form them into something, then it cannot exist without your body and its materials. Probably most forms in nature are that way. In the case of your soul, we have something more to go on. Your soul lives part of its life even now outside of matter, or apart from it somehow, when it understands. Is that any indication that its existence is independent of matter, too?

Your Immortal Soul

It is as certain as anything can be, Cebes, that the soul is immortal and imperishable, and that our souls will really exist in the next world.

—Socrates, Plato's *Phaedo*

"Just the Flu"

My longest-running friendship is over forty years old. It began on the first day of first grade, first thing in the morning, with the first person I met at the bus stop, Matt McSorley. We introduced ourselves. We talked over a few essentials, determined that we had a sufficient number of things in common—Lego, baseball, anxiety about school— and became fast friends before the bus arrived. Matt's was the first house to which I was invited for a sleepover. I was thrilled to learn that there was no official bedtime under his parents' regime. I could stay up until midnight if I wanted to. And I did want to. Having no experience of midnight, I was resolved to find out what it looked like. Matt, accustomed to such liberty, took no interest in this experiment and turned in around nine thirty. I stayed up watching *Starsky and Hutch* and observed the clock for as long as I could, but the latest time I noted was around ten forty-five. Next morning I woke up in a bed I had never climbed into. At breakfast I savored my first English muffin and asked Mrs. McSorley if I could have a second one. (What delicious things! Why didn't my mother know about them?) After breakfast, Matt and I and his four-year-old brother, Mikey, built something or other out of Lego bricks and played *Stratego*. I know I saw Mikey more than just that one time, but it is the only time that really sticks in my memory. The other thing about Mikey that sticks in my mind is that he one day came down with the flu—"Just the flu," as I am told one doctor put it to his concerned mother. Matt and I had the same flu. Its main symptom besides a fever was a severe headache. Mikey's case was different, however. He wasn't getting better and wound up in the hospital. The doctors warned his parents that he would appear to improve and feel better, but that this illusory recovery would not last. It happened just as they said. He seemed to feel better, to be himself again. Not long after that, Mikey died.

I remember my mother explaining it to me. My first reaction was that this news made no sense. Mikey was alive and well the last time I had seen him. Surely it takes a lot longer to die than that. And, far more importantly, Mikey was a kid. Kids don't die. Death is for old people. I actually thought it was impossible for Mikey to be dead. There had been some kind of mistake. Or someone must have hidden him away somewhere. I'm not sure how long it took me to absorb this strange response to that tragedy, the first one I ever knew. Matt could not afford the luxury of mere bewildered disbelief. He lived in a house with that gaping absence in it all the time. He was reduced to tears easily and often now. And his mother always seemed to be wearing sunglasses, regardless of the weather or the time of day. Imperceptive and egocentric as my six-year-old self was, I could see that Matt and his mother (Matt's father was less often home and left less impression upon me) had been permanently changed by this abrupt severance from someone who shared life with them. Matt would eventually smile more often, I suspected. Mrs. McSorley would probably stop wearing sunglasses on rainy days. But other, more hidden effects of their loss would surely persist and evolve through various forms for the rest of their lives.

Many of us seem to have as much difficulty believing in our bodily mortality as in our spiritual immortality. If death is not just for old people, at least it is for *other* people. It is not for us and for those we hold dear. Thus do we (mostly involuntarily) keep death at an acceptable distance when it is not knocking on our chamber door, and thus can we tolerate its existence and find it bearable. This fragile and temporary arrangement is easiest to maintain when we are in good health ourselves, along with everyone else we care deeply about.

A professor friend of mine once invited me to address one of his classes as a guest lecturer. I was asked to speak on God and the soul. What can one say about these things inside an hour? Not much. I abandoned any idea of trying to present evidence for the existence of God or the immortality of the soul, and decided instead just to draw out some of the consequences of believing or disbelieving in these things. One consequence of disbelieving in either one, I said to the students, is that perfect happiness becomes an impossibility. We cannot be perfectly happy so long as we are burdened with our mortality, and we cannot even hope for perfect happiness if our life is purely this mortal one.

A student raised her hand and objected that she was perfectly happy already. I do not recall how I responded to this. Mostly I remember being caught off guard. Outside the pressure of such moments, though, I know well enough how to reply. Perfect happiness requires not only that we *think* we are in a good way, but also that we really are. If we think we are well-off, but really we are not, that is practically the definition of false happiness. Think of clueless meth addicts or problem gamblers who believe they are getting a lot out of life and have everything under control. If we think ourselves perfectly happy on this side of the grave, it is only because we have something in common with these self-deceivers. It is only because we can tune out our mortality and vulnerability, and effectively disbelieve it, that we can ever be so silly as to think ourselves perfectly happy in this world.

Picture a gathering of family and friends celebrating a wedding, an anniversary, a political triumph, or some other cause for common rejoicing. For the moment, they are enjoying all the good things in life. They are young, healthy, wealthy, good-looking, educated, successful, well regarded, and genuinely fond of one another. Only there is a time bomb under the head table, and every last one of them will be dead within the hour. They think themselves perfectly happy. Would you willingly give up your knowledge of the bomb in order to take part in their blissful ignorance?

And yet our situation is essentially the same as theirs. Our future death is a time bomb we cannot diffuse, and in most cases we cannot see what time remains on the clock. This very moment might mark when my life is exactly half over and done with, so far as I know. Or it might mark the beginning of my final twenty-four hours. Most of us cannot even know, for most of life, what shape our death will take. And this goes not only for ourselves, but also for all whom we hold dear, and the order in which they will succumb to death is something we must discover through painful experience. This is perfect happiness? Even if some period of distraction from our true condition is something we can reasonably hope for in this world, it certainly leaves much to be desired. It is not all we could wish.

We are odd creatures, we humans. We are capable of the deepest-reaching affections for each other, and for life itself. No other earthly creatures besides us can contemplate living forever, desire it, discover its possibility, or else be tormented by its impossibility. And yet we rank among the most fragile and temporary things in existence. The life spans of many animals may be even shorter than ours, but many also live longer. The longest-lived organisms are not even animals, but forms of vegetative life devoid of any interior awareness, let alone affection. Behind my house sits the old stump of an enormous pepper tree that the builders of my development had cut down in order to open up the view. Around the rim of this stump there sprouts up every spring a corona of pepper tree shoots, and if I let it go long enough, it becomes a weird, imposing pepper tree "bush". Once a year I hack away at it, since it is no longer a real tree, and since it does indeed threaten to obscure a sweeping view of far lovelier trees in the distance. I have been doing this for nearly a decade. No manner of violence by saw or by hatchet seems to discourage that immortal stump. Why should this be? If a pepper tree stump is less worthy of longevity than a child like Mikey McSorley, then it is somehow backward that the stump should get to live longer. Can that really be the whole story that nature has to tell in this matter? Are we at once the beings most able to crave individual immortality, and least able to attain it?

The truth is not so bleak. You and yours are of course mortals, doomed to dissolution one day. But this will not mean the annihilation of every part of you that is distinctively you. Your essential form, and your mind and will, which are seated in it, are indestructible and immortal. At least these deepest parts of you, which make you to be you, will live on forever.

Life outside Work

Can your soul exist without your body? At first that sounds impossible. Can a form exist apart from what it forms? Can the shape of the clay exist without the clay? If I begin with a spherical mass of clay and mold it into a cube, where has its old spherical shape gone? A ridiculous question. Of course it has simply ceased to be. The previous shape of the clay cannot extricate itself from the clay and skulk away to the corner of the room. It was precisely the shape of this clay, and nothing else. When the shape of this clay is no longer the shape of this clay, why, then it simply is no more.

Why say anything different about the life-giving form of your body? Once your body has ceased to be, how can "the form of your body" still exist?

A form such as a shape is a mere property, not a substantial form that causes its owner to exist. The spherical shape in the clay causes the clay to be spherical, not simply to be. Your form, your soul, is quite different. It is a substantial form. It causes you not just to be in some particular respect, but simply to exist as the substance that you are. Your soul gives existence to your body, and so far as that goes, we have a reason why your living human body cannot exist without your soul, not a reason why your soul cannot exist without your body.

Still, how could "a form of a body" be without that body? Does the substantial form of a mushroom exist after the mushroom is destroyed? Not very likely. In fact, if a form of a certain body is nothing but that, a form of such a body, then it clearly cannot exist when such a body is gone.

Is your soul anything more than the form of your body? Your soul is the form of your body and lives much of its life, your life, in it. But even while your soul gives life to your body, it also lives a life beyond it, too—an intellectual life, for example. Most of your activities take place in and by means of your bodily organs. Your acts of understanding, since they are universal, are an exception. Bodily organs cannot form universal ideas of things, and so your intellect, your power of forming universal ideas, is not in your body, but only in your soul. Some of your acts of loving and desiring, too, when they are not purely emotional but based on your understanding of what is good and bad, right and wrong, take place in your soul and not in your body. Since the activity and power of your soul is not entirely in your body, then neither is its existence and life entirely in your body. Your soul, in other words, is *not* just the form of your body. And therefore, when it ceases to be the form of your body, it does not by that fact cease to be.

Is that going too far? The dependence of your thinking on your brain might give us pause. As long as your soul exists in your body, it depends on the functioning of your brain in order to think, or at least to think well. That is not because your brain is the organ in which you do your thinking, however, but because it is the organ in which you sense and imagine particular examples of things from which to extract universal ideas. This kind of dependence does not make your intellect dependent on your body in order to exist. Your eyesight cannot function, either, unless visible objects present themselves to it in the light. But it can exist without those objects. What it cannot exist without is the organ that supports it. Since there is no organ that houses your intellect, its existence is independent of your body. Your body cannot be alive or be you without your soul. But your soul can be, and have its intellectual power, without your body.

Workaholics are in danger of finding themselves without a life when they retire, since their work was their whole life. Retirees who kept up a healthy life outside of work during the years of their career are another story. When they retire, they cease to be employed and withdraw from their professional life. But they do not simply by that fact cease to be or withdraw from life, since their life at work was never the whole of their life. Your soul is like that in relation to your body. Its life is not completely immersed in your body. It has a life outside of the work of making your body be you.

The shape of a piece of clay, on the other hand, is nothing but the shape of the clay, so it has nothing to be or to do apart from the clay. Probably the other substantial forms in nature besides yours are like that. The form of water cannot exist apart from the hydrogen and oxygen that it forms into water. The form of water has, is, and does nothing outside of the materials that it causes to be water. Anyway, it offers us no reason to think otherwise. Even the form of a horse, alive and remarkable as it is, does not seem to perform any activities except in and by means of the materials of the horse. The horse can sense, imagine, remember, feel hungry or afraid, whinny and gallop, but these activities take place in its body and brain. If it is right to speak of the *soul* of a horse, then it is a soul that does everything it does in the horse's body, and so its existence is only in the body of the horse. When the horse dies, its soul is gone, as the shape of a piece of clay is gone when the clay is re-formed into something new.

Your soul is different. Like the soul of the horse, it gives being to your body and is the source of its powers. Unlike the soul of a horse, that is not all it does for a living. It also has its own powers of understanding and willing that are not in your body or from your body. When your body ceases to be, your soul ceases to be its form. But it does not by that fact cease to be.

Your Indestructible Side

Are we now justified in concluding that your soul is immortal? Almost, but not quite yet. Our reasoning has shown only that the destruction of your body cannot cause the destruction of your soul, and that your soul is capable of existence without your body. Your soul is the sort of thing that can continue to exist after its business of being the form of your body is concluded. By itself, that is no guarantee that your soul will go on living forever, or that it won't one day suffer its own destruction by other causes.

Plato wrote a dialogue called the *Phaedo*, in which he recounts the last conversation of Socrates. Socrates was in prison, soon to drink the hemlock that would carry out the death sentence that an Athenian court had imposed on him, so his friends were present to comfort him (although it was in fact he who comforted them) and hear his thoughts one last time. Appropriately enough, the subject of the conversation was the immortality of the soul. In the course of their discussion, Socrates and his friends considered a number of arguments on both sides of the question. They earnestly desired to know whether the soul is immortal or not, because they did not want this to be the last time they got to speak with Socrates, just the last time in this life. At one point in the conversation, Socrates argued that the soul can exist after the body. Nearly everyone present rejoiced, thinking this meant that the soul is immortal, and that they now knew this for certain. One fellow, however, Cebes by name, remained unconvinced. Cebes worried that maybe the soul will die anyway, even if not together with and because of the death of the body. He compared the body to a coat. You can outlive your coat. When your coat wears out, you live on and buy a new coat. But eventually one of your coats will outlive you. Could your soul be like that? Could it survive the death of your body, only to go on and suffer some kind of destruction of its own later on for other reasons?

There are lots of ways to destroy things, of course, and little kids discover most of them. Things can be cut, burned, crushed, shattered, shredded, erased, reformatted, and on and on. Most of them obviously could not apply to your soul, since your soul has no shape or size or parts. It is whole in every part of you, and nothing like that can have shape or size or parts. So your soul can never fall apart, at least. But might there be some other way for it to suffer destruction? That is our question now. To answer it, we must become more familiar with what destruction really is.

Destruction is not complete annihilation. It is the forming of something new out of the materials of the thing that is destroyed. It is basically recycling. When I was young, the side door to my parents' house opened out onto a very small, uncovered deck with a railing. They decided to tear it down and build a new, larger porch with a roof. The wood that once was the old porch first became a scrap pile, and later my first tree fort. Sometimes the destruction of a thing means re-forming its materials with a new form worthy of a name, such as the form of a tree fort. Other times the destruction of a thing means re-forming its materials with a new form or forms unworthy of any special name, as when we rearrange the parts of an old deck into a disorderly pile. Either way, we always produce something new out of the materials of the things we destroy, even if not something very noble or nameworthy. Nature behaves the same way. The destruction of a living thing, for example, can produce a corpse, or else new life. Natural destruction is never simple annihilation, but always the production of a new thing as well, since the destruction consists in the replacing of an old form in certain materials with a new form incompatible with the old one.

Whatever is destroyed is therefore a combination of two things: materials and a form of some kind. The porch is wood plus a certain arrangement. A car is steel and other materials in certain shapes and arrangements plus the working order among these things. The animal is its natural materials plus the soul making them to be that animal. Destruction of such a thing is just the replacement of its form with a new form that cannot abide the continuing presence of the old form in the same materials.

That means that destruction is usually a two-for-one deal. Not only is the original formed thing (the porch, the car, the animal) destroyed, but also its form as well. Suppose you are paying someone to tear down a house. Once the demolition team goes to work, you can be sure that the form of the house (the structurally sound arrangement of its materials that form them into a house) will cease to exist every bit as much as the house itself will. You don't need two wrecking crews, one to demolish the house, and another one to demolish the form of the house. You would be understandably upset if the demolition team, on their itemized bill, charged you separately for the destruction of the house and for the destruction of its form. They might charge you separately for hauling away the materials, but that is another matter. It would be outrageous to charge you once for the destruction of the house and again for the destruction of its form, as if these were two separate destructions. The destruction of the form of the house is not a separate destruction, but a free side effect, or part and parcel of the destruction of the house itself.

These general observations are all we need to answer our question. Is it possible to destroy your soul? Your soul is a form. Is it possible to destroy a form? Not in the way that it is possible to destroy a house, or anything else that consists in materials having a certain form. To destroy something like that, we must replace the form it has with another one. But what would it mean to do that to a form? A form does not itself have a form, but simply is a form. So it is not possible to take away or replace the form it has, since it has none. You can shape a piece of bronze, but you cannot also shape the shape. That's meaningless. You can remove a shape from a piece of bronze, but you can't remove a shape from the shape. That's also meaningless.

The only way to destroy a form is as the free side effect of replacing that form in some thing that it forms. When you replace the shape of the bronze with another shape, you have effectively destroyed the old shape, since it is no longer the shape of that bronze, and it was never anything but the shape of that bronze. In this way alone does a form lie open to destruction. If a form is nothing but the form of the thing it constitutes, and that thing is destroyed by the replacing of its form, then the old form is gone. Nature provides no way of destroying a form if it is one that does not depend on the existence of the thing it forms. You can't re-form it into a new thing, since it does not have a form but simply is one, and you can't destroy it as a consequence of destroying what it forms, since its existence does not depend on that thing. There is no way to destroy such a form. It is naturally indestructible.

Yours is just such a form. Although it gives existence to your body, it does not depend on your body in order to exist, since it is not only the form and life of your body, but also has a life of its own apart from your body. So the replacing of your soul with some other form in your body's materials will stop your soul from sharing its existence with your body, but cannot destroy your soul.

This conclusion ranks among the most magnificent in all philosophy: your soul cannot be destroyed. Like any other form, it cannot be destroyed by being re-formed into something else. Unlike any other form we know of, it also cannot be destroyed by re-forming the body it forms. Thanks to its intelligent life outside your body, and its nature as a pure form, your soul is an indestructible, immortal thing.

The Fate of the Soul

Your body is to your soul somewhat as your arm is to you. You can live without your arm. And so long as your arm is a part of you, it possesses no life or being of its own, but only yours. It is you who live and exist in that arm. That is how your soul is related to your body. It can live and be without your body. But it can also communicate its life and being to your body, so that the body exists and lives by your soul. Unlike "the rest of you minus your arm", however, your soul is not a thing composed of parts, or of matter and form, but it is a pure form, and so it is of an indestructible nature.

The indestructibility of the human soul provokes some of my students to raise a certain question. How can the soul be indestructible if God can destroy it? Or if God cannot destroy it, what sense does that make, if he made the soul in the first place? Can he make something that he is unable to destroy? This question is a bit out of order here, at least philosophically, since our own souls are far more familiar to us, more accessible in our ordinary experience, than any divine being. As long as we are proceeding by the light of reason, not by the light of a divine revelation, we ought to ask about God in light of what we know about our souls, not ask about our souls in light of what we know about God. If the existence of your soul does not depend on your body, but does continuously depend on God giving it existence, then your soul is not a self-existent, self-immortal thing. Nonetheless, if God is good and by choice gave your soul an existence that is not naturally destructible, that would not be a reason to worry that he would one day withhold existence from your soul, but a reason to think he specially set it aside from other natural things for an existence that is everlasting. I will return to that idea toward the end of this book.

We have come far in discovering what kind of being you are. Your body is of course a real part of you—so is your soul. Yet you are not a ghost haunting a machine, nor are you somehow two beings, but instead you are just one, since your soul and your body are complementary constituents of one complete human being. Your soul is the essential form of your body, making its materials to be such a body and to be alive. Your soul is not *just* the essential form of your body, however, but holds its head above matter, so to speak, enjoying a life and activity outside matter in addition to its job of forming your materials into you. Your soul, consequently, is not destroyed by the destruction of your body.

Nor will your soul ever cease to be. It is not a destructible thing, but is naturally immortal, since it is a form that does not depend on the existence of the thing it forms. You as a whole are mortal. The chief part of you, your soul, is not.

All this leaves us still with much to wonder about. What is existence like for a soul after death? Will it ever be rejoined to matter and thus form a new body? Whatever the fate of a soul may be, it will not find itself reincarnated in a new body entirely different from the one it now possesses. You cannot "come back as another person", let alone come back as an aardvark or as a carrot. Your soul is your form, after all. What it does is form you. Even if we could take hold of the very shape of Michelangelo's David and somehow wrest it free from the marble it forms, we could not then place that shape in some other material and get a bust of Homer Simpson. The David shape, just because it is a David shape, forms its recipient material into a David, and nothing else. A human soul, and in particular the form of you, is a similar case. The you-form, when joined to matter, forms (drumroll please) *you*. If your soul were not the very form of your body, but instead were like a little person in its own right that could inhabit a body as a driver sits behind the wheel, then just as a person can switch from one kind of car to another, or even pilot a plane or ride a bike, so too your soul could, conceivably, hop from one kind of body to another between lives. As things are, that is entirely impossible. Your soul is your form. For your soul to be in matter is for it to form a human body, and yours in particular. The idea that you might be reincarnated as another person or as an animal comes from a radical misconception of what you are and what your soul is.

But the question remains: What is the existence of the soul like after death? Is it comatose, inert, without the help of the brain to present it with raw materials out of which to extract objects to understand? Is death an everlasting sleep of a real, indestructible, but forever inactive soul? And if your soul is indestructible and will never *cease* to be, did it also never *begin* to be? Or if it began to be with your body, what caused it to come to be? Where did your soul come from? Due to the general similarities between you and other living things, it is likely that there is a common cause at work. For that reason it will be useful to look into what you have in common with other living things before asking about the origin of your soul.

These questions will occupy us for the next few chapters. While many of them will take us to the very borders of philosophy, and their full answers would require us to overstep those boundaries, we will find that the light of reason has many worthwhile things to say to each.

Eyes Are for Seeing

If "that for the sake of which" exists in art, it exists also in nature.

—Aristotle, *Physics*

Early Astronomy

Upon a bitter cold, clear, moonless night in the middle of a New England January, my father set up our telescope on its wooden tripod in our front yard. This was my first lesson in astronomical observation. I remember seeing my breath turn to white clouds that tore away and disappeared in the breeze, and feeling the pleasant numbness of my face (the only part of me exposed to the winter air). That night I saw the rings of Saturn for the first time, impossible to discern by the naked eye.

Brrr! The breeze picked up. With it came the sharp cracklings of a thousand icicles high in the nearby treetops that swooshed back and forth like black waves under the starry sky. Now this was living! It made me feel alive to be outside in such weather for so noble a purpose. Who else in the whole wide world was so zealous as these two astronomers, father and son, braving the wind on a frosty, midwinter's night just to catch a glimpse of those celestial worlds above? No one else, I felt sure. Those silently twinkling sparks, wild and aloof, stood there just for us two explorers alone.

The rings of Saturn were wonderfully alien and exciting, but the naked-eye patterns in the heavens fascinated me, too. I began scanning the sky for anything significant, and lo! I made my first momentous discovery:

"Dad! Dad, look!" I cried, pointing overhead. "Right there! See? Those three stars make a straight line and they're perfectly spaced!"

This amazed me, and I was very proud of this scientific finding of mine.

"Hmm?" My father had been peering into the telescope and now turned his head to follow my pointing finger. "Oh," he said, "you've found Orion's Belt." He pointed out the remainder of the prominent constellation and explained who Orion was. When I later looked it up in a book, there it was, the same pattern my father had shown me, belt and all. Although I continued to enjoy observing the stars, I quickly found I could learn about them much faster by reading books written by people equipped with better telescopes and deeper knowledge than I could hope to attain by my own efforts. My reading taught me that each star, tiny as it may appear, is really a sun, and like our sun is a giant plasma ball containing an ongoing nuclear explosion held together by its own gravity. So it befell that I knew the answer to an ancient question before I had ever had the chance to ask it—"What is a star?" I remember being subsequently puzzled by the nursery rhyme:

> Twinkle, twinkle, little star
> How I wonder what you are

What was there to wonder about? Stars do not *really* twinkle. The twinkling is just a trick of our atmosphere. And everyone who bothers to look it up knows that a star is a giant plasma ball containing an ongoing nuclear explosion held together by its own gravity. Even the dictionary said it. I never wondered what stars were. I wondered why anyone would wonder.

Many years later, when I was in college, I began to understand why those who had not been spoon-fed facts about the stars could wonder about them in so basic a way as to ask what they are. Without telescopes, Internet access, or the discoveries of geniuses like Copernicus, Kepler, and Galileo, what might previous generations have theorized about the stars?

One thing they wondered was whether or not the stars were alive. Their apparent twinkling makes them look alive, as if they are fluttering around up there. Also, the whole sky appears to wheel counterclockwise around Polaris, the pole star. We do not feel the earth's rotation, and nothing in ordinary experience or pre-Copernican thought compels us to think the earth rotates or moves in any way except during an earthquake. The most natural interpretation of our ordinary experience is that the earth is sitting still. If that were true, then the stars would have to be rotating around our world, which would mean they are moving very fast, and apparently all by themselves. This, too, could be construed as evidence that the stars or the heavens are alive.

Many of the ancients believed this was the case. Imagine, now, what that would mean. In this pre-Copernican understanding of the world, the stars were fixed in an enormous, self-moving sphere, like so many spots on an animal. The name of this living crystalline ball was the "sphere of fixed stars". Other living beings, the lesser spheres on which the planets rode, revolved within its embrace. The heavens were thus full of life and unceasing activity. The biggest, fastest, most all-containing and everlasting things were these living beings, and life was the norm in the universe. Inanimate things existed only in one insignificant spot in the cosmos, down here on earth, sitting inside all those nested, living, celestial containers. Life on Earth was mortal, whereas the celestial animals were everlasting. As a consequence, they were also entirely *other*, sharing no materials with the destructible things found down here at the bottom of the world. If the heavens really were alive, then the distinction of the living from the nonliving, and the priority of the living to the nonliving in the cosmic order, would be sharp and clear.

We today can hardly think such thoughts, having been raised on truer accounts of the stars that preclude these fantastic possibilities from the start. We know that there is no real reason to believe they are immortal living beings made of indestructible stuff. Stars are not alive, and their existence begins and ends. They are also made of the same ultimate stuff as we are, and indeed our materials came largely from the processes that go on inside them. If, in the grand scheme of things, living things really are essentially distinct from and superior to nonliving ones, this truth must emerge from facts about life as we know it here on Earth, and from more nuanced comparisons than those of size, speed, and longevity.

Are living things essentially distinct from nonliving ones? Or is that idea as antiquated as the geocentric vision of the world that seemed to support it? To answer this question, we must say what a living thing is. Since you are a living thing yourself, the question falls under our overarching question about what you are. In the measure that we are in the dark about what a living thing is and what distinguishes it from a nonliving one, we are in the dark about ourselves.

Then why ask this very general question about what you are only now? You are a living thing endowed with sense and intellect. We have talked about the more distinctive side of you, sense and intellect, quite a bit. Shouldn't we have asked first the more general question of what it means for you to be alive?

As we shall see, we could not have begun with this question at the outset, since defining a living thing will rely on some of our previous work—for example, that you are not a collective, but a single being. That is one reason I have postponed the question of what a living thing is until now. But there is another reason as well. I have a special reason for asking what a living thing is. The answer will reveal a peculiar purposefulness in you, in all your parts, and in every living thing—an unconscious purposefulness. Quite apart from your deliberate intentions, your parts are up to something. They are not just mechanical things obeying mathematical laws, since their behavior cannot be understood apart from the good results they produce. That especially is what I intend to show. In the language of Aristotle, one thing in nature is for the sake of another, as eyes come into existence for the sake of seeing, to make that future good possible. This fits with my general aim of pointing out some of the ways that human nature and nature as a whole have more to them than the vocabulary of modern science alone can express. But learning about the purposes of nature will also prove useful for answering the question that arose at the end of the last chapter about where your soul came from, something we wonder about especially after discovering it is immortal. The goal-oriented character of living things that we will discover in this chapter, and a similar character in the cosmos as a whole that we will discuss in the next, are clues that we can trace back to the cause of your soul and of the whole natural world.

Toward a Definition of *Life*

So, what is a living thing? What is it to be alive?

Biologists have something to say about this, and it would not be right to launch our own investigation into the question without first acknowledging them. Biologists tend to study living things from an outsider's view—a souped-up outsider's view, that is. With the assistance of microscopes, the techniques of biochemistry, and other such devices and methods, they have made countless discoveries about living things that could not have been made otherwise, and certainly not by mere consultation of our own experience of being alive. Some of these discoveries touch on living things in general. For example, so far as we can tell, all living things consist of one or more cells. We might accordingly define a living thing as something made of one or more units called cells.

This definition undeniably advances our understanding of living things, but it does not say (nor does it try to say) what people meant by *alive* before the advent of modern biology. The word must have meant something. If a "living thing" is "something made of one or more cells", but a "cell" is "the basic unit of which living things are made", then there must be some way of saying what a "living thing" is that does not require a reference to cells, or else our definitions will be circular.

Biologists also study activities of life, and some of these are common to all living things—obtaining and using materials and energy, for example, and growing, reproducing, and responding to an environment, to name just a few. So some biologists define living things as things that perform some or all of these activities.

Sometimes people object that these activities are not unique to living things. A crystal can be said to "grow", for example, and a fire in some sense "consumes" and can even "reproduce". This is no real problem. Clearly a fire or a crystal does not *grow* in the same sense of the word that you or a dog or an aspen can grow. Analogously, we can define *reproduce, obtain and use energy*, and *self-repair* in ways that would bring out the unique manner in which these activities are attributed to living things. Properly understood, any one of these activities would be common to all species of living things and unique to living things, and could therefore serve to define living things. For example, we might say this:

A *living thing* is a thing capable of growth; that is, it is an individual (as opposed to a collective) that can increase its own size by taking in foreign materials and distributing these within itself to make them into parts of all its parts.

Have we now successfully defined *living thing*? Not quite. The description above does circumscribe living things. It includes all living things we know of and excludes all nonliving ones. And that is enough for most purposes of the biologists, who are understandably anxious to get into the details of living things. But the description does not really say what it means to be a living thing. Being alive does not mean "being a thing that can grow", even if it is true that all living things do at some time in their lives grow, just as being alive does not mean "being a thing that can heal itself", even if that description happened to fit all living things and only living things. "Growing" and "healing itself" are obviously not synonyms, either. Why should being alive be defined by one of these rather than the other?

There are many activities called living. What we seek is the special attribute that entitles them all to be called living. What is the quality common to all these activities and absent from nonliving activities? In order to discover this common something-or-other that qualifies an activity as a living one, we may draw up a representative (though not necessarily exhaustive) list of living activities to survey. We should feel free to include some activities that are peculiar to certain specific organisms, as long as they definitely qualify as living activities. Here is such a list:

- Metabolizing
- Growing
- Healing
- Reproducing
- Walking
- Sensing
- Understanding
- Desiring

What common feature in all these activities sets them apart from nonliving activities? For starters, all of them originate within the being whose activities they are. Wind is active and can do things, but it is not alive. Why not? Because the motion of air does not originate in the air itself, but entirely in the sun, or some other outside influence working on the air. The movement of wind is therefore not a living activity. And which is more obviously alive, a horse or a spot of mold on a bun? Clearly the galloping horse. But why? What is the stand-out difference? Just this: the horse undeniably moves around of its own accord. Much more noticeably than the mold, the horse initiates activities within itself. The mold, too, originates its own activities, just less obviously. When mold grows, for example, it is growing itself. It is not the bread on which it grows that causes the mold to grow, although the bread provides needed materials.

One distinctive quality of living activities, then, is that they originate somehow within the one performing them. Living things are self-movers.

There is something else common to all the activities we describe as *living*. Living activities benefit the being whose activities they are, whether by benefiting its parts, or the whole of it, or its species. Take self-repair, for example. All familiar living things do it. You heal from scratches and get over colds. Even a tree will heal from the proper pruning of a limb. This is self-beneficial behavior. The very phrase *self-repair* means not only that the repairing action originates in the thing being repaired, but also that the thing doing the repairing is the beneficiary of the action. The taking of nourishment sustains and energizes the thing that takes nourishment. Growth and development increase and complete the thing that grows and develops. Locomotion gets the self-moving thing where it wants to go. Sensing and thinking apprise an animal of many things advantageous or dangerous to it. Reproduction seems a more selfless living activity (although animals are induced to do it by a desire for pleasure), but even it serves the reproducer in a way, by continuing the existence of its type. If it will not live on, at least others like it will.

Using these common features of living activities that set them apart from nonliving ones, we can now take a second stab at a definition: "A *living thing* is a being that originates its own self-beneficial actions." A living thing is a thing that takes action for itself, we might say. That seems to bring out what we mean by *alive*. Whatever initiates its own self-beneficial action (and is not moved to do things purely and simply by an outside influence) is somehow alive.

Does this definition really succeed in setting living things apart from nonliving ones? Some artificial things seem to move themselves for their own benefit. Consider a Roomba (a brand of robotic carpet vac). After vacuuming the carpet for a while, it goes to recharge itself.

Is it therefore *alive* by the definition above? Do we have to bite the bullet here?

No. The Roomba parts ways with the living at the very first opportunity. It is not truly "a being". It is truer to say that it is many beings, connected to each other in various ways. A robotic floor vac is not an individual thing as you are, but a collective of individual things (bits of steel, copper, rubber, and plastic) whose individual properties we human beings have exploited by bringing them together in such an arrangement that their net behavior is beneficial to us. The same goes for a computer or a car. The old-fashioned name for a car—*automobile*—implies that it "moves itself". That would appear to make it alive by the definition above, except that there is no true "itself" in the case of a car. In the nature of things, apart from human purposes, the car is only a *they* and not an *it*. In this respect, it is like a horse and carriage (another old-fashioned name for a car is a "horseless carriage"). The horse and carriage is really many beings linked together, not one individual. We tend to speak of such a multitude as an "it" and in the singular because of its purposive unity: the parts of a car are stuck together (by us) with a view to a single principal purpose—namely, transportation (for us). A car or a horse and carriage is really many things, some of which act on others, with the result that the whole collective moves "itself". A living thing, on the other hand, is truly a single thing, some of whose parts act on others, with the result that the whole individual moves itself.

The Roomba and the car fail the test for life in another way. A living thing acts toward its own benefit—maybe to the benefit of others, too, but at least sometimes to its own benefit. A Roomba does no such thing. Nor does a car. All the tendency for the car to be driven resides in the will of the driver. My car "itself", or the collection of artificially shaped substances that I call my car, is indifferent (or else hostile) to the goal of getting me to work on time. My Roomba recharges "itself", but not because of any real inclination in it to keep my carpet clean. So far as the world outside my head is concerned, the Roomba's benefit to me is only a net side effect of the many physical tendencies and interactions of the bits and pieces composing it—just as a horse is indifferent to getting me to work on time, although it might happen to do this when its horse behaviors can be harnessed for that result. The natural substances that go by the collective names of my *car* and my *Roomba* have no special inclination to serve the purposes for which I employ them, no more than a rock has a tendency to function as a paperweight.

In contrast to all of this, a living thing has its own built-in agenda, arising from what it is. A horse embryo grows into a horse, and that is its own program of action, not one that someone imposes on it. Unlike an artificial thing, the body of a living thing is an individual natural substance with a power and inclination for living activities somehow built into it. The business of living is not irrelevant to a living body. On the contrary, the parts of a living body are means to an end, and deserve to be called its instruments or tools. The definition of a living thing can therefore be reformulated like this: "A *living thing* is a natural being made up of tools for itself." We can say it even more shortly if we are willing to dabble in a little Greek. The Greek word for "tool" is ὄργανον, from which we derive our words *organ*, *organic*, and *organism*. An ancient Greek carpenter would have called his hammer or saw an *organon*. So a living thing, we may say, is an *organic* natural being, one that is composed of parts that are its tools for carrying out its self-beneficial activities, for making its living in the world. This fits with the biological discovery that all living things are made of cells, which are themselves like tiny organs, specially made for carrying out the activities of life. The smallest forms of life, the single-celled forms, are also "organic" in the sense of being composed of tools for performing self-beneficial activities. Their "organs" are their organelles, their walls or membranes and other structural components, and also those smallest tools of all, proteins.

Are Eyes Really "for" Seeing?

This idea of tools in the definition of *living thing* deserves closer scrutiny. Is it some kind of metaphor? Is it strictly accurate to call an eye or a hand a "tool"? They are not detached tools like a knife or a fork. They are naturally conjoined to their owner. We can easily remedy that just by noting that we mean attached tools when we say a living thing is composed of tools.

There is a more pressing difficulty, however. A tool is by definition something for performing a specific task (or tasks). There can be no doubt that we use our hands and eyes to perform specific tasks. The tricky part is whether our hands and eyes are really *for* those tasks. I can use a stone as a paperweight or as a doorstop or as a weapon. Does this prove that stones are for those tasks, that stones, by their very nature, are tools? That seems farfetched. Better to say that I employ stones for my purposes, but the stones are in themselves not for those purposes at all. They are indifferent to my wishes, with no intrinsic orientation toward serving them. The tools in my garage are no different. A *wrench* is by definition a tool, but the chunk of steel I call a wrench, considered purely in itself and apart from human beings and their purposes, is just a funny-shaped chunk of steel, neither a wrench nor a tool. When I call the things in my garage *tools*, I am saying something not about their attitude toward me, but about my attitude toward them.

Could the same thing be true about your eyes and your hands? Could it be that you use them for seeing and grasping, but these are only your choices regarding how to use them, and not what they themselves are intrinsically "for"? People use their noses to hold up their glasses. Are noses therefore for holding up glasses? Some people like to get nose piercings. Shall we say that noses are for nose piercings? That skin is for tattoos? And if not, then what justifies our saying that eyes are for seeing? Just because we can use them for seeing, and just because we choose to use them that way, does not mean they are in themselves really for seeing.

To make matters worse, plants do not possess any conscious desires, any wishes, and so it seems they can never put their parts to use for accomplishing something they want. Only animals desire things. Like us, other animals can put their parts to use in order to get what they want. An elephant moseys down to the river because it wishes to quench its thirst. It makes its legs function as means to that end. But a tree does not "wish" to use its leaves for photosynthesis. Then what can it mean to say that the tree is made of tools—that is, of parts that are for certain uses? The word *for* implies a purpose, a goal that will satisfy desire. It would seem that where there is no desire, there can be no question of anything being for the sake of anything else. Consequently, our definition of living things does not seem to apply to the plants.

Worse still, it does not even seem to apply to ourselves. When we grow our eyes, we do so every bit as unconsciously as plants sprout their leaves. Do we grow our eyes "for seeing" and "in order to see"? If we say yes, does that mean we grow our eyes by choice, that we design them with our future eyesight in mind? That is quite ridiculous. But if we say no, then it seems we must revise our definition of living things, since all their parts (even our own) come to be not for the sake of serving some future purpose, but mindlessly, unconsciously, automatically, in answer to no desire at all. That seems to prevent their parts from being for anything, so far as the nature of things goes.

On the other hand, the alternative is to say that an animal is a mass of meaningless tissues that are inherently indifferent to the life activities of that animal, and that they only happen to be useful for performing them. While that is essentially the view that many a materialist philosopher will take, there is something very fishy about it.

Is there any middle road? Is there a way to say that the body parts of a living thing are somehow really and truly for performing the life activities of their owner, even though it did not bring its parts into existence by conscious desire?

Yes. There is something just short of conscious desire, but similar enough to it in a general way that it can supply a purposive sense to the word *for*. That something is natural tendency.

Even apart from living things, we see that there is such a thing as unconscious tendency or inclination. In the most literal sense, a ball at the top of an inclined plane is inclined to roll down the ramp. This is not a conscious desire, to be sure, but a present tendency to a definite future action. It is not equally inclined to roll up the ramp. The ball has no wishes, but there is something in the ball that is analogous to desire—namely, its present orientation toward a definite future outcome.

We often employ the language of desire when speaking of the unconscious tendencies of inanimate things. The ball *tries* to go down the ramp, but your hand stops it. Opposite magnetic poles *like* each other. A stone *seeks* the center of the earth, and water *prefers* the path of least resistance. A stubborn floorboard won't stay in place, because it *wants* to bend up at one end. There is something playful and distinctly anthropomorphic in such talk. These expressions nonetheless exist for a good reason. We are noticing a kinship between natural tendencies and conscious desires. A conscious desire is itself nothing else than a specific kind of tendency, the kind that follows on awareness. When we become aware of a thing's fittingness to our-selves, its agreeability, we incline toward it with the special tendency called desire.

Unconscious tendencies, found even in nonliving things, can take the place of conscious desire in supplying a meaning to the purposive words *for* and *to*. The squeezed rubber ball has a distinct tendency to get back to its original size, for returning to its original size. This general idea of what a thing is "for" involves no notion of conscious desire, but only a specific end state to which a thing is inherently inclined. In itself, and not just in how we choose to view it, there is something orienting the ball toward a particular future condition, and when it gets there, that orientation or tendency rests. This is not exactly desire and satisfaction, but something analogous to them: tendency toward something, then arrival at it and the relaxation of the tendency.

Invoking the idea of unconscious natural tendency, it is fairly obvi-ous that your eyes are for seeing, and that they came into existence for seeing. Your eyes, open in the light, tend to see by their own interior constitution, not because of an outside force, and you grew your eyes by your own inherent tendencies. We would nevertheless be mistaken if we thought there was nothing remarkable about this. Consider the implications. When you were first growing and devel-oping, you were an unconscious thing with a tendency to produce your own consciousness. That is a strange thing. Moreover, if your future eyesight was the real goal or object of some tendency present in the earliest version of you, then we must admit that future benefits can be the reason for present actions even in a thing without aware-ness or any idea of the future. Because of how strange this is, many thinkers try to wiggle out of it, especially those wedded to a scientific determinism that says the past explains the future, never the other way around. For that reason, however obvious it may be that your eyes came into existence for the sake of seeing, it is worth explaining why saying so is not just projecting our human way of behaving on nature's way.

How should we go about finding criteria for deciding when an outcome is the object of a tendency, and when it isn't? We can find these by considering certain unintended outcomes of our own actions, then asking ourselves how an outsider could tell they were unintended. Suppose, for example, you go grocery shopping and bump into someone who owes you money and who has been trying to avoid you. Or suppose that while digging a new septic tank in your backyard, you find gold. Although both outcomes are desirable to you, neither was the object of any tendency that was actually driving you to go shopping or to dig in your backyard. Even someone who does not know you can figure that out. Why? Because these are extremely rare outcomes of the kinds of actions you were performing. People who go grocery shopping do not usually bump into people who owe them money. Those who dig a hole for a septic tank do not, as a matter of course, find gold as a result. Also, there is no definite causal relationship between these outcomes and the kinds of events that led to them. Not only is bumping into a debtor a rare outcome of grocery shopping, but bumping into a debtor is not the sort of thing that depends on grocery shopping.

Rare outcomes not resulting from any regular process are generally not the object of a specific tendency. Instead, objects of real tendencies will be regular outcomes of some definite kind of action or series of steps. Is that enough? Can we rest assured that where we find a regular outcome of some definite process we have also found the object of a tendency in the one carrying out the process? Not quite. Sometimes an action nearly always produces a certain outcome, and in the same way every time, but it is still not the object of any tendency in the one acting, not the thing its action was for. For example, when surgeons perform a certain type of surgery, a certain type of pain or disability might always result. That does not mean there is some pain-producing tendency in the surgeons, as though that were the very goal and object of the surgical procedure. The pain is a mere side effect of the real thing toward which the surgeons are acting— namely, the removal of a malignant tumor or something of the kind. This outcome of the surgeon's action fits much better with what a surgeon is. When pain is the object, that fits better with the definition of a torturer.

Putting together these criteria, we get a three-part test for determining whether an outcome of action is really the object of a tendency in the one acting. Whenever the outcome in question (1) always results from that kind of action, or at least results whenever all conditions are right and nothing interferes, and the outcome (2) results in the

same way each time, at the end of a definite process, and the outcome
(3) is the most appropriate of all the results, the one that most agrees
with the nature of the acting cause, then the outcome is an object of
a tendency in the agent. Perhaps an outcome can be a real object of a
tendency without meeting all these criteria, but whenever an outcome
meets all three, the agent that produces it does so out of a tendency
toward it.

According to these criteria, your eyes came into existence for seeing. Human eye development leads to the human act of seeing in
nearly all cases, and indeed in all cases where all the requirements
of eye development are present and no external influence interferes.
The growth of human eyes is a regular process too, producing the
ability to see by going through the same kinds of steps in every case.
The end result, seeing, also fits well with what a human being is, a
visual animal. That you are rightly described as a "visual animal" is
clear because the desire to see is something inborn in you, not the
result of a decision you made. Everyone desires to see, and desires it a
lot—even those among us who have never seen show signs of being
visual animals. Unless the process is halted somehow, or something
necessary is missing, everyone at least begins to develop the usual
apparatus of vision. Sometimes those who cannot see repurpose the
visual parts of their brains in order to elevate touch to a nearly visual
height of perceptual accuracy. The desire to see is therefore a natural, built-in desire, not a personal option. Maybe we can combat
that desire when other, stronger desires consume us, as Oedipus in
his misery no longer wished to see and stabbed his own eyes. These
exceptions only prove the rule, since they are always violent, not a
mere lifestyle choice like a tattoo. And it cannot be a coincidence,
or a side effect of some other objective, that a being endowed with a
natural desire to see is also endowed with a natural ability to produce
organs capable of seeing. Then we must say the opposite. A visual
being, such as yourself, produces parts capable of seeing precisely
because such parts will make seeing possible.

If the process we call eye development were *not* for making vision
possible, what would we have to say about it? Since it is a regular
process, it is still the result of some natural tendency, even if not
a tendency to vision, but to something else. Therefore something
other than seeing would be more appropriate to the agent driving

the process. But no outcome of that process is more appropriate to a visual animal than seeing. Therefore the agent causing the process would have to be something other than the visual animal. But to what else could we attribute the process of developing eyes? The parts of the animal—its molecules, or something of the kind. In other words, to rid ourselves of the idea that there is a real tendency in an animal to produce organs for the sake of seeing, we must get rid of the animal and replace it with its parts. This is to imagine the animal, or you in particular, as a collective, and to ignore the evidence that you are in fact an individual being. That is itself revealing: denying the existence of natural, built-in purposes in your parts is tantamount to denying the existence of you.

Living things are made of tools after all, and saying so is not an instance of anthropomorphism. To say that eyes are for seeing, and that living things are made of tools for living, is not a naïve or romantic description that could be put in more exact and less frilly terms. It is just an honest acknowledgment of the facts.

As we drew the line between you and the beasts, we have now drawn the line between the living and the nonliving. This does not imply that we will always be able to say on which side of the line any given thing falls. Viruses are a notoriously tough case, for example. But if indeed they do not grow (do not, as individuals, take in nourishment and increase in size), and if they do not develop their own parts, but instead these are manufactured separately inside a victim cell and then assembled like so many parts of a Roomba, then it is reasonable to conclude that viruses are not alive, but are side effects, parts, or rogue versions of the mechanisms of life. Prions might be a similar case. The difficulty and uncertainty of cases like these does not affect the exactness or certainty of the line between the living and the nonliving, however—no more than the difficulty of telling whether $1,000,000,000! - 1$ is prime or not affects the exactness and certainty of the line between prime and composite.

We have progressed once more in our understanding of your nature. You are a living being, an organic being, one whose parts by their very nature, and not merely by your choice, incline to certain actions that befit and benefit you. And once again our progress provokes new questions about you. If your parts are inherently purposeful, what must we say of evolution, which many thinkers propose as an alternative to the apparent purposefulness of the parts of organisms? And what does the purposeful character of animate nature imply about the origins of the natural world? Is the world itself purposeful? Is it just a happy accident that the human soul can mirror the universe, and in its own way become a little universe? Or was the natural process of our universe's development, in some definite way and from the very beginning, heading toward that result?

Sometimes experience suggests that the affinity between the human soul and the universe runs deeper than we might think. If our eyes are for seeing, might it also be true that the universe is for being seen? And is it by choice and upbringing alone, or also by nature, that our cognitive powers rejoice in finding patterns and unities pervading the multitudes of things? I was very much struck when, on a cold winter's night in New England, our feet crunching in the snow while walking from the house to the car, my seven-year-old son, Max, cried out in excitement: "Dad, look! Those three stars are right in a row!"

"Well, would you look at that!" I said, smiling in the dark. "That's amazing!"

I I

The End of Evolution

A man is a little universe.

—Democritus

The Swale

I was one of those first graders routinely picked last by any captain of any team at recess. No one complained when I stole away from athletic activities to see what was happening in the swale. The swale (as we all called it, don't ask me why) was a shallow drainage ditch that ran behind my elementary school. Teachers didn't like me playing near the swale, but the students outnumbered the on-duty teachers at recess by something like a thousand to one, if memory serves, so enforcement kept to a happy minimum.

The swale was always full of water, maybe two feet deep in the cooler seasons. I watched orange and vermillion leaves drop onto its surface in the fall. In winter, I brushed away the snow and walked on the dark ice beneath, listening to it crack and watching the silvery bubbles trapped beneath it as they darted out from under my every step. But the real magic happened in that first spring semester of all my school years. Sometime in April or May, I found strange things afoot in the newly thawed swale. Nested in the algae and weeds were hundreds of crystal-clear spheres, each one with an unidentifiable black speck at its center. What were these? After a few days, the black specks were bigger—and wiggling. "Eggs," I thought. But what kind of eggs? What were the little black specks inside them? One sure way to find out was to keep careful watch over them for many recesses to come.

199

Each day, the black specks grew larger. Eventually, they nearly filled their gelatin chambers. One day I could find no eggs, but instead the swale teemed with tiny black tadpoles. They grew to be muddy-colored speckled blobs, like fat little fish sporting shimmering tails. Then they sprouted hind legs. They began bobbing to the surface for a breath of fresh air, and my merest movement would send them dashing off for safe hiding places in the underwater shadows, their tails fearfully undulating behind them. At last the forelegs came, and although many retained their tails, their faces became recognizably froggish. I was sad when the tadpoles were no more, living now the more secretive and cautious life of frogs.

This experience brought home to me the concept of development. What is at first inarticulate and seemingly almost nothing (like one of those little black specks), can yet have inscribed within itself a definite future trajectory and target. The ensuing process is a working out, an execution of a predetermined course, and so the end result is a fulfillment, a completion, an arrival.

It is nature's developmental powers that will next occupy our attention. Up till now we have been asking the constitutional question of what sort of being you are. We now move on to the historical question of where you came from. We have by no means exhausted all there is to say about what you are, but we have said enough about it for one book, and enough to provoke us positively to wonder what your astonishing nature might imply about your origins. You are part body and part spirit, a mammal with a nonmaterial mind capable of grasping eternal truths. Where in the world can a being like you have come from?

I am not talking about your parents, of course, but about your ultimate origins. Now the theory of evolution is the most accepted account of your ultimate origins among those professing to know them in the light of reason. Rather than leave it out of our reckoning, it seems wise to come to grips with it, somehow, in our search for where you came from. Evolution will not be the final word on your origin, however. *Evolution* is supposed to name an origin of you within the world, not outside it, and therefore, as we will see in the next chapter, your evolutionary origin could never be your absolutely first origin. Nonetheless, if—and I will stress this *if* below—some version of the evolution story is true, then it describes a first origin of sorts and, excepting only the Bible, there is hardly an origin story that exerts greater influence on current thought about the human race.

Evolution is of course an enormous and hot-button topic. Countless books have been written on it, and continue to be written on it. How can anything of value be said about evolution within the narrow confines of a single chapter like this one?

By keeping a limited focus. In what follows, I will ask only a single question: Is evolution compatible with the purpose-driven, goal-oriented natures of living things and their parts? Is it possible to believe in mainstream evolutionary science and at the same time to acknowledge that a tadpole grows limbs because they are useful for hopping and swimming, and develops eyes because they are good for seeing?

To answer this particular question, it will not be necessary to decide whether the evolution story is the truth. That is why the matter can fit into a single chapter. The truth about evolution is extremely important, of course. Nonetheless its importance does not affect all questions. Whether evolution is the truth or not, two and two still make four. Similarly, whether evolution is the truth or not, your human nature, and every nature of every living thing, is inherently oriented toward certain beneficial goals, and nature itself is laden with purpose. These facts about you stand even if Neo-Darwinists are right. If we fail to see this, then we will not have the proper conviction about these facts concerning you and the rest of nature. We will be liable to think we cannot know anything for sure about your nature without first settling the hairy and ongoing questions about evolution. We will regard everything said in the prior chapters of this book as hanging in midair, awaiting a verdict to be handed down in terms of sticky details of biology, biochemistry, geology, and so on. That would be a huge mistake. In the foregoing pages lurk no hypotheses or theories, but only simple facts about you drawn from your own experience of being you. Many of these facts are seldom noticed. Few people have noted their consequences. We have taken the trouble both to notice those facts, and to spell out their consequences. It would be a shame if we lost sight of these things, of their independent force and certainty, due to worries over evolution not really critical to them.

If the compatibility of mainstream evolutionary science with a purpose-driven world can fit inside a chapter, it still takes some work to see. At first blush, the two seem strikingly incompatible. A creature with a visual nature like yours, as I explained in the last chapter, makes eyes for itself because it is somehow inherently oriented toward seeing. The Neo-Darwinian story of evolution, on the other hand, seems to speak differently. According to it, your eyes came into being because random genetic mutations and genetic recombination occurred down through many generations of living things, and natural selection accumulated the mutations with survival value, and *voila*, you have eyes. On this account of things, the notion that eyes are the products of an unconscious tendency toward seeing would appear to have no place. The random mutations and new combinations of traits are the chief or even sole innovators of organs, and they are precisely random—that is, driven by mechanisms not specifically correlated with any particular need, the very opposite of anything purposeful.

Holders of the Neo-Darwinian view of evolution usually present it as the alternative to a purpose-driven world. The theory liberates us from Lamarckism—the idea that giraffes, for example, have long necks because their ancestors found it useful to stretch their necks to reach the highest leaves on the trees, and then kindly passed on to their offspring this beneficial trait (stretched necks), acquired by their own purposeful efforts. Too bad inheritance doesn't usually work that way. Acquired traits are not generally passed on, at least not macroscopic traits in multicellular creatures. If a mom and dad make a habit of working out in the sun, their children are not born buff and tan. Genes seem to abide by rules that operate independently of their owners' self-beneficial accomplishments. If Lamarck's ideas had only proved right, then we could indeed say that purposeful action shapes offspring and drives evolution. As it is, that job is customarily assigned to random mutations.

So it is not immediately obvious that evolution and the goal-oriented natures of things can get along. More than that, some things coming under the umbrella of Neo-Darwinism definitely do not fit with the truth about you and nature. The term *Neo-Darwinism* (and perhaps even the term *evolution* itself) often carries materialism and atheism as connotations, if not as strict parts of its definition. These elements are not the scientific theory itself, however, but a pair of opportunistic parasites from philosophy badly done. Materialism (the philosophical idea that matter alone exists) is false. Your own intellect is a counterinstance. In the coming chapter we will see that atheism is also false.

The positive claims of Neo-Darwinian science (for example, that natural selection acting on random mutations is the chief mechanism driving the formation of new organs and species) do not logically entail atheism or materialism. It is the other way around. If you want to be an atheist or a materialist, you will need to find purpose-free explanations of nature, since purposefulness, or orientation toward what is good, seems to imply an intelligence at the back of it all. Atheism and materialism therefore logically entail something like Neo-Darwinian mechanisms, and then add to these the idea that they are the only causes in town. But the converse is not true. Neo-Darwinian mechanisms do not logically entail atheism or materialism. Nor do they do away with the idea that eyes really are for seeing, as we shall see.

So let us now ask ourselves, does assigning random mutations a large role in the formation of living things preclude the idea that organs are inherently purposeful, that eyes, for example, are truly and inherently for seeing?

And once we have learned the answer, we may ask a similar question concerning the cosmos as a whole: Does the theory of a "multiverse" that randomly spits out different kinds of universes eliminate the possibility that our universe is intrinsically oriented toward producing life?

Dandelions

Did eyes come into existence for the sake of seeing? The Neo-Darwinian account does not seem to permit this understanding of nature. According to it, eyes are entirely the handiwork of random mutations and other mechanisms not specially responsive to the needs of organisms. Random mutations that contributed to the formation or improvement of eyes also contributed to longer survival of the mutants. Those randomly improved mutants were therefore rewarded by natural selection with more frequent reproduction. Eyes were built by random events. Their usefulness for seeing is not why they came to be. Their usefulness for seeing is merely the reason they stuck around and are with us today—or so goes the story.

Do random mutations and natural selection therefore provide us with a vision of nature purged of all tendencies toward benefits to the living?

Not at all. Natural selection cannot simply do away with the tendencies of living things toward what benefits them. After all, natural selection operates by rewarding better survivors with more frequent reproduction. That means it entirely presupposes, and therefore cannot replace or even explain, the basic ability and tendency of living things to survive and to reproduce in the first place.

And that is just the beginning. Even for things that could be explained by natural selection acting on random mutations, these mechanisms can never be the whole explanation, but only a part of an explanation. It is easy to take natural selection as more complete an explanation than it really could be, even if it were responsible for everything that mainstream biologists say it is. Suppose random mutations and natural selection were indeed responsible (in their way) for every single part of a horse. Do we now have a "complete explanation" of the horse?

We must proceed with care. You could give a grammatical explanation for every part of *Moby Dick*. Every sentence in it admits of grammatical analysis. Does it follow that an understanding of the book purely in terms of the rules of grammar is a complete understanding of the book? Not in the least. That would be an understanding of the whole book, but not the whole understanding of the book. Other kinds of intelligibility are at work in it, too. Other, nongrammatical rules shape all its parts—those of logic, rhetoric, style, intelligent plot, theme, and believable characters, for instance. The rules of grammar do not answer all questions about *Moby Dick* even if they answer certain questions about all its parts.

Random mutations and natural selection are like the rules of grammar. Even if these principles explain every part of you, they do so only in a particular way. To name but one of their limitations, they are essentially historical explanations. They are genealogies of how you and your parts got here. They do not explain why you and your parts behave thus and so right now in the present.

Why did the chicken cross the road? Are random mutations making it do that? Ridiculous. Is natural selection forcing it to run? A silly personification of natural selection. No, the poor chicken is running across the road because the neighbor's dog is chasing it and it is in terror for its life. There is within the chicken a presently existing tendency to use its eyes and legs in order to preserve itself, regardless of how its eyes and legs and self-preservative tendency have (or have not) descended from past antecedents. The fact that its parts have come down from random mutations in the past (if that is a fact) simply is not the reason that they function well in the present. They function well in the present because of what they are right now, quite independently of how they got here. My car is no doubt the result of many generations of engineering and reengineering with a selective eye toward improvements and probably some lucky discoveries. That explains in some way how my car came to be. But that explanation does not replace the presently operating mechanical principles that are the real reasons why my car functions as it does today. Why does depressing this pedal stop the vehicle? This question is answered not by reference to how and when foot brakes were first invented, but by the principles of hydraulics. If a whirlwind whipped through a junkyard and by a great stroke of fortune left behind a car exactly like mine, it would drive exactly like mine, despite the radical difference in its origin. "What a thing is" and "how it got here" are not the same question. And it is what a thing is, not how it got here, that chiefly explains its present behavior.

Suppose, if possible, that natural selection and random mutations fully explain the natural behaviors of a living thing right now in the present, thus doing away with any need to suppose in organisms any presently existing, unconscious tendencies to do what is self-beneficial. Since you yourself are (on this hypothesis) also the product of natural selection and random mutations, the same must apply to you—your actions are all fully understandable in light of natural selection and random mutations alone, leaving no room for explaining your actions by any other causes, such as your present tendencies. Now this does away with your conscious present tendencies just as much as your unconscious ones. If you did not grow your parts because of any tendency in you toward the benefits those parts would eventually provide, then for the very same reason neither do you ever get up out of your chair because of any desire in you for something to drink. You get up solely because of natural selection and random mutations. Does that sound like a poor explanation? Absurd, even? It should. You experience your desire to drink. You experience that desire influencing your decision to get up. These things, I humbly submit, are facts. These obvious facts about you—that your present desires and tendencies influence and to a large extent explain what you do and become—do not necessarily rob natural selection and random mutations of their role in explaining where your desiring powers came from historically. But your present desire does explain your present behavior in a way that natural selection and random mutations never could.[1]

Your natural and unconscious activities are no different in this regard. When you grew your eyes or your ears, this process was not a series of random mutations going on in your cells. It was the execution of an extremely definite tendency, the very opposite of random. The history behind that tendency might involve a good number of chance events. But it does not follow in the least that the outcome of the tendency is therefore the outcome of chance. My wife and I met by chance, as I suppose most couples do. It does not follow that we got married by chance or had children by chance. Those were the results of choice, not chance.

This brings us to an important principle: an effect can be the product *both* of causes that tend to produce it *and* of causes that merely happen to produce it without having any special tendency toward it. A child, for example, might be the offspring of parents who were trying to have a child, but the very same child can also be in some way the consequence of a car accident or jury duty or some other accidental cause of the parents' meeting (to say nothing of the infinity of past contingencies without which they themselves would never have come into existence). From an effect's dependence on certain causes that had no intrinsic tendency to it, we cannot conclude that no causes had any tendency to it. Eyes can be both the products of causes precisely productive of eyes right now in the present and also the products of past chance events without which eye-producing causes would never have arisen in the first place. Nor

---

[1] Nor do biologists think otherwise, so far as I am aware.

does it follow, just because eyes somehow arose from a multitude of chance events, that eyes themselves are nothing more than accumulations of amendments—no more than it follows, just because you came to be as a result of an infinity of highly contingent chance events (what were the odds that your parents would meet?), that you yourself are a mere bundle of random events.

Evolutionary mechanisms and the presently existing natures of organisms answer essentially different questions. The present nature of an organism answers questions such as, what is this individual? Why does it do what it does? What cause, acting right now in the present, is responsible for this? Why is it growing eyes? Evolutionary explanations, on the other hand, try to answer questions such as, how did this species arise in the first place? Of all the possible species, which ones get to exist, and where and when, and under which of the many adaptive forms possible to them? We must distinguish historical questions from constitutional ones.

We now have the answer to our first question. Between goal-oriented nature on the one hand, and natural selection acting on random mutations on the other, there is no real conflict, but only an apparent one. The mere absence of conflict does not lend positive support to the Neo-Darwinian conception of nature, of course. It just means that if the Neo-Darwinian view is false, then in order to find this out we must roll up our sleeves and do some serious empirical work—we cannot refute it from our armchairs simply by reflecting on the fact that a horse grows eyes because of its innate and unconscious tendency to equip itself with eyesight.

Still more needs to be said, however. If (and I once more stress *if*) natural selection and random mutations and genetic recombination are capable of everything Neo-Darwinian theory suggests, if they are the main force by which living things adapt to their environments and develop new and beneficial traits and parts, then these Darwinian mechanisms must be among nature's means to its ends.

This sounds oxymoronic at first. How can randomness serve as a means to any specific end? And yet it is not so strange as it sounds. We ourselves often employ randomness as a means for getting a good result that we cannot shoot for in any other way. Suppose I am an overnight guest at someone's house, and I wake up thirsty in the middle of the night. The room is totally black, and I have very little memory of the disposition of the furniture, and of the locations of the light switches and doors. Cautiously, I stand up and begin to make random movements with my hands in an attempt to navigate my way out of the room. In one sense these movements are without purpose—my hands do not reach for any particular object as they wave back and forth. In total darkness I cannot simply make a single, object-specific reach for something helpful. So instead I make many wide, flailing sweeps with both hands. Moving them in this random fashion increases the odds that they will touch upon walls and furniture before I bump into them with my face, and increase the odds, too, that I will find something useful like a light switch or a doorknob. The moment my hand lands on a doorknob and I recognize what it is, I grab hold and turn. The preceding random movement of my hand was not specifically in search of a doorknob, but in search of anything advantageous. My blind fumblings were neither object-specific nor definite in form. They were in this sense "random". But they were nonetheless for the sake of something.

Nature employs similar means all the time. A dandelion's mechanism of seed dispersal is not controlled or directed in the sense in which my reaching for a doorknob (when I see it) is controlled and directed. It is more like the random sweepings of my hands in the dark. And just as my random movements were at the service of my tendency to get out of the room, so the dandelion's random seed dispersal is at the service of its tendency to reproduce. Just as eyes are precisely for seeing, so too dandelion seeds are precisely for making new dandelions. The dandelion naturally strives toward reproducing itself, and for this it needs a way of getting some of its seeds to good ground. But where good ground will be on any given day is unpredictable, and the dandelion cannot simply observe where the good ground is, since it is destitute of all powers of observation. No matter. That there will be some good ground within a certain radius, for most dandelions, is a fairly good bet. The more seeds a dandelion produces, and the more randomly (and hence widely) its mechanism of dispersal spreads them around, the better the odds that a sufficient number will land on the one little patch of good ground just over there.

Even if all nature's main adaptive mechanisms fall into this general category of the shotgun approach, they remain instruments of nature's tendencies. The adapting organism is like the dandelion; its uncontrolled and undirected mechanisms of genetic variation are like the dandelion's method of seed dispersal, and the presently favorable, naturally selectable future trait among all those traits that are next available to the organism is like the little patch of good ground.

Empirical evidence might force us to admit, now or in the future, that some natural mechanisms of genetic modification are more like reaching for the doorknob than like flailing about with our hands in the dark. Perhaps random mutations, upon closer inspection, are too wild and sloppy a method for nature to have used for all its main accomplishments. Trial and error can work for some things, but it can also be too clumsy or too slow for many jobs. (If I need a specific antidote for a deadly snake bite, it's no good mixing ingredients at random in my kitchen; if that is the only method at my disposal for finding an antidote, I had better just say my prayers and make my peace.) Whether random mutations are competent or not to solve all of nature's problems, it remains true that living things have problems and strive to solve them. Even unconscious creatures such as plants and the unconscious parts of ourselves exhibit definite tendencies to self-beneficial results. This general point does not stand or fall with evolution—it remains open to the truth or falsehood of evolution, and in this way more general truths leave those in the particular sciences free to do their jobs.

None of this means we should rest in complacent indifference to the debates over natural selection and random mutations in the history of life—far from it. The world of purpose-driven natures and the questions about how they arose do not exist in parallel worlds that never meet. The questions "Are there unconsciously goal-oriented things out there?" and "How did they get here?" are closely related. But they still differ, and the answer to the second does not settle the first.

Destination Mind

Living things grow, and many of them develop and change. These processes are automatic, natural, and unconscious, and yet they tend toward what benefits and completes the individual organism.

According to modern physics, the universe also is growing in some sense, and certainly it has undergone significant development since its inception. It loosely resembles a living thing. It is natural to wonder whether its growth and development might be in some way analogous to that of something alive. Could it be that the universe's development has been inherently headed toward something, and is in that sense *for* something? Does its "evolution" involve any kind of preset destination? The very word *evolution* implies something of the kind. Its origin is the Latin verb *evolvere*, meaning "to roll out, to unroll, to unfold", which calls to mind a gradual disclosure of something hidden at first but implicitly present from the very beginning. Is that a good name, or not, for the behavior of our world?

The most astonishing beings in the universe are living ones, and they seem to have come along after a great deal of cosmic development. Might they be the predestined products of cosmic evolution, the built-in target of the growth of the natural world?

"Fine-tuning" arguments have been around for some time now, amassing impressive evidence that this universe of ours is "just right" so that life-friendly conditions would arise. Tinker with the value of this or that physical constant just a wee bit, and no stars can arise, or only those that are hostile to life, or various elements necessary to life as we know it will not arise or not in sufficient abundance, or they will not be able to form stable compounds—or some other nasty consequences will ensue and make life literally impossible. The universe, it seems, is tailor-made for living things, and we should look for a cause of this fact.

Thinkers wishing to avoid a world in which life is a target for nature have replied to these fine-tuning arguments with the theory of a "multiverse". Ours, they say, is just one universe among countless ones coughed up by a universe matrix called the "multiverse", a kind of nursery giving birth to all kinds of universes. A "universe" in this way of thinking does not mean "the whole shebang" (that is now the "multiverse"), but only one glob of it that is defined by its particular array of physical constants. In one random glob of multiverse stuff over here, for example, the speed of light might be half of what it is in our universe, and the ratio of the force of gravity to the electromagnetic force might be double what it is for our world. In another glob, these numbers will differ again. The special set of numbers makes for one special universe. Each universe glob is born with its physical constants in some haphazard ratio, so that practically every conceivable ratio among physical constants is represented in some universe or other, at least eventually.

In the last decade or two, Stephen Hawking and others have proposed the idea that a multiverse dispenses with the need to ascribe life orientation to the evolution of our universe. According to this hypothesis, our universe and its life-friendly physical laws are in fact just a local phenomenon. Our laws are only a specification of much more general laws, the true laws of physics that govern universe formation, by which all or nearly all possible universes come to be, each with its own outcomes of the general laws, almost none of them capable of sustaining life. Our particular universe's uncanny friendliness to life, therefore, is not the result of nature's fundamental orientation toward producing it, but only the outcome of the multiverse diversifying itself at random into nearly all possible combinations of determinate physical laws and constants.

The multiverse can thus be compared to a computer program randomly spewing out all possible sequences that consist of n characters (where n is some number of our choosing). If n is sufficiently large, our program will chug out words and whole sentences and even poems and plays. If it really generates the letter sequences randomly, and never fixates on any portion of them, then it is just a matter of time before it churns out "Jack Sprat could eat no fat", and "Three cheers for the multiverse!", and the Gettysburg Address. But clearly the machine would not really be trying to tell us anything by these "sentences". They would in fact be meaningless sequences of characters with only the appearance of meaning to us meaning-seeking creatures. So too this local universe of ours is admittedly hospitable to life, but don't let it fool you into thinking this was somehow the target of our multiverse's behavior.

Some critics have replied that the whole idea of a multiverse is pure adhockery, invented on the fly to wiggle out of the fine-tuning arguments. Nor is it just Bible-thumpers who have said so. Thomas Nagel, a prominent philosopher and an atheist, asks whether there are any alternatives to (1) the idea that the world is inherently oriented toward life and mind and (2) the idea of an intervening God as explanations of the possibility of conscious life. His reply:

Well, there is the hypothesis that this universe is not unique, but that all possible universes exist, and we find ourselves, not surprisingly, in one that contains life. But that is a cop-out, which dispenses with the attempt to explain anything.[2]

Others say that a multiverse is a very natural or even necessary implication of quantum physics, or of some other legitimate branch of science. Whichever is the truth, the multiverse hypothesis does not logically prevent the production of living things from being a goal of the universe. Champions of the multiverse (they sound like superheroes, right?) would have it that the true laws of physics are not specifically aimed at life. Why not? Because those laws produce universes randomly, not consciously and purposefully, and most universes it spits out are hostile to life. Consequently, they conclude, there is no sense to saying that the multiverse, or the cosmos as a whole, has any special tendency to produce living things.

Sound familiar? This is like inferring that since most of the random movements of my hands in the dark never amount to anything, therefore these movements are not for the sake of finding anything. This is pure nonsequitur. Nothing prevents us from supposing that the multiverse is like a dandelion. The randomly generated universes are like the randomly dispersed seeds. The universe with life-friendly laws is like the seed landing on good ground. The growth of the new dandelion is like the unfolding of the life-friendly universe into life-friendly stars and life-friendly planets, and in the end, living beings. The rarity of the outcome does not exclude it from being the very purpose of the preceding activity, just as the miniscule amount of gold compared with the tons of worthless dirt that gold miners dig up does not prove that they must have been after dirt, not gold. Therefore, even if (an enormous *if*, I suspect) the multiverse exists and behaves as Hawking and others suggest, that does not really help us decide the question one way or the other. For all it shows, the multiverse could still be like the dandelion, or like someone fumbling around in the dark—a thing with a definite tendency to certain results that it must shoot for with a shotgun approach precisely because of the blind manner in which it operates.

---

[2] Thomas Nagel, *Mind and Cosmos: Why the Materialist Neo-Darwinian Conception of Nature Is Almost Certainly False* (New York: Oxford University Press, 2012), p. 95, n. 9.

So which is it? Is the built-in target of nature's tendency just "all possible worlds", with no special orientation toward any of them? Or is its target instead certain worlds, life-friendly worlds, so that its tendency to produce all worlds is just a means to that end? Is it more like the computer program, or more like the dandelion?

It is more like the dandelion. The whole of nature (or "the multiverse"), like the dandelion, is a natural thing acting out its own inner tendencies. It does not behave purely in accord with some arrangement superimposed on its materials from the outside, as the materials of the computer do. Also, the outputs of the program are inherently meaningless, only by chance resembling words put forward by someone to express something, whereas living things embody real purposes—their own—and so we have in their case a real, not an apparent, meaningfulness to explain.

In fact, the same reasons for saying that a dandelion disperses seeds in all directions for the sake of finding the good ground apply in a general way to the whole of nature. If it does indeed produce all kinds of "universes", it must do so out of a tendency for producing the ones in which life is possible.

Why? Well, the dandelion, too, is a blind and unconscious thing. The way to tell whether a given outcome of its activity is a mere side effect or is instead the very thing toward which the activity tends is by checking that outcome against the three criteria from the last chapter. One outcome of a dandelion's dispersal of seeds could be that one seed gets in my eye and causes me to get into a car accident. But that is a mere side effect of what the dandelion is really up to. How do we know? For one thing, that outcome almost never happens. It is not a usual outcome of dandelion activity. Nor does "causing a car accident" fit or agree in any specific way with what a dandelion is. Another outcome of a dandelion's dispersal of seeds is that new dandelions come into existence. Now that is no mere side effect, but is the true and inherent destination of dandelion seeds, since new dandelions (1) always result from the production and dispersal of the seeds (so long as necessary conditions are present and nothing interferes), and since (2) new dandelions come about by the same steps every time after the seed dispersal, and since (3) new dandelions are an outcome that specifically fits or agrees with what dandelions are— "making new dandelions" cannot be purely incidental to something else that the dandelions are really up to.

Living things meet these same criteria for being no mere side effects but the very objectives of nature's tendencies. The multiverse (if it exists) does not merely happen to produce life-friendly worlds. It must do so. It cannot avoid them forever. So say the believers in the multiverse themselves, as I understand them. Believers in the multiverse typically want to avoid saying that the emergence of living things in our universe is a cosmic coincidence, a fluke, since that is obviously a dodge. So they make the emergence of life instead the inevitable outcome of a process that they think cannot be inherently tending toward that outcome, for the bad reason that the process produces lots of other things as well.

Not only are living things an inevitable outcome of the natural behavior of the multiverse, but on top of that, whenever they do come about, they must come about in the same way, at the end of the same kinds of steps and in the same order. Whenever the action of the multiverse does issue in life, it must have gone through the same kind of ordered process, at least in a general way. The multiverse must first make a world whose physical constants are "just right". That is Step One. Then that world must form certain basic atoms, and stars. That is Step Two. Then those stars must produce all the other elements needed for living things. That is Step Three. And so on. It cannot instead begin with penguins and then make stars and nitrogen only later on. Living things, in other words, are not a fluky outcome of nature's development, but are by nature the furthest thing it can tend toward by its own building process, even if it does not always get that far down the line, and even if it usually does not. On that score, nature is again like the dandelion.

The world of nature is like the dandelion in the third way as well. Many outcomes of the dandelion's action are admittedly mere side effects of its true tendency, even if these side effects come about in a regular way. The dandelion expends itself in reproduction, for example—this flower is undone in the process of going to seed. That is a regular result. But it is not the object of the dandelion's behavior. It is not trying to do itself in. That is just the cost of doing business. We cannot understand all the specificities of dandelion seeds as though they were just the flower's way of destroying itself, of coming to an end. The real object of all this work is the production of a new dandelion. That goal alone can explain the need for all the specificities in the seeds. The production of a new dandelion is also an effect that fits the cause. It does not make sense to say that what dandelions do for a living is commit suicide or die, even if they do all end up dead (an event, sadly, that I never witness in my own front yard). Dandelion action must tend somehow toward dandelions, whether to the maintenance, repair, growth, or reproduction of them. Producing a new dandelion cannot be a side effect of what the dandelion is really tending toward, as though dandelions had something better or more dandelion-relevant to do than to make dandelions.

Our universe, some have said, is headed toward maximum entropy, maximum disorganization, heat death. That would be the "end" of the universe not in the sense of its objective, but in the sense of its finish, its kaput. That is like the dissipation of the dandelion. What, then, could be the outcome in relation to which this unraveling is a side effect, like a price to be paid? Well, if the dissolution of things is the death or decay of the universe, then the organization of things is its coming to be, its development, its maturation. That is the object of nature's program of action—namely, to become all natural things, and in natural order. In this order, living things come last. But they are also the universe's best products, furthest from the disorder into which it must eventually fall. Each living thing is to some degree and in some fashion inclusive of other beings within itself. A living thing not only has a world—it *is* a world, a little cosmos, a microcosm. This is truest of all in our own case, the only kinds of creatures that try to fit a model of the whole universe into our heads. And to the extent that the world gets reproduced in our own understanding, it thereby shares in our own souls' immortality. If the life of a dandelion is not essentially toward its death but toward its share in immortality by making other dandelions, then, correspondingly, the development of the world is not essentially toward its disorder but toward its share in immortality by making other worlds—namely, living things, and especially ourselves. As the business of the dandelion is to make new little dandelions, the business of the universe is to make new little universes—rational beings like us.

If all of this sounds a little bit fanciful, self-centered, or else like a plausible interpretation of the universe but one which the facts do not force, then consider the alternative. Assume, if possible, that nature's materials are perfectly indifferent to the forms of life, with no tendencies to them, not fulfilled by them in any way. The form of a living thing would therefore be no more natural to nature's materials than is the form of a stapler or a flyswatter. It would be a mere imposition on matter, an irrelevant accident. Forms of life would therefore be like artificial forms, conferring a new shape or arrangement to matter, but not constituting its very substance. The form of you, for example, would not cause your materials to be the substance that they are—namely, you—since on this view of things you would not be a substance, but a mere arrangement of substances that have their own individual existence independently of your form, even while existing in you. This would make you a mere collective of substances, contrary to your whole experience of being you.

Multiverse or no multiverse, the form of a living being is not related to its materials as the form of a desk or a chair is to the wood it is made of. Wood is indifferent to those artificial forms. They do not cause it to be wood, but only to be structured in some special manner toward which the wood has no particular tendency. Wood can receive those forms, but not by any internal drive of its own. In contrast, the form of a living being is to its materials more as the forms of roots, trunk, and branches are to wood. Wood is not indifferent to these forms, but takes them on in the course of its own development, in its own process of coming to be. Nature is related to living things like that, since nature's raw materials become various substances, and eventually living things, by their own inherent tendencies. Or so at least the believers in the multiverse must say, if they wish to avoid positing a god who built living things in the manner of a mechanic.

A false understanding of what a living thing is will therefore lead to a false understanding of the universe, and a true understanding to a true one. If we think a living thing is like a robot, an aggregate of many substances, only then are we free to think the world of nature is indifferent to the production of living things. Once we realize that a living thing is a single substance whose form gives being to its materials, we see that nature's materials are completed by taking on the forms of life. Inanimate nature is not indifferent to living things, but is completed either by taking on their forms, or else by making their forms possible.

Are we in danger of taking a middle stage for a final one? The nineteenth-century German philosopher G. W. F. Hegel is often thought to have believed (perhaps unjustly) that the whole of human history, and even of natural history, had by a natural process led to the emergence of the modern German state, and to him in particular as its herald, and that therefore all things before him had been for the sake of this final, end-all, be-all result. And yet, amazingly, the world has moved on. Are we in danger of the same sort of egocentric silliness? Might not evolution move past man and on to bigger and better things?

While it seems right to say that human nature has not yet finished expressing itself and achieving its own perfection, we have already encountered a decisive reason to deny that evolution can usher in some more ultimate form of life than the human form. Perhaps the human body can improve (although it seems more likely that what will really improve is our understanding of it and our power to heal, preserve, enhance, and also deform it by means of advances in science, medicine, and technology). But there can be no natural form beyond the human soul, or anyway the rational soul. The rational soul is an ultimate form.

Why? Because it is immortal, capable of existing apart from matter, and capable of knowing all things in some way. There is no "beyond" that, in natural forms. We can perhaps imagine better brains that serve our intellects better, make us far smarter, but that is a difference of degree in the kind of body that is at the service of the soul, not a difference in the nonmaterial intellect itself. If there could be different kinds of intellectual souls, some of which were smarter than others (a doubtful matter, but let it be for the moment), then as a general class intellectual souls would still be the ultimate kind of form in nature, and evolution could not surpass them or make adjustments to them. They are the only all-inclusive forms, the take-all-things-in forms. Nor could evolution be responsible for introducing new and better kinds of intellects, since evolution is a process in matter, whereas intellects are nonmaterial.

Cosmic evolution cannot surpass intellectual souls. They represent a destination more than the middle of a journey. They are evolution's end. Strictly speaking, they must lie a step beyond evolution's reach, as I hinted just now. Your intellectual soul is capable of being and acting outside of matter. How can random mutations, or any kinds of changes in matter, produce that? At most, nature can bring forth lower forms of organic life with a definite trend toward sense life and then specifically the sense life that can serve an intellect. This it does before any human intellect exists. Why? Why this series of preparations for an intellect that does not yet exist, all made by a universe without any understanding of its own? It would seem impossible for anything but intellect to ordain things to the good of intellect.

There is also the odd fact that the evolution of the universe is from lesser natures to greater ones, from the lifeless to the living, from the senseless to the sensitive, from the mindless to mind. Unless we are to get more out of less, which is just a sneaky way of getting something out of nothing, it seems we must admit a force behind evolution that is superior to all its products.

A Totally Original Thought

The world is like a vast orchestra tuning up.

—Hans Urs von Balthasar, *Truth Is Symphonic*[1]

Beyond Nerf

My mother was the one to tell me there was no Santa Claus. And it didn't come as a blow. What happened was this. I had just come home from the house of a friend up the street—I'll call him Todd—and I told my mother how impressed I was with Todd. He had been a much better boy than I had been. My mother wanted to know why I was so certain and matter-of-fact about this. I explained that Todd had gotten far more toys than I had that Christmas, and everyone knew that Santa gave more presents to better boys and girls, and none at all to bad ones; so I was a good boy all right, but not anywhere near as good as Todd. That tore at her heart a little, I guess. She told me right then and there that there never was a Santa Claus, and that Todd had gotten more presents than I had simply because his father made a lot more money than a philosophy professor does.

That had the ring of truth to it. And I didn't shed a tear. Somehow it came as good news that the person who had been eating the cookies I was leaving out for Santa on Christmas Eve (and who was always very careful to leave some perceptible crumbs behind) was dear old Dad all along. Yes, it was good news, all things considered. Not least because it meant my (purely relative) toy poverty did not reflect on my merit as a human being.

[1] Hans Urs von Balthasar, *Truth Is Symphonic: Aspects Christian Pluralism*, trans. Graham Harrison (San Francisco: Ignatius Press, 1987), 7.

The same news was not always so welcome to my more toy-laden friends. Not that I burst their bubbles. My mother made me promise to say nothing to them, and I obeyed. No, my friends all found out in their own ways. One of these, Frank, was utterly devastated one day to discover, in a drawer in his parents' dresser, all the lengthy, painstakingly crafted letters he had dispatched to Santa since he had learned to spell. There they were, each one addressed to "Santa's Workshop, North Pole". I'm not sure he ever forgave his parents.

By no means do I wish to judge them. My own parents encouraged me to believe in Santa Claus in a wink-wink sort of way, and I look back on the thought of Santa in my earliest years with pleasant nostalgia. But my experience with Todd, my recollection of poor Frank, and perhaps certain grinchy quirks in my personality, kept me from encouraging my own kids to believe there is a Santa. I didn't tell them there was a Santa, and I didn't (at first) tell them there wasn't. But rather than ask the kids to write to Santa, I let Amy solicit Christmas wish lists from them when they were very little, making it plain that the lists were being submitted directly to Mom and would never be forwarded to the North Pole (we posted them on the fridge). She invited the kids to be as wishful and extravagant as they liked, as long as they realized they probably wouldn't get everything on their lists.

Max and Evelyn were capable of producing very extravagant and entertaining lists, indeed. Evelyn even rolled hers up at the ends so that in order to read them one had to unravel them first, like official proclamations of a king. Ben, the youngest, learned to write later than the other two, and although his wishes in prior years had been as bounteous as his siblings', his very first written Christmas wish list was parsimonious and short. It was all on a single tiny slip of paper, smaller than a gas station receipt. On the right is a facsimile of the original. That last bit says "a turanchoolu", Ben's variant spelling for "a tarantula". Not long before composing this list, he had caught his first tarantula with help from me, so he knew they were to be had free of charge.

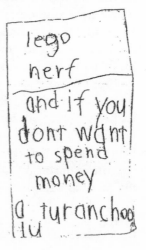

Maybe some Lego bricks, maybe some Nerf toys, but then again, maybe just a bug captured in the wild if we didn't think we could afford either of the first two vague possibilities. Why so conservative? Clearly, Ben had overheard me and his mother talking about how tight money was for us that year. The family budget was a larger concern than any that Ben would have had just of his own accord. It was a concern he had gotten from others, even if it really was now his concern, too.

The question before us in this chapter bears on just this sort of thing: a concern that goes beyond the thing concerned with it. All the things on Ben's list were things he wanted, even the tarantula. But the whole list was also considerate of the needs of others beyond himself. The natural things in the world all have their own agendas, their own natural objectives, their own wish lists, we might say. And yet, even in the course of their natural and unconscious pursuits of the things on their agendas, many of them are also zeroed in on something beyond themselves. Unconscious and unintelligent beings, for example, in a law-abiding way and as a matter of course make consciousness and intelligent life possible. Why does the universe tend to serve the interests of intelligence? Why do even conscious beings develop their own consciousness unconsciously, as a horse embryo develops eyes for seeing? Why, in ourselves in particular, do our own bodies mindlessly provide organs for the needs of our minds? Are all these mindless agencies thus concerned with mind purely of their own accord? Are they in no way indebted?

When those who are not grown-up share grown-up concerns, that is because they are influenced by the grown-ups. When things that have no mind share a concern for mind, could it be because they are influenced by a mind?

Wiser Than Man

Many people think of the raw material of the world as though it were "just stuff". But there are serious problems with the "just stuff" idea of nature. For one thing, we often learn how to achieve our own ends better by looking to nature for guidance. Medical science, for example, is still learning from the human body how to take care of it—the human body was taking care of itself long before there was an art to help it along. The very stuff of nature behaves in accord with mathematically elegant laws that mathematicians and physicists admire. There must be something to saying that nature is wiser than man, if nature can still teach us a thing or two. And yet nature has no mind of its own. That is the odd thing. Although nature has no mind, it is marvelously capable of making minds possible.

Why does it strike us as strange, as something demanding explanation, that the universe by lifeless processes paves the way for living things, and by mindless processes prepares for mind? Why are we not equally surprised by its turning into atoms or stars or piles of dust?

Living beings are better beings than nonliving ones, conscious beings than unconscious ones, and intelligent beings than nonintelligent ones. If nature's raw materials become all these things by some internal drive in them, that is like wood growing itself into a house or a ship. It is a striking case of self-improvement, of something becoming a nobler thing than what it was before. This implies that the lifeless, mindless, unimproved thing at the beginning is not all there is to the story of its improvement.

The clincher is that the human mind is nonmaterial. Even aside from the philosophical reasons for this conclusion that we have explored in previous chapters, most people suspect or believe the human mind is nonmaterial. Then why should the material world be inherently oriented toward mind? Why does matter preoccupy itself with the nonmaterial? Matter cannot even become mind, if mind is nonmaterial. How strange, then, that matter should be all about mind. Obeying the laws inscribed within it, matter mindlessly becomes the organs of sense and imagination, which in turn serve the human intellect by providing it with things to understand. Matter also assumes myriad forms that are abundantly intelligible, often exactly, mathematically intelligible, thus furnishing the human mind with plenty of food for thought. Matter, by its lawful behavior, becomes both the organs that support human thinking, and the things for us to think about.

On the one hand, there is the nonmaterial human mind in need of sense organs. On the other hand, there is also a material world handy, and it is capable of becoming just such organs.

This is no accident. This is an orchestrated affair.

The Original Idea of You

Lifeless orientation toward life, and mindless orientation toward mind, are not self-explanatory things, nor mere coincidences. Wherever we find them, they are due to a cause. And we find them in the universe, in its most basic materials, in many of the particular natural things they become, and in you in particular. I do not mean that you are lifeless and mindless, of course. But your body unconsciously and automatically grew and now maintains the organs for sensation and imagination. Your soul is also involved in the work, since it makes your body to be alive and to be you, but it, too, does this automatically, naturally, unconsciously—as much when you are asleep as when you are awake. Your soul animated your body and endowed it with the power to develop organs useful for understanding long before it could actually understand. It is not just your body, but even your intelligent soul, that unconsciously paves the way to consciousness, and mindlessly serves the interests of mind.

There must be a cause for this strange behavior, and it is not your own understanding. Your mind is more product and beneficiary of the symbiosis between matter and mind than cause of it. So what sort of thing is responsible for matter's orientation toward mind, and for your soul's mindless, but mind-beneficial, organizing of matter?

Whatever the cause, it not only oriented matter and the human soul toward one another, but produced them both. Matter's orientation toward mind is not forced on it, but comes out of its own inherent nature and properties. The human mind's relationship to matter, its natural dependence on sensation, is also built into it. Since their mutual orientations are due to the constitutions of matter and mind, therefore to cause their orientations is to cause their constitutions. An archer can cause an arrow to tend toward a target without being the maker of the arrow. That is because the arrow has no inherent tendency of its own to head toward the target, so the archer can simply impose this new tendency on the premade arrow by force. If instead the arrow had its own built-in tendency toward the bull's-eye, that tendency could not be imposed on the arrow by force, but would have been built into the arrow's constitution by the cause that produced it. Matter and the human mind are like that. Their complementarity, their unconscious tendency toward each other, is built into what they are, not imposed on them. Therefore the cause responsible for their natural tendencies is also the cause of their very natures. It is the maker of matter and of the human soul.

There is, then, a common cause of both matter itself (nature's raw material) and the human mind. Is this cause of matter and mind a material thing or a mind?

It must be a mind. The reason we need to explain matter's trend toward mind in the first place is that mind is so notably superior to matter. Matter's orientation toward mind makes it like a child with grown-up concerns. The ultimate cause behind this will not be yet another thing that seems to be concerned with things above and beyond itself, and whose behavior therefore requires a further explanation. The only thing that is of itself capable of explaining an orientation toward the benefit of mind is a mind. The cause of matter and mind is therefore a mind, not matter.

More general principles about causation fit with this result. In *Who Designed the Designer?* I developed in some detail the argument for the existence of an intelligent primary cause of all things.[2] If I were to try to cram it into a paragraph, it would go something like this. There must be a primary cause, a first reason, for anything that requires a cause and a reason: If the room is bright because of something shining its brightness into the room, and the shining thing is just a mirror that derives all its brightness from something else, that cannot just go back forever through a series of mirrors, but must start with a light source, a thing that is bright all by itself and does not need to be lit up by anything else, like the sun. The same goes for the cause responsible for the existence of matter and the human mind. If it happens to need a cause, there must nonetheless be a primary cause of their existence, a thing which itself needs no help in order to exist and to possess the power of causation. This primary cause, moreover, must be a mind. It is the cause of both matter and the type of mind that depends on matter, but mind is superior to matter, and the effect cannot surpass its cause. Therefore there exists a mind that is the first cause of things.

The ultimate origin of you, body and soul, is a mind. But it is not a human mind. Your parents might have had some idea of conceiving

[2] Michael Augros, *Who Designed the Designer? A Rediscovered Path to God's Existence* (San Francisco: Ignatius Press, 2015).

you, but even if they did, theirs was not the original idea of you. They are not the reason that matter has an inherent orientation toward the human soul, for example. They are themselves the result of that orientation, not its origin. Instead, the first idea of you was someone else's.

Is this being, which is the cause of matter and the human soul, a nonhuman mind conjoined to a nonhuman body? Could it be some kind of alien biological engineer, for example?

Impossible. If it had a body that was necessary to its mind, then just as your mind depends on your body in order to understand other things and to influence them, the same would be true of this hypothetical alien. It could not be a cause of anything except by means of its material body—and yet (as we just now inferred) the cause we are talking about is the cause of matter itself. Our alien might be very smart and powerful, but since its causal power depends on its body, and thus depends on matter, it cannot be the cause of matter itself. By means of its body it cannot be the original cause of the very materials that make up its body. That is circular and unthinkable. It seems we cannot explain odd creatures such as ourselves, whose materials serve the needs of their nonmaterial minds, by introducing yet another such oddity into the picture. Only one alternative remains. The mind responsible for matter's mindless orientation to mind, the maker of matter and of the human soul, is a purely nonmaterial being. It is a pure mind, without a body, and with no need of one.

This fits well with its being a primary cause, not a secondary or derived one. A mind that depends on matter's mindless orientation to mind is one that depends on a prior mind responsible for that orientation. Such a mind is therefore a derivative mind, a thing produced. The first being—first cause and first mind—is therefore not a mind that depends on matter in any way, but is purely nonmaterial. Its simplicity is the reason it is first and needs no cause. The reason a mind needs a cause is not because it is a mind, but because it depends on many things coming together to form a unity—for example, if it is a mind combined in some way with a body. That combination requires a cause, a combiner. The first cause plainly does not depend on a prior combiner, and consequently does not depend on any kind of combination. It cannot consist in a combination of mind and body, then, but is simply a mind. Asking what made the first mind is therefore an illegitimate question, founded on a misconception. It is like asking what number does 1 come from. Not from any number, of course, since it is the first and simplest number, and all other numbers come from it in one way or another.

Is it right to talk about this first intelligent cause in the singular? There are many different species in the world, and in some ways they seem to be at war with each other. They are engaged in the great fight for survival. Might the universe be the product of warring minds? That is a very ancient idea, and some philosophers have embraced it. But it is wrongheaded. Many species cooperate in various ways, for one thing. For another thing, competition, opposition, and the destruction of one thing by another are not necessarily opposed to holistic unity. Certain types of unity demand these things. A good piece of music is not only compatible with but absolutely demands certain contrasts and requires the replacement of one sound with another. The idea that there must be one mind responsible for the zebras and cheering them on, and another one responsible for the lions and championing their cause, is like supposing that behind a painting full of stark contrasts there must be a pair of rival artists, one with an unaccountable preference for dark colors and the other with a taste for light ones. Sheer diversity does not point to a unifying cause. But a balanced diversity does. And it is a balance and an order of diverse natures that we find in our world. Zebras and lions are not unrelated pet projects sent to combat one another like the robot competitors on *BattleBots*. Things like zebras make things like lions possible in the first place, and make sense of the lion's own instincts and physiology. The universe, as its name implies, is unified; in fact, it is a unified diversity of things. And the primary cause of unifying diversities is not diversity, but unity. The first cause of the unity of the world is therefore one.

Our reasoning has now brought us to a single, intelligent, purely nonmaterial cause of matter itself and of the human soul. A thing of that description deserves the name *god* if anything does, so I won't shy away from the name anymore.[3]

---

[3] Nor will I hesitate to refer to god with the masculine pronoun, although he has no sex and includes in himself certain feminine characteristics as well as masculine ones. For my reasons for this choice, see chapter 7, p. 120, of *Who Designed the Designer?* Also, in philosophical contexts, I tend to write *god* with a lowercase *g*, since a philosophical proof for the existence of a divine being does not by itself establish, for example, that such a being has spoken to

No Mere Designer

A carpenter causes a house to come to be, but not to continue in existence afterward. The carpenter can die in a car crash the day after the house is finished, and the house will live on. A singer, on the other hand, does not just get a song started and let the song finish by itself. The song depends on the singer for as long as it goes on. Which type of causation is more like god's, the singer's or the carpenter's? Did god get you started, but now you just exist of yourself independently of him? Or is god causing your soul to exist even now, at this very moment?

The answer to this question turns on the difference between things that can continue to be without the help of their initiators and those that cannot. What is this difference? A fire can continue to burn without help from the fire starter. A house can continue to stand without help from the one who raised it. In cases like these, the cause does not produce the entirety of the effect. When campers start a fire, they start with tinder, kindling, fuel, and air that they did not make but only found and arranged. Once the fire is started, the natural properties of these things take over and continue the combustion as long as they are able. When carpenters build a house, they start with wood that they did not make, that they only redispose. Once the house is standing, the natural properties of the wood, which exist independently of the carpenters, take over and sustain the posts and beams in their new disposition, which is why the house continues in being without further help from those who brought it into existence.

A song is quite another matter. Not only does the special arrangement of notes in it derive from the singer, but each note itself, the very sound from which each is made, comes from the singer, too. There is nothing in the song that is not from the singer. Consequently, nothing of the song is independent of the singer. So there

---

Moses and Elijah or sent his only Son into the world for our salvation. Since God with a capital G seems to be a proper name, and not just the name of a certain kind of being, and hence it implies some historical and personal interaction between us and God, I refrain from capitalizing the word as long as I am speaking precisely about what we can know of god by means of general philosophical principles. "god" means the divine being as Plato or Aristotle could have thought and spoken about him; "God" means the same divine being, but named as someone who revealed himself to us in special ways in the course of human history.

is nothing in the song that can take over for the singer and continue the song.

Which is more like the present case? Are god's effects more like a house, made of materials he did not make and which exist independently of him, or are they more like a song, the whole of which comes forth from the singer, not just part of it?

Clearly his effects are more like a song. God is the cause of matter itself, since he is the cause of its inherent orientations, and he cannot cause those without being the author of matter itself. And he is the cause not just of certain types of materials, the way brickmakers produce bricks and a sawmill produces lumber. God is the author of the most basic material (or materials) in nature, whatever that may turn out to be, since the basic stuff of the world is inherently oriented toward life and mind. This means there is nothing in a material thing that is not from god, and therefore nothing in it that has its own independent capacity for existing, or any power of retaining what is given to it. What is in a material thing entirely apart from and independently of god's power is exactly nothing. And nothingness has no power of any kind, neither to exist itself, nor to keep something else in existence.

The same goes for the human soul. God made each soul, since he is the cause of its mindless tendency to serve the needs of its own mind (by growing a brain, for example), and this tendency of the soul is not an added disposition but lies in its very constitution. Now a soul cannot be kept in existence by its materials, since it is not made of any. Consequently, there is nothing in a human soul that is independent of god's causal action, and the human soul is therefore more like a song god sings than a house he built.

Since neither matter nor your soul has any way of continuing to be apart from the influence of the divine cause, each of these effects continues in existence because of the divine action. God, in other words, causes you, your body, your soul, and the material world itself, not only to come to be, but simply to be, as long as these things exist.

He is a maker of the entirety of things, of their totality, materials included. He supplies not only forms and arrangements of things, but the very stuff of which they are made. There is no material that exists independently of him, that waits for him to stumble upon it and impose on it some of his designs. He is the designer of the fundamental stuff of the world, and that fact alone explains its inherent capacity for becoming intelligible things and intelligent beings such as ourselves. He is no mere designer. He is a creator. Someone who finds a preexistent material and conforms it to his plan may be called a designer, but not a creator, since such a one originates only a part of his product, not the whole of it. God is much more original than that, producing the whole of each creature, such as you or me. He is quite literally the most original thought there is.

Why God Bothers

Is god a thing to be pursued and loved? Or a thing to be feared? Is it good news, or bad, that we and our world are the product of someone's thought?

Our gut reaction might depend on our prior experience of human beings above us in power or knowledge. What has been our experience, on the whole, with parents, teachers, bosses, political figures, religious leaders, and people behind the desk at the DMV? Pleasant? If so, then we might welcome the fact that the world is under someone's direction. If not, perhaps we will not be so fond of the idea.

Of course, which of these subjective responses is closer to fair should be judged by the character of god himself, not by our experience with incomparably inferior minds who all too often take themselves too seriously. How can we find out about the character of god? The world around us is filled with terrible and puzzling events, some due to human choice, others to the behavior of nature (so-called acts of god). But such particularities must be parts of a grander design, and though we might be incapable of fitting these pieces into the whole picture in the correct way, we might be able, in a rough and general way, to discern god's motive in having created the universe at all and us in it.

The first question is whether it is right to suppose he had a motive. Could it be instead that he had no choice in the matter? Could he have made the world naturally, automatically, as a tree blossoms?

Were that the case, god would be less perfect than us, our inferior. We prize our freedom of choice, particularly when it comes to sharing something of ourselves with others. We like to have a say in whether we will do so, and with whom, and how and when. If that is a perfection, an advantage and not a limitation, then it must belong to god most of all. Besides, the ultimate cause of things must be a mind in order to explain the world's natural orientation toward mind. And it is characteristic of a mind, as opposed to mindless things that always act automatically and by nature, to be capable of acting by choice.

God made the world by choice, then, and for a reason. What reason? Why was this universe something worthy of his choice? Does it fulfill some need of his?

We tend to imagine so, since we are such needy creatures ourselves. The pure nonmateriality of god might even appear to make him a rather thin, ghostly thing, one whose overall situation might somehow improve if he could just manage to create some honest-to-goodness tangible, material things—things, in other words, that seem to us more real than he is himself.

This kind of mistake has a name: *anthropomorphism*. We are naturally self-centered, since it is naturally ourselves that we perceive first, most, and best. We therefore tend to make ourselves the measure of things without realizing it, judging that as things are for us, so they are for other beings. If we need bodies and sensible things in order to be complete and happy, and if our minds depend on our senses and seem to be lost without them, we easily slip into imagining that god must find himself in a similar situation. And—poor god!—he has no body, no sense organs, but is just a pure mind, floating out there in an abstract fog devoid of anything vivid or firm.

That is of course nonsense. All the firmness, vividness, and detail for which we rely on our senses god has in his understanding. It is our understanding that is poor, vague, and abstract, not god's. Eyesight is especially noteworthy among our senses for its power to take in, all at once, effortlessly, without confusion, a million crisp details. But eyesight was entirely god's idea. It is a safe bet that his ideas of things are every bit as effortless, all-embracing, and vivid as human vision, or rather much more so, and that he perceives nonmaterial things such as himself with that same immediate vividness, not by some laborious reasoning process such as we must resort to.

All this means the divine mind is very different from ours. His thoughts are not our thoughts. Without effort, hence without reasoning, without a multitude of different ideas, but with a simple gaze of his mind, he knows all things. Nor does he "take them in", as if learning from them. Things do not exist until he makes them. They exist first in his knowledge, and only because he wills it do they exist in themselves. We also can think up a thing and then make it afterward, whether a table, a meal, a painting, or a song, so that our thought precedes the thing we thought up. But though our thought precedes the thing we make, the materials in the thing we make precede our thoughts, and all our thoughts derive from our experience of things we did not make. God is too original a thinker for that. No things precede his thought, but all of them come from it. We have no direct experience of such a mind ourselves. That is why we must reason to its existence and attributes. But if only we reason well, we can see that god cannot be the sort of thing that has needs, let alone needs that can be fulfilled by bodies, or by souls such as ours that are born into the world knowing nothing. He has nothing to learn from us, nor from creatures in general, since they are entirely the products of his thought. The world comes from his knowledge, not his knowledge from the world. What could god stand to gain from things he makes in their entirety? All they have comes from him, so they can hardly turn around and offer him something profitable in return.

God therefore cannot have made the universe in order to gain something for himself. He has nothing to gain. He also has nothing to lose, since it is impossible for him to lose anything he has. He is a self-existent immortal, eternally in possession of a perfect interior life. As far as he is concerned, all of us and our whole world are completely gratuitous and unnecessary. The world could have gotten by without us, and god without the world. If we are tempted to feel resentment upon thus learning that we are on a cosmic scale superfluous, each of us just one among billions whom god could have done without, we should bear in mind that he makes each human soul by his personal choice, since matter cannot produce or become a nonmaterial soul. There is something rather uplifting in that. God picked out each one of us, setting us aside from the infinity of souls he might have made but chose not to. My wife didn't have to marry me. She had her pick among suitors, and she was happy before she met me. But she chose me. I am happier as things stand than I would be had she no choice but to marry me, or if she had married me mainly to get something out of me and not to make a free gift of herself to me. I wouldn't prefer god to be less giving and free and generous than my wife.

With nothing to gain for himself, but also nothing to lose, god remains free to create or not. And he chose to create. For what reason? All choice is based on seeing something as good. What does god see as good? Himself first of all, since existence belongs to him before it belongs to anything else, and also because he is the best of beings (a creator must be superior to what he creates). God's own goodness must therefore be the motive of his action, since that good is best and most intimate to himself, and again since all other things are good only by their derivation from and resemblance to him. On the other hand, his goodness as it exists in himself is not exactly a reason for him to create, since that already exists before he creates and cannot be improved by creating. Well, then, if creating does not promote his goodness as it exists in himself, what remains? What is left to be desired? To extend it to others—to increase the divine goodness not intensively but extensively. If god cannot increase his own goodness or his enjoyment of it, he can at least increase the number of those who can participate in it and enjoy it.

This motive behind god's choice to create does not mean he was lonely without creatures. Loneliness belongs to those whose inner richness is not self-sufficient, who depend on others to be happy in one way or another. We need others of our kind just to survive in the first place, and to reproduce, and to learn and acquire all good things. We also need others of our kind in order to enjoy more fully those goods we already possess, so that we might have them not only in ourselves, but also in and through one another. If you see a gorgeous sunset, you think it a shame if you are the only one to witness it, and you are happy to have a friend nearby to enjoy it with you. You feel that you are not, by yourself, an adequate enjoyer of the beauty of the sun, and you yourself enjoy the sun more fully when you see others enjoying it, too. God does not need even that. He possesses his own goodness fully, without needing to see creatures possess it, too, in order to enjoy it perfectly. But there is also something selfless in your wish for others besides yourself to enjoy the sunset with you. When there is a friend beside you to enjoy the sunset, aside from any gain to yourself, you see that this is a gain for your friend, and the beauty of the sun is now reflected in and enjoyed by another beholder. That is good, even aside from being a gain to you. So it is that god chose to create, to magnify his goodness in others, not in himself.

God's motive in making us and the world can therefore be summed up in a single word: love. We must beware of being deceived by the cold-sounding word *mind*. That is just one inadequate word we have for describing what he is. *Love* is another, and each makes up for limitations in what we mean by the other. God is a mind who is also an act of love of his own goodness and of those who might share it. He is not, as the word *mind* alone might suggest, some grand accountant, a cold calculator, an indifferent observer. Since he acts by choice, and hence out of recognition of what is good and beautiful, he is more like a poet, albeit one who can make characters so lifelike they are actually alive, and can enjoy the creations of the poet along with him. He loves first of all his own goodness, as is only right, since it is first and objectively the greatest, and all other things are good only by coming from it and returning to it. But he also loves the world he made and especially us, those for whom he made it, since we are all his handiwork. To the degree that artists feel they have succeeded, they love their works as faithful expressions of the profound or beautiful things they have conceived within themselves. Their works are like their children. And so we are to god. Indeed, since you have an immortal and intelligent part of you, you are like a little god yourself. Only rational creatures, capable of knowing god and loving him in return, can in that full way reflect the divine goodness within themselves. Every creature exhibits something of the divine wisdom and goodness. But exhibits it to whom? God does not need to see himself in a mirror. The reflection is for others to see. It is for us to see. God would therefore not have bothered making a universe without intelligent life, since that would be a job only half-done, a mirror in a world of blind things, a symphony played to an audience of stones. God's motive behind creation therefore implies something about us. We, and any rational creatures like us, are the principal things in creation. We are the sharers, the potential coenjoyers of divine happiness.

Could this communication of himself in the world of nature be his final word to us? An unlikely proposition. The world is an announcement to us of the perfection of god, of his everlasting, all-containing, imperturbable, and blissful enjoyment of living an infinitely intense yet effortless life. He would not announce to us this hidden life of his in order to show off, to rub our noses in it. He has no need of being admired or envied. As his act of creating us in the first place, so his revelations of himself to us in his works must come instead from largesse. He would not make us aware of his perfect and endless joy only to let us know that he has it and we do not. He cannot be eating candy in front of us, as it were. He is inviting us in.

What, then, is the personal character of god? Our only universally admitted evidence is the universe, or nature. Its ever-present, quiet beauty, neither insisting upon being noticed, nor hiding under a carpet or in an obscure library or science journal, is invitational, not elitist, nor oppressive, despotic, or suffocating. Its very wildness and freedom suggests a playful joy behind it, which we may take an interest in, hope to share in, or not, as we decide. Maybe god should be the object of fear in the sense of awe or reverence. But he seems to address himself to us, at least to start with, not imperiously but quietly. His first way of speaking is through goodness and beauty, in the mode of exhortation more than in the mode of command, and by implanting natural desires leading us to him, such as the desire to see the world, and the desire also to understand it, especially those noble desires called philosophical wonder and scientific curiosity.

It is nonetheless a long and slow journey for many of us even to learn of his existence, and for most of us an even slower journey to learn genuinely to care about it, and to desire some greater share in it. For most of us, myself included, it is a journey of many years to learn to think of him more truly as he is—less like Santa Claus or Zeus or the Man Upstairs, and more as the only thing in existence that can satisfy our deepest desires to live and exult in splendors and to deserve it. It is good that he is patient. The first things to capture the attentions of our hearts tend to be impoverished imitations of his goodness indeed. We like soda and Jolly Ranchers before we savor fine wine. We relish comic books before Shakespeare, and long to see a movie sooner than we long to see god. Slowly and by degrees do we climb toward god in our affections, if we choose to make the climb at all.

Faced with the solidity and gorgeousness of his world, we cannot reasonably doubt that he is worth it. All that we strive to enjoy and become by increasing and multiplying our encounters and understandings, the author of life without any toil already is, always was, all in one act, all at once. Can we doubt that he wants to share this life of his, the existence and transcendence of which we can read out of the things that he has made? God acts under no compulsion. By choice he willed to communicate to us a likeness of himself and a share in his own power, understanding, and goodness. He neither gains nor loses by the enterprise. It was not self-interest or natural necessity that moved him to produce this life-filled world. It was generosity.

He is a giver of gifts. The graces of the universe bear witness to the fact. Ubiquitous, astonishing, needless and gratuitous, beauty covers our world from end to end. Were it not for the weakness of our mortal condition—our understandable tendency, in dark times of trouble and grief, to forget blessings bestowed—a mere glance at the stars would dispel all doubts about the goodness of our maker.

13

Know Thyself: Audrey's Problem

Trust thyself: every heart vibrates to that iron string.
—Ralph Waldo Emerson, "Self-Reliance", 1841

The Different Answer

In this book you have probably noticed a higher-than-expected number of references to triangles. One excuse I offer for this is that triangles (and such) are much shallower things than our own souls, and much more imaginable, and consequently we can clamp them in the vise of mathematical certainty. Not only can we get a firm grip on triangles and other mathematical things, but they are also fundamental to our world, and accordingly they provide matter for analogies to deeper truths that might otherwise elude us.

So it is that the very word *mathematics* comes from the Greek for *learnable*, and Plato posted over the entryway to his Academy a sign reading "Let no one ignorant of geometry enter here." The natural world is somehow quantitatively, hence mathematically, intelligible, and no doubt that has something to do with the world being the handiwork of a mind, and in particular, a mind having us in mind. The world is startlingly intelligible to us. God is not subject to our mental limitations and preferences, but he is surely aware of them. Probably he made a world subject to mathematical laws in order to make it intelligible to minds peculiarly mathematical—to our minds, in other words.

Were nature ever-so-unmathematical, however, I still would have sprinkled mathematical illustrations throughout the foregoing chapters if only because mathematics is so marvelously clear and exact, and thus furnishes excellent examples of our understanding of things, and also because I sometimes have occasion to teach the elementary parts of it, which means I often have it on the brain.

A specific purpose brings us back into the company of triangles now. We are about to compare and contrast the kind of knowledge we have attained about you to what is called "exact science" or "hard science", much of which is mathematical. With an eye to that goal, I ask you to bear with me through a short mathematical tale. Really it is a tale about students, with math as mere background. The story contains, we will see, a general insight needed for rectifying some of the most common misconceptions about science and common sense.

The story goes like this. I once was teaching a certain group of students the first book of Euclid's *Elements*. Together we had learned some basic theorems about congruence among triangles. If you are not a math lover yourself, perhaps you will nevertheless recall from high school that two triangles are called *congruent* when they are exactly the same shape and size, which means all their corresponding sides are equal, and all their corresponding angles are equal, and they contain equal areas to boot. Congruent triangles are carbon copies of each other. Even if you have not thought about geometry for decades, you will probably remember that given enough equalities among the corresponding sides or angles of two triangles, it will follow that all the remaining corresponding sides and angles will be equal as well, and so the two triangles will be in complete agreement—that is to say, congruent. For example, if in one triangle a pair of sides and the angle between them are respectively equal to a pair of sides and the angle between them in another triangle, then the two triangles are entirely congruent, as are triangles ABC and DEF in the accompanying figure.

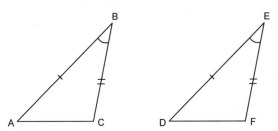

After my students had seen the proofs for this congruence theorem and a couple of others, I asked them a question. Suppose two sides in a triangle and some angle *not* between them were equal to two sides in another triangle and some angle *not* between them—what then? Would the two triangles have to be congruent? If, for example, in the triangles GHK and PQR we knew that

$$GH = PQ$$
$$\text{and} \quad GK = PR$$
$$\text{and} \quad \angle GKH = \angle PRQ$$

then would triangle GHK have to be congruent to triangle PQR?

A young man dashed up to the blackboard. "Yes!" he shouted, scribbling up a diagram like the one I'm supplying here:

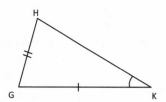 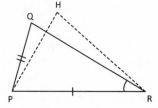

He said that we could pick up triangle GHK and plop GK exactly on top of PR (since they are equal). After doing this, if H did not land right on top of Q, then angle GKH would not be equal to angle PRQ after all—but it is, since that was one of the given conditions, and so point H must really land right on top of point Q, making the two triangles completely coincide, proving their congruence.

The young man took a bow (no, I'm not making that up) and took his seat.

Every student in the class accepted this proof—everyone, that is, except for Audrey. She alone was not convinced. "I think we made a mistake," she said. She stood up, approached the blackboard, and drew a circle around center G, with radius GH, cutting line HK at Z, as seen in the diagrams on the next page.

"See," said Audrey, "this new triangle GZK has two sides and a nonincluded angle equal to two sides and a nonincluded angle in triangle PQR, but even so those two triangles are not congruent."

A babble of discordant voices broke out, offering various reasons why her objection was illegitimate. "You're not allowed to change

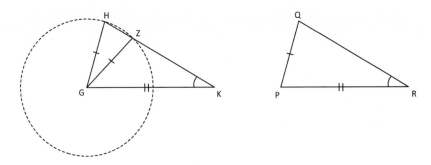

angle GHK," someone shouted; "The circle you drew can't cut HK *twice*," insisted someone else; "We *proved* that HK is equal to QR," said a third, "so it's not fair to go and use a smaller line like ZK instead."

"Oh," said Audrey, replacing the chalk in its tray and staring blankly for a moment at her diagram. Then she shrugged her shoulders and said (not sarcastically but with honest resignation), "Well, I guess we proved it after all." And she resumed her seat at our discussion table.

She had of course been entirely in the right with her brilliant construction of circle G. Her triangle GZK shares base GK with triangle GHK, and its side GZ is equal to side GH, and both triangles share the angle at K. Despite all that, the two triangles obviously have some unequal sides (such as HK and ZK), and some unequal angles (such as HGK and ZGK), and clearly have unequal areas. They are not congruent. The given conditions I had asked about therefore do *not* guarantee congruence.

Audrey, and Audrey alone, had seen this and had even seen why it was so. And yet, the moment the majority of the class—that formidable authority—spoke out against her, she renounced her own insight and signed up for their nonsense. I intervened at this point and asked the students to help me understand why Audrey's triangle could not exist, or why, if it did exist, it did not discredit our original attempt to prove a new congruence theorem. After some discussion, it became clear to everyone that Audrey had been right, and that the majority of us had been too hasty and had merely succumbed to the first plausible drawing laid before us. She had made an uncommon use of certain commonsense principles and consequently arrived at something beyond common sense, proving that sound commonsense thinking and the common consensus do not always coincide. Her classmates had nonetheless prevailed upon her to fall back in line with them.

Here we have an instance of an astonishing and seemingly impossible fact about the human mind. We are so constructed that even when we see the truth for ourselves, and see it quite clearly and correctly, through perfectly decisive evidence, we can be talked out of it. Sometimes others talk us out of it. Sometimes we talk ourselves out of it. Sometimes we are talked out of it because of social pressures—we discount what we see with our own eyes and minds because we cannot believe everyone else can have gotten it wrong, or because we are afraid that we might be ignorant or incompetent, as in the case of the tale "The Emperor's New Clothes". Other times we are talked out of the truth we have seen because we discover objections to our conviction that we do not know how to answer. We have been fooled so many times before (into thinking we knew something when it turned out we did not) that we are readily persuaded that this must be one of those times, and so we repudiate what we initially thought.

Socrates gave his life, both in the ordinary and extraordinary sense of that expression, to the cause of helping people learn to recognize when they really knew something and when they really did not. Often his encounters brought him into contact with people who thought they knew something when really they didn't. Some of these people, such as the "Sophists" (the self-styled "Wise"), were renowned for their knowledge and received money as well as applause for it. Socrates made enemies of them when he showed in public that they did not really know the things they professed to know, or not nearly so well as they thought. Other patients of his philosophical art were quite ordinary people, not particularly renowned for their knowledge, but who nonetheless professed to know things they really did not know. Many of these believed they knew quite well what it means for a human being to be good. But Socrates showed over and over that this is far harder to understand in any clear way than we are apt to realize. Even among the educated, very few people take the trouble of thinking through, from first principles, what sorts of habits and actions perfect a human being, and which ones do not. Instead, most people tend to adopt uncritically the moral principles of their culture, or else of some smaller subculture, and they mistake their agreement with other people and authorities for their own understanding of the truth of things. It is not wrong to accept moral principles from others, of course, especially when we do so from those wiser than we are. But it is a mistake to think this sort of acceptance is the same thing as knowing for ourselves.

That is one version of the problem to which Socrates devoted his life. Sometimes we think we know something perfectly well when really we do not. Not only Sophists, but most of us (probably all of us, at one time or another) delude ourselves and others in this way. But there is another version of the problem. There is Audrey's problem. Sometimes we think we do *not* know something when really we *do*. That is the version of the problem I wish to place in the spotlight. In particular, I am interested in exploring why people allow themselves to be talked out of many things they really do know about themselves simply because they mistakenly believe that science—that formidable authority—says otherwise.

We are profoundly social creatures. In one way, knowing and understanding are things each individual must do for himself, but in other ways even the activity of knowing is a community enterprise. No thinker who gets anywhere worthwhile is entirely independent. We depend on one another to supplement our thoughts with things we were prone to overlook, and to teach us truths we had no time or ability to discover on our own. Such cooperative effort saves us the trouble of repeating the mistakes of others, saves us a great deal of time, saves us from reinventing the wheel. Even once we have really understood something, we often look to others to be sure we really understand it. It is not enough to know. We must also know that we know. The procedures by which we come to know are many and often prolix, presenting us with any number of opportunities to take a wrong turn. When we have worked out a long calculation, and even gotten it right, we may worry that we slipped up somewhere, so we check our answer by redoing it, or by comparing it to a rough estimate, or by asking other people what they got for a result. When everyone else in the class got the same answer except you, you worry. That can be a sign that you went off track somewhere. But it also happens—and almost as often—that the one person who got a different answer is also the one person who got it right.

The understanding of you that we have worked so hard to achieve in this book is like the "different answer" in a math class. Of course it is a common enough belief that you have an immortal soul created by god. Among those who strive to understand what you are, however, which is to say, among the philosophers and scientists who make it their business to say what a human being is, there are relatively few who affirm that you have a soul at all, let alone an immortal one. Many do not deny it, either, but only subscribe to uncertainty or else agnosticism concerning such things as your immortal soul. But among those who profess to know about the matter, there are also those who deny you have any such thing, and probably more who deny than affirm. That you possess an immortal soul and a noncorporeal intellect, that you and all nature derive from god, such things are common beliefs, but are exceedingly uncommon knowledge.

We cannot help but wonder why. Is this picture of you uncommon among seekers of knowledge because it is erroneous? Did we wander off the true path somewhere in our reasoning about you? Or is the picture correct but impossible to prove, a matter only for faith, or some sort of untestable hypothesis? Lest nagging doubts like these harass us, we would do well to understand why ours is the "different" answer.

The chief cause responsible is not far to seek. It is the widespread belief that modern science alone, with its sophisticated tools and techniques, provides true insight into nature generally, and into what you are in particular. The name for this belief is *scientism*. According to the *scientistic* (not to be confused with *scientific!*) outlook, you cannot be *known* to be anything other than what modern science can say about you. All true knowledge of you is the outcome of work done by someone in a lab coat. Severer forms of scientism go further, denying you to *be* anything other than what modern science says you are. What is common to all forms and degrees of scientism, however, is the idea that all nontrivial knowledge of you must be the fruit of specialized empirical research. Your personal experience of yourself, and particularly your insider's view of you, cannot be trusted to reveal anything worthwhile about you. We must, at the very outset of serious inquiry, replace your ordinary experience of yourself with an extraordinary experience of you—with images of brain activity produced by MRI, with protein structures revealed by means of X-ray crystallography, with cycles of chemical reactions, and other such particulars, if we are ever to form a high resolution (and therefore true) picture of you.

A book such as this one, according to this way of thinking, contains no real insight into what you are, precisely because it begins from your own experience of yourself, which is entirely unscientific and consequently untrustworthy. All the work in the foregoing chapters is just so much "folk psychology", an elaboration of the ordinary (hence illusory) view we all have of ourselves. To break the spell of ordinary experience, to tear aside the curtain it places between us and the truth about the world and ourselves, we must get serious—we must get scientific. And *scientific* means beginning from scratch, jettisoning all our ordinary experience and all the concepts of the world and of ourselves that it engenders, and starting over from technically enhanced experience alone.

This is scientism. And it is by far the main reason why the "homemade" science of you (as exemplified in this book) receives so little public fanfare and even less recognition in academic circles, and so I propose to examine it closely in this chapter. It is worth saying why this is worth doing. After all, if you have gotten this far in this book, in fact if you have picked up this book in first place, chances are you are not much enchanted by scientism. If you are, and you have nonetheless struggled patiently through this whole book waiting for me to address objections to your ordinary experience, then the importance of this chapter for you will be obvious. If not, if the whole idea that your ordinary experience can be sidelined and replaced by something else strikes you as silly, a serious consideration of scientism is nonetheless eminently worth your time for four reasons.

First, however little attraction scientism may hold for you, it is immensely influential in modern culture—not only in academia, but in popular media, in fiction as well as nonfiction. It is worth understanding the age you live in just because you live in it. Knowing how people think means knowing how to sympathize with them and how to talk to them—and maybe how to help them.

Second, you will possess the general Science of You as outlined in this book more fully if you see it in the context of other forms of knowledge. Scientism forces us to consider carefully how the knowledge of you that is developed out of ordinary experience relates to modern science. Are these two pictures of you opposed, as scientism asserts? Or is one of them part of the other? Or are they two parts of some larger enterprise?

A third reason to consider scientism carefully is that it means coming to understand yourself better. You have been the subject of this whole book. We are now asking one final question about you. You are so made that the world and you yourself appear to you in certain ways in your ordinary experience. How true and indispensable is this ordinary experience of yours? How does the validity of your common sense stand up to accusations that it is untrustworthy since it lacks the exactness of scientific observation? The main accuser of your ordinary contact with reality used to be modern philosophy. Nowadays it is not modern philosophy, nor is it modern science, but a certain philosophy about modern science—namely, the view that modern science discredits your experience and simply replaces it. The enemy is not modern science, but the false assessment of it as a complete and adequate understanding of reality. That false assessment of science is not the same as science itself. That deserves emphasis. *Scientism is not science.* It is a particular idea about what science is. Science, on the other hand, is not an idea about science, but a unified network of well-correlated theories about nature. It is a genuine and profound way of understanding nature, including you, even if it can never by itself be the whole understanding of nature.

A fourth reason for thinking carefully about the thesis of scientism is that it is not enough to see *that* a commonly believed position is wrong in order to break free of it. To become liberated from a common error, we must see why others find it so alluring. Until we understand the intellectual appeal of scientism, we will not understand why ours is the "different" answer to the big questions about you. And so long as we don't fully understand the more common answer, it will retain some power to make us doubt ourselves.

Science and *Philosophy*

Before we begin, we must take a moment to define two terms: *modern science* and *the philosophy of nature*. We cannot understand scientism without a clear and general grasp of modern science, since scientism is the claim that modern science is the sole trustworthy knowledge of nature. And if scientism is false, then there must be another knowledge of nature besides the kind we find in modern science. The other knowledge of nature that we have been pursuing throughout this book has a name: *natural philosophy*, or the philosophy of nature. In order to understand scientism, in other words, we must understand modern science, which scientism makes a certain claim about, and natural philosophy, the kind of knowledge that scientism overlooks.

The word *science*, or at least its Latin origin, *scientia*, existed long before modern science. It meant any sure and exact knowledge of things resulting from careful and rigorous procedures of reason. So far as that definition goes, mathematics is a science. Indeed in centuries past, mathematics would have been put forward as the prime example of a science, and even today mathematics is called by some a *science*. But when we speak of *science* today, we generally mean modern science. And what about it makes it modern? Why do we think science was somehow born with Galileo? What further defining characteristics do we need to add to "sure, exact, reasoned knowledge" in order to set modern science apart from science generally, and from mathematics in particular?

We must add two further ideas to the general idea of science before we get the specific idea of modern science. One of these is "empirical observation". The other is "testable statements". And these two ideas go together. Modern science is science that tests its statements against empirical observations. It may use many other techniques besides, but this feature especially characterizes it and sets it apart from other ways of knowing nature. If we can understand empirical observation and the testing of statements, we will have a fair idea of the general nature of modern science.

What does *empirical* mean? The word *empirical* comes from the ancient Greek word for experience, ἐμπειρία. The derivative English word *empirical* is more specific than that, however. When people talk of empirical observations, for instance, they do not mean merely "things known through sense experience". *Empirical* usually implies something significantly narrower. My wife asks me whether we have any milk in the fridge. I peek in and take a look. That is not "empirical research". Why not? According to common usage of the term *empirical*, the objects of empirical observation are (1) objects of careful observation—that is, of deliberately sought experience as opposed to things passively experienced; (2) objects of external sense experience, things seen from the vantage point of an outsider; (3) objects of repeatable experience, as opposed to a unique, one-time event; but furthermore, (4) objects of experience are considered supremely and quintessentially *empirical* when, in addition to meeting these first three conditions, they are also measurable attributes of things ascertained with the assistance of instruments of measurement and detection (such as thermometers and voltmeters) or by means of special techniques (such as setting up an experimental group of subjects and a control group).

So much for *empirical observations*. What now of *testable statements*? The kind of statement I mean is to be found outside natural science, too, in the world of criminal detection and similar fields. If Mr. X has been murdered and no one witnessed the deed, then "Mrs. X did it" is an example of a testable statement, one that we cannot directly experience, but which we can reason to in some way from things we can directly experience, from empirical evidence. We might reason like this:

If Mrs. X were the killer,
then her alibi would not hold up,
and she would have had access to a .40 caliber Sig Sauer P229
    pistol,
and she would have to be able to lift two hundred pounds,
and traces of her husband's blood would be in the trunk of her car,
and she would have a motive.

But her alibi in fact fell through (under interrogation, her sister
    admitted that she was not really with her that night after all),
and her husband had a registered Sig Sauer P229, now missing,
and she is a competitive weightlifter,
and though the trunk of her car had been cleaned with bleach,
    traces of her husband's blood were found there nonetheless,
and she had recently discovered that her husband had taken a lover,
    and she has been well known for her violent fits of jealousy.

Conclusion? Mrs. X probably did it. Why? Because the assumption that she did it explains a significant body of data otherwise difficult to explain. That is detective-style reasoning: if statement S were true, that would neatly explain lots of otherwise puzzling or coincidental facts, so S is most likely true.

Many of the great statements of modern science are statements like "Mrs. X did it", and the form of inference supporting them is hypothetico-deductive reasoning (a fancy term for what I have just called detective-style reasoning). Since empirical evidence in science most of all means quantitative evidence, most great statements of science verified by empirical methods are statements about the quantitative relationships of things. For example, Sir Isaac Newton reasoned like this:

1. If the moon is kept in its orbit because it is falling toward the earth just like a giant stone, then its acceleration toward earth, when adjusted (by an inverse square law) for a location near the surface of the earth, would be the same as that of any ordinary stone.

2. And indeed the moon's acceleration toward earth, when adjusted (by an inverse square law) for a location near the surface of the earth, is exactly the same as that of any ordinary stone.

Therefore the moon is kept in its orbit because it is falling toward the earth.

Strictly speaking, the conclusion should say, "Therefore we will suppose, until such time as contrary evidence forces us to say otherwise, that the moon is kept in orbit because it is falling toward the earth." That is always understood in modern science, so it is not always explicitly said. But it must be at least in the backs of our minds. Why? Why doesn't the argument above absolutely demonstrate that the moon is falling toward the earth?

The reason is because this kind of reasoning is not formally airtight, which is clear if we consider, for example, this instance of it:

1. If you are stranded on a desert island, then you are absent from my classroom today.

2. And indeed you are absent from my classroom today.

Therefore you are stranded on a desert island.

This is of course fallacious reasoning, while Newton's imposing argument is anything but fallacious. It might even conclude beyond a reasonable doubt. Why the difference in cogency, if these two reasonings are formally identical? Just as there can be more than one conceivable reason why you would be absent from my classroom, and being stranded on a desert island is merely one possibility among the many, isn't there also more than one conceivable reason why our moon would stay in its orbit around the earth, whereas Newton's theory offers just one of the possibilities? Yes, but Newton's theory also explains countless other empirical data in the universe, and it predicted many others quite unknown beforehand that were verified afterward. That is far more than we can say for the hypothesis that you are stranded on a desert island.

Now that we have a rough sense of the characteristic way that modern science operates (it advances testable statements and corroborates them by checking their empirical consequences), we need one last piece of terminology before we put scientism under the microscope. The way we have studied you and nature in general in this book has made little use of empirical data (though plenty of use of experiential data), and little use of detective-style reasoning. So although it might be genuine knowledge, it is not modern science. It is something else. One name for that something else is philosophy—in particular, the philosophy of nature.

So what is "natural philosophy", exactly? In one sense, the expression simply names the whole rational inquiry into nature, of which modern empirical science is the larger part. In this sense, modern science itself can be called "natural philosophy". Thus Newton's most famous book, in which he propounded the theory of universal gravitation, was entitled *Principia Mathematica Philosophiae Naturalis*, or, in English, *Mathematical Principles of Natural Philosophy*. So the whole study of nature can be called natural philosophy. The whole study of nature can also be called *natural science*, of course, and that is more in keeping with current usage.

But what now about the part of the study of nature that is not especially modern, but is instead perennial? What about that part of the science of nature that consists in observations and inferences such as those in this book? What shall we call that?

That kind of knowledge has always been called philosophy, too, and still is today. By calling the modern study of nature *science* and the perennial part *philosophy* I do not mean to imply that modern science is unphilosophical, or that natural philosophy is unscientific. Far from it. But I use these convenient labels ("modern science" and "natural philosophy") to distinguish the part of natural science that exploits empirical methods and testable statements on the one hand, and the part of natural science that instead exploits universal human experience, common to us all, on the other hand.

Which brings me to the positive description of natural philosophy. It is not merely a knowledge of nature "not using modern methods", but has methods of its own. For example, as opposed to special empirical observations, which belong primarily to those few who take the trouble to make them (and which the actual observers may then report or describe or show to the rest of us in some way), there are other forms of experience common to everyone, and these I call universal experiences. For example, not everyone has the experience of "Jupiter's moons moving" or of "clocks ticking more slowly as one ascends a mountain". Those are not matters of everyone's experience. But anyone with any experience at all has an experience of "motion" or of "something moving". It is that kind of inescapable experience, common to all of us, that the philosophy of nature makes the most of, clarifying such experiences and drawing out their logical consequences.

As a consequence of this difference in the kinds of experience that modern science and natural philosophy exploit, we find a second difference. Modern science strives to be as empirical as it can, and therefore as far as possible keeps to an outsider's view of things, even ourselves. Unlike much of modern science, the philosophy of nature takes full advantage of our insider's view of ourselves, since that type of experience is common to us all, and contains a wealth of implications, as we have seen for ourselves in previous chapters. (Some experiences are not perfectly universal among us, but at least belong to all adults who are both whole and healthy—the experience of seeing, for example; these, too, are wellsprings of the philosophy of nature.)

How are these two studies of nature related, modern science and natural philosophy? Some would have it that they are simply unrelated, or related only in the most tangential of ways as are geometry and literature, each of which can get along just fine without the other. More often we find people adopting an either/or stance toward them. Some philosophers have spoken as if empirical science is a superficial knowledge of nature, a kind of bean-counting knowledge, while philosophy is the genuine article. Since that view is quite rare and not very reasonable, we will examine instead the contrary view that any "philosophy of nature" is just a poor and lazy attempt to do what empirical science alone is truly competent to do. This is the idea of scientism.

This view, I have said, is quite commonplace in our universities and institutions of research, and it is not hard to find on TV. All sci-fi shows try to operate on *scientific* premises. But some operate also on *scientistic* ones. And just as a sci-fi show can operate on a scientistic premise without ever enunciating that premise, let alone defending it with arguments, so too can mainstream academia. And this is for the most part how things are done in practice. Scientism, in other words, does not live in the world as an explicitly formulated and formally defended thesis, but more as an unspoken, hardly thought about background assumption. Sometimes it is openly defended, but rarely. Such defenses are unnecessary, since most academics, most scientists, and indeed most philosophers have certain leanings toward scientism, whether conscious or unconscious. This itself is important to understanding scientism. In many cases, it is not so much a deliberately embraced theory as a naturally adopted outlook in the absence of any obvious alternative.

Nonetheless, once we hold scientism deliberately before our minds, it is not too difficult to discover formidable reasons that seem to justify it entirely. All of them may be found in print, at least as far back as *Novum organum*, the great and revolutionary work of the seventeenth-century English philosopher Francis Bacon. Bacon, gifted with impressive insight and foresight, saw the limitations of the philosophy of nature as it had been practiced up to his day, and envisioned a new way of investigating nature for the future, free from those limitations. He was not a pioneer or father of modern science as was Galileo, by making specific scientific contributions of great significance. He was more a herald of modern science, an explainer of its possibilities, and of the need for it. In commending to us the new science, however, and tempering the love of the old, he sometimes went overboard, tending to disparage natural philosophy completely. He threw out the baby with the bathwater.

14

Know Thyself: The Five Half-Truths of Scientism

All knowledge, and all science, must be built upon principles that are self-evident; and of such principles, every man who has common sense is a competent judge, when he conceives them distinctly.

—Thomas Reid, Essays on the Powers of the Human Mind

Certainty in Modern Science and Philosophy

What are the rationales for scientism? Why would anyone think it right and necessary to reject our common experience of the world and of ourselves? Why embrace modern science and reject a commonsense philosophy rather than acknowledge both together?

The main reasons are these five:

1. Modern science seems certain, philosophy uncertain.
2. Modern science is objective, philosophy seems subjective.
3. Scientists agree with each other, philosophers do not.
4. From common experience alone it seems we can get nothing but common knowledge, which hardly deserves to be called science.
5. Science gives control over nature, philosophy does not.

Taking these up one at a time, let us now discern what is true and what is false in each.

The very word *science* conjures up in the hearer an idea of exactness of knowledge, of precision and certainty. The application of mathematics especially yields "hard science", where "hard" is opposed not to "easy" but to "soft", to squishy things that are not so sure or decisive or exact (sociology, for example). Long before modern science found its legs, Thomas Aquinas defined *scientia* as "cognitio perfecta", *perfect knowledge* of some particular thing. This means knowing some truth with either certainty or precision or both, and knowing it as the result of some rigorous procedure of thought.

Now it may appear that any science of nature, even by this very general definition of *science*, would absolutely have to be founded on empirical observations. Science implies certainty; ordinary experience does not. Who doesn't see that more ordinary forms of experience often leave us in doubt? Whether the star I am looking at is just a single star or is instead a double, whether Venus has phases, and whether the sun is a perfect sphere or not—these questions are left doubtful by the naked eye and are settled by such instruments as telescopes. Empirical observation, in other words, because it is more carefully procured and technically assisted than ordinary experience, is more certain, more trustworthy than ordinary experience, and should therefore stand in judgment of it. Correspondingly, the knowledge founded on empirical observation (namely, modern science) is more certain than the knowledge of nature founded on ordinary experience (namely, natural philosophy), and should stand in judgment of it. Natural philosophy would therefore seem to be nothing more than easy, primitive guesswork about nature, whereas modern science is labor-intensive question settling about nature—which alone deserves the name *science*.

The skies over philosophy grow black! They get blacker still when we consider that ordinary experience is not only in many cases doubtful where empirical observation is sure, but it is often wrong or illusory besides. It is not hard to rattle off propositions into which students of nature, prior to the advent of modern science around the time of Galileo, have duped themselves. Here are a few of the usual suspects:

- The earth sits still at the center of the universe.
- Heavier things fall faster than lighter ones.
- Light does not travel, but is instantaneous.
- Water is infinitely divisible and homogeneous, hence an element.
- Human vision is perfectly continuous, with unlimited temporal resolution.

Philosophy's rap sheet goes on and on. So it would appear that the philosophy of nature, beginning as it does from common experience and ideas accessible to everyone, is really just "armchair dabbling", or ivory-tower thinking, a lazy project that should not be called science.

There are nuggets of truth in this indictment. Empirical observations not only bring to light new things beyond the reach of ordinary experience—quasars, black holes, skin cells—but they are also indispensable for settling many doubts about things in ordinary experience, and for correcting countless misconceptions we form about things based on that same incomplete experience of them. Philosophers of nature generally agree to these points.

This corrective and judgmental capacity of empirical observation in regard to ordinary experience is, however, confined within definite limits. It is not absolute. It is restricted to those times when ordinary experience moves us to believe, suspect, hypothesize, or guess at something beyond its ken. Outside of such cases, ordinary experience is not only certain, but more certain than empirical observation, since ordinary experience is itself a component of every empirical observation, but the reverse is not true. When scientists read thermometers or columns of data registered on computer monitors, they must use and trust their eyesight the same way everybody does—in a completely natural, prescientific perception of reality. Since ordinary experience is thus prior and foundational to empirical observation, empirical observation cannot stand wholly outside of all ordinary experience and judge it or replace it, because it always needs and uses it, always assumes its trustworthiness, and always will. Every empirical observation, in other words, be it ever so sophisticated, depends on the reliability of our unreflective and unassisted use of our senses.

Modern science no doubt brings to light many counterintuitive truths, things that seem to strike against common sense, that do violence to how we tend to imagine the world around us and ourselves. Quantum physics is full of examples. But there are certain inflexible limits to how strange quantum strangeness[1] can be. If quantum theory became so strange that it overturned all the ordinary certainty we have about what we are doing when we use scientific equipment,

---

[1] I am using "strangeness", here, in a purely nontechnical sense, as in "weirdness" or "unexpectedness". The term also has a scientific meaning.

about what we think and imagine when we use words to make scientific observations, form concepts, and make inferences, then there would be nothing so strange about that sort of strangeness after all, because it would only be another example of a self-refuting mistake. The whole basis for believing in it will be removed if it displaces our ordinary certainty about what we are doing with our hands, mouths, and minds, whether to conduct experiments in the lab or to make meatloaf in the kitchen. Quantum physics cannot afford to be so strange, in other words, that it undermines our experience of ourselves and our actions (internal as well as external) to the point that we cannot be sure whether we are really thinking, sitting, talking, and existing. All of science's counterintuitive results must leave such ordinary knowledge of ourselves intact, inviolate, since such ordinary knowledge forms part of its own credibility. Heisenberg's uncertainty principle does not mean everything is uncertain. If it meant that, then it itself would be uncertain, and we could ignore it with impunity. Einstein's principle of relativity is not an endorsement of intellectual relativism. Then the principle itself could not be absolutely true, but would be true only for people who thought it was, and false for other people, and it would be of no scientific importance. Science often finds out things that run directly against our initial expectations based on ordinary experience of the world and ourselves. That is arguably what science does when it is at its best (and the same holds true for math and philosophy as well). But it does not overturn our ordinary experience itself. It uses it, needs it, in addition to other kinds of experience that supplement or enhance it. Those who say otherwise are confused about what science really says, or else about what ordinary experience really says—they are poor scientists, or poor philosophers, or both.

This one-way dependence of empirical types of experience on ordinary experience holds certain consequences for the concepts of modern science. The concepts we deliberately form with the help of empirical observations depend on the concepts we naturally form out of our universally shared experiences. *Mass* is a concept of modern science, and not everyone has formed such a concept—it is defined by a body's resistance to acceleration, with Newton's First Law of Motion in mind. Not everybody has formed the idea of *acceleration* as it is intended in the definition of mass. Acceleration can be positive or negative, can consist in a change of direction or speed or both, and is defined as the derivative of velocity with respect to time. It is possible to live a long and happy life without thinking any of those thoughts. But the commonsense notions of *resistance, motion, size,* and *distance* are inescapable notions common to us all. We seize on these things quite naturally in our unassisted experience of the world. And even if we add certain mathematical ideas to these fundamental ideas common to us all, the fundamental ideas themselves still enter into our scientific concepts. Without such prescientific concepts, the concepts of science lose all their meaning.

No one reaches healthy adulthood without these universal conceptions. We don't need to be taught them. We cannot be taught them. All instances of teaching, indeed all communication and meetings of minds, presuppose and use them. They are the lingua franca of all human understanding. As to certainty, there can be no doubt which concepts are surer. Concepts of modern science such as *mass, space, field, atom, electron, gene, cell*—these continually evolve together with our scientific advancements. The modern atom has little in common with the "atom" of Dalton, less still with the "atom" of Democritus. But what the unassuming Joe-on-the-street means by *body*,[2] which idea any physics teacher must presume you possess and can never give you if you don't, is the same in everyone's mind from century to century. If we had no such concepts in common with the ancients, their statements would not seem to us wrong or doubtful, but utterly devoid of meaning—we could make nothing of them. As it is, they can talk to us, and we can agree or disagree, thanks to the common inheritance of every human mind, the concepts born of universally experienced things.

It is both a hopeless task and a needless one, then, to try to emancipate ourselves entirely from our ordinary experience and the concepts to which it gives rise, and to replace these with empirical observations. We can fool ourselves into thinking science can function without recourse to ordinary experience and universally shared conceptions. This self-delusion is possible only because our use of these common funds of knowledge is so ubiquitous, continuous,

---

[2] A body, in the general sense I have in mind here, means "a thing having length, breadth, and depth", without specifying any method for measuring these dimensions.

natural, and effortless that we need make no fuss over them in order to apply them. Our dependence on them consequently escapes our notice, particularly when we are deeply preoccupied with a particle accelerator or a probe sent to Mars or some other spectacular and demanding instrument or technique aimed at knowledge. But what scientist can make progress without everyone's ordinary idea of motion, or of number, or of causation, or of whole and part? Or what scientist can get by without trusting sense experience and self-awareness in quite the ordinary way we all do when reading something on a computer monitor?

The type of experience at the foundation of modern science depends on ordinary experience, then, while ordinary experience is independent of special empirical observation. The special concepts of modern science, too, are dependent on (and less certain and stable than) the primary concepts arising out of ordinary experience, and this dependence is also one-way. And there is more. The basic statements of modern science are also less certain than the basic statements arising out of our common concepts, and we find once more a one-way dependence here. Compare, for example, the following pairs of statements:

1. A. What moves has speed.   B. Light moves at 186,000 miles per second.

2. A. What acts against its own tendency is influenced by a cause.   B. A body that reverses direction is being influenced by a force or field.

3. A. There must be elements.   B. The chemical elements are those listed on the periodic table.

In each pair, the first statement is more certain than the second, and the first can be true and known even if the second were false or unknown, but not the other way around. In each case, the certainty of B depends on the certainty of A, and yet B is a statement of modern science, while A is known independently of any special empirical observations.

There is also a way in which statement B is in each case superior to statement A—namely, by giving us more information. Statement B tells us more about reality, or at least about certain particular realities, than A does. Precisely for that reason, however, we are in each case more certain of A than of B. The less we say, or the less specific we are, the more certain we can be of what we have said. (The police are more certain that *someone* committed the murder than they are that *a white male* did it, and I am more certain that *something* is wrong with my car than that *the transmission is going*.) What one statement loses in content by being more noncommittal than another, it gains in certainty. In this way, the statements expressing self-evident truths of universal experience surpass the certainties of modern science.

So far, philosophy exceeds modern science in the certainty of the experiences, concepts, and basic truths from which it begins. Its method of reasoning from these is also more certain. Modern science is characterized by "detective-style" reasoning—that is, hypothetico-deductive reasoning (like the Newtonian example about the moon that we considered earlier), which form of reasoning does not force its conclusion even if all the premises are true. Inductive reasoning, also commonly employed in modern science, does not force its conclusion either. Induction takes us from particular cases to a general statement like this:

- Energy is conserved in *this* system, here.
- Energy is conserved in *that* system, there.
- Energy is conserved in every system that any competent scientist has taken pains to study.
- Well, then, energy is conserved in *every* system.

This conclusion is subject to revision in light of future counterinstances, should they ever come along. No number of instances suggesting a general rule can guarantee that the rule is general in the way we might think. Not even an infinity of instances fitting a pattern can do that. For example:

- 3 is odd.
- 5 is odd.
- 7 is odd.
- A whole infinity of numbers are odd.
- Well, then, *every* number is odd.

This particular example of inductive reasoning, like the "desert island" example of hypothetico-deductive reasoning I introduced earlier, is of course invalid, because it is based on a biased sampling of all the numbers. But "Energy is always conserved" is not, so far as we know, based on a biased sampling of types of energy. And there is another difference. The Law of the Conservation of Energy carries with it immense unifying and explaining power, making sense out of piles of otherwise seemingly unrelated or unintelligible phenomena of the natural world. It also predicts many things, and these predictions thus far have all checked out (this is the hypothetico-deductive technique again). Unlike the conclusion that "all numbers are odd", the conclusion that "energy is always conserved" is a crucial piece in a big puzzle that fits beautifully with many other well-confirmed ideas, and when all are taken together they represent a coherent, simple, elegant understanding of practically all empirical phenomena. It is part of a great convergence of ideas in modern science. The invalid examples about numbers and desert islands nonetheless show that these ways of reasoning are not inherently airtight. The convergence cannot give us perfect logical certainty that our conclusions are true, but only that there is a strong case for them, that they are either the truth or something closely related to the truth, because of their power to unify and explain.

In contrast to the way modern science characteristically reasons, the philosophy of nature typically reasons deductively; that is, its principal inferences are such that if their premises are true, then their conclusions absolutely must be true as well. We cannot deny their conclusions without denying at least one of their premises. For instance, in the philosophy of the soul, we might wonder whether any knowing power in us can know both universals and individuals, such as "man" and "this man", or "triangle" and "this triangle". At first blush, we might think we know universals by our intellect and individuals by our senses, so that in no way do we know both universals and individuals by any single knowing power in us. But that would be a mistake, and we can prove it like this:

> The power in us by which we know that "Socrates is a man" knows both universals and individuals in some way.

Our intellect is the power in us by which we know that "Socrates
is a man."

Therefore our intellect knows both universals and individuals in
some way.

Say what you will about the premises, the conclusion follows necessarily from them. Deductive reasoning like this (and there are many
forms of it) leaves us with no choice but to accept its conclusion so
long as we accept its premises. This is the go-to method of reasoning
in the philosophy of nature. It is used in modern science, too. But
modern science will not shy away from the hypothetico-deductive
argument, either—whereas the philosophy of nature has little use for
this form of reasoning, since philosophy tends to begin from statements that are self-evident, and that do not need to be tested by
looking for their empirical consequences. For example, it is evident
that we know the truth of statements such as "Socrates is a man", in
which there is an individual, Socrates, and a universal term, *man*, and
it is evident that we understand the statement by a single knowing
power in us that knows and relates both those terms. We will not
need to test this. We will only use it, reason from it. And since it is
true, whatever follows necessarily from it will also be true.

By these four metrics, then, modern science is not as certain as the
philosophy of nature. (1) Empirical observation depends on unaided
and ordinary experience, not vice versa. (2) The concepts of modern
science depend on the most fundamental concepts arising out of everyone's ordinary experience, not vice versa. (3) The basic statements of
modern science depend on the basic statements arising out of the concepts of ordinary experience, not vice versa. And (4) some of the most
characteristic forms of reasoning in modern science are less logically
rigorous than those that characterize natural philosophy.

What shall we say about the many "illusions of ordinary experience" that we must look to modern science to correct? How do we
reconcile these with the superior certainty of universally experienced
things compared to that of empirical observation?

None of the "illusions of ordinary experience" adduced earlier is
a true example of a universal experience or a self-evident principle
coming out of such experience. They are all in fact theories—guesses
people made, facile explanations that suggest themselves to account

for things we do experience. Take for example the idea that "the earth is at rest." Do we really experience the nonmotion of the earth, its nonrotation? Of course not, since it is in fact moving. What is really going on just at the level of our experience is that "we do not feel earth rotating." That is not the same as saying that "we feel that the earth is not rotating"—unless saying that "I do not know that I have cancer" is equivalent to saying that "I know that I do not have cancer." That I do not experience the rotation of the earth, do not feel it spinning me at nearly 1,000 miles per hour in a circle, is true and certain, not an illusion, and it is a matter of ordinary experience. I step beyond this sure fact of experience, however, the moment I suppose that the earth is in reality sitting still. Its being still would explain why I do not feel any rotation in it—but other things besides its nonrotation might also explain this, too. I have ventured into the realm of theory.

My sense of touch does not (or not in any obvious way) discern any rotation of the earth, and my eyes show me the sun and my eastern horizon now moving apart. My senses are faithfully reporting what is happening, within their limited abilities. But my mind wishes to understand and readily offers an explanation—the earth is still and the sun makes a circuit around the earth each day. This interpretation suggests itself to me so naturally, with so little effort from me, that I probably do not even notice that it is an interpretation, and I simply mix it up with the bare facts themselves. Consequently, when I later find my interpretation was mistaken, I am prone to blame my original perceptions, as if they, and not merely the manner in which I had attempted to understand them, had been false. This is all the more tempting if what leads me to discover the falsehood in my geocentric outlook is not the mere act of mulling over my original perceptions, but the shock of quite new experiences—experiments with pendulums demonstrating the rotation of the earth, for example. I can easily come away from this thinking I had learned my lesson: ordinary experience of the world is simply not to be trusted, but only technically assisted, mathematically precise experience of the world is reliable.

This would be a grave injustice on my part. My sense of touch did not really tell me the earth stood still, but only that if it was moving, it had to be moving in such a way, and I along with it, that for some reason I could not feel it. And that is perfectly true. And physicists must respect this datum and must accordingly revise any theory of the motion of the earth from which it would follow that we could all feel it, and feel it so strongly that most of us would have motion sickness. That would fly in the face of ordinary experience, and for that very reason no serious scientist would accept such a theory. Nor did my eyes tell me that the sun was truly moving and the earth truly sitting still, but only that there was relative motion between them, without making any claims about which one was "truly" doing the moving. On that point, my eyesight had nothing in particular to say.

It is my mind, not my senses, that said the earth is absolutely at rest. If I said it may be regarded as being at rest, I might even have been right. But if I say that it is absolutely still, and cannot be regarded as moving, this little theory of mine is wrong and can be disproved by Copernican considerations, Foucault pendulums, and so on. In such cases, modern science is not so much correcting ordinary experience or natural philosophy as it is advancing us beyond the inadequate empirical science of prior generations. It does not replace or correct the ordinary fact that we do not feel the earth's rotation, but respects and preserves this fact, and is obliged not to contradict it. If any astronomical theory of the earth's rotation entailed the consequence that we should feel it, that it should make us all dizzy and sick, that would be a piece of badly done science. Geocentrism is therefore not an instance of natural philosophy in the special sense I defined earlier—it is not a conclusion deduced from conceptually evident truths, but a guess at a best explanation, hence an instance of the hypothesis forming that is characteristic of modern science (albeit poorly done).

The examples earlier adduced ("Heavier things fall faster", "Illumination is instantaneous", "Water is an element", "Human vision is continuous") are all guilty of the same confusion. They therefore illustrate precisely the opposite of what they are usually intended to illustrate. They show not the upsettable nature of ordinary experience or of natural philosophy, but the upsettable and progressive nature of our scientific theories. Since we can hardly ever be sure of being in possession of all the relevant empirical data concerning some question, we can rarely be sure that our explanation of the data we have considered is in fact the true explanation.

There is also such a thing as "armchair philosophy", of course. What makes it deserving of the reproach implied in this label, however, is not that it is philosophy, nor the fact that it is done in an armchair and without consulting reality in the specific form of an empirical observation. What is deserving of scorn is the attempt to settle certain questions from one's armchair when it should be perfectly plain that those specific questions cannot be settled just from there. If I wish to decide, without abandoning the comfort of my living room and without consulting any empirical evidence, whether intelligent life exists on other planets, or how a cell determines which proteins to manufacture when and where and in what quantities, I suppose I am welcome to try. But I am fooling myself if I call the result "knowledge". It is at best an educated guess—and the less educated the less use I have made of the relevant empirical evidence so hard-won by others. The ordinary experience we all share simply does not contain the answers to such questions, not even implicitly.

If instead I tried to decide, again from my armchair, whether twin primes eventually run out or instead go on forever, no one would accuse me of being "an armchair philosopher". Perhaps I should not try it solo, but there is not some special experience of reality, relevant to my inquiry, which I am lazily choosing to ignore. It is reasonable to think the answer to the twin prime question lies implicit somehow in the basic concepts of number, prime, infinite, and the like, and no amount of deep-sea diving or space travel will elucidate it. It is a question of drawing out the deeply hidden implications of concepts already known to everyone, rather than a matter of acquiring new and revelatory experience of the sensible world.

Likewise, what we have thought through together in this book was not an exercise in armchair philosophy, but a careful unraveling of some of the deeply hidden implications of our ordinary experience of ourselves and the world. Like a mathematical proof, which begins entirely from elementary number facts known to everyone and then painstakingly works out their unforeseen consequences, the kind of enterprise we undertook went forth entirely from common knowledge about ourselves. All of us, even those who try to hold the contrary, know we possess minds capable of understanding universal truth. But not everyone has seen the implications of this, such as the nonmateriality of the human mind, or the further implication, the immortality of soul.

The foregoing distinctions and comparisons provide a framework for determining the true relationship between ordinary experience, modern science, and natural philosophy. Ordinary experience has its certainties and its uncertainties, and empirical observation and science can in many cases supply certainty where ordinary experience cannot. But the portion of ordinary experience that is necessarily common to everyone, what I have called "universal experience"—the contents of which are such things as the experience of change, of whole and part, of unity and number, of cause and effect—such experience is certain, as far as it goes, and never depends on empirical observation for its certainty. The dependence goes the other way. Therefore natural philosophy, whose foundational experiences, concepts, and statements are stabler and more certain than those of modern science, and whose characteristic method of reasoning is more rigorous, is a surer knowledge than modern science. This does not mean it can do what modern science can do. But it does mean that modern science cannot replace natural philosophy, or stand in judgment of its conclusions, although it might sometimes clarify the way in which they are true.

Besides all this, natural philosophy also talks about certain things that no strictly empirical science can, such as the human soul. Natural philosophy attends to the "insider's" data indispensable to perceiving and understanding the soul, whereas empirical methods conscientiously ignore such data as far as possible. For this reason, too, science grounded chiefly in empirical observation could never replace natural philosophy. Knowledge of things approachable purely from the outside cannot replace knowledge of things that must be known from within. Certainties about stars and stones could not replace certainties about souls.

The "insider's view", however, brings us to the second reason some people are slow to acknowledge a philosophy of nature.

Is Philosophy Subjective?

Modern science is rooted in empirical observations that different people can make of the very same thing. Any number of different scientists can read the same thermometer, the same weighing scale, the same clock, or study the same line spectrum. Taking these kinds of observations as our foothold in nature, we thus remove observers from their own observations as far as possible, as well as extend the range of their experience. Were thermodynamics to begin from how hot something *feels* to scientists, not only could they never compare the temperatures of things with mathematical accuracy, but they could never study anything dangerously hot or cold. Their own body temperatures, moreover, would be mixed up with their perceptions of how hot or cold things were. To one scientist, A might feel warmer than B, while to another B feels warmer than A, leaving us with nothing to say about how the temperatures of A and B compare in themselves apart from our scientists. We want to know how the objects in nature themselves are, not how Walter or Sheila perceive them to be when they mix up the objects' qualities with their own. The science of nature, in other words, must be objective and must as far as possible prevent the knowing subjects—the scientists—from including themselves as part of the object observed. So it is essential to the science of nature, one might conclude, to begin from observations of things from an objective viewpoint not somehow mixed up with the thing to be observed, and hence no serious science of nature could begin from one's own "inside view". This, however, is just what the philosophy of the soul purports to do, and therefore it seems to be methodologically flawed at the start.

Those who object along these lines sometimes add that were we to begin from what we find within ourselves, this subjective viewpoint could not reveal to us anything general or universal and objectively true, but only our own idiosyncrasies. What you can experience only in yourself cannot be examined by others and verified by them. Consequently, any such philosophy is really a private enterprise, each one of us finding by introspection a group of personal phenomena no one else can ever witness. Can you imagine what would ensue if that sort of thing were allowed in science generally? We would then owe respect to any quack scientist who claimed to have overthrown a well-verified result by a single, unrepeatable experiment performed once in private. Private experience, locked up in one individual's mind, cannot be admissible in the court of science without turning science into a free-for-all in which all participants can say whatever they like.

Much of what our objector says here is true. A certain removal of ourselves from our observations of things that can be observed in the same way by many observers considerably broadens the reach of our study, and prevents us from mistaking our own qualities for those of the objects we hope to understand. It is also true that the same objects of experience must be available to many different people if we are to study them as a common project, and not merely report unverifiable personal experiences to each other in a sharing session. None of this, however, means that your "insider's view" sheds no real light on you, or that the knowledge founded on it is unscientific or bogged down in your idiosyncrasies.

For one thing, the danger of falsely mixing up your own qualities with the thing you aim to understand is considerably mitigated when the thing you wish to understand is yourself. You cannot mistake your qualities for your own, since they *are* your own. I did say, in earlier chapters, that there is a danger of anthropomorphism in attempting to understand both animals and plants beneath us and god above in terms of things we first experience within ourselves. If we say the plant "feels" or the rat "reasons" or the computer "thinks" or god "learns", we have either used a metaphor or else we have overstepped. We have remade the thing in question in our own image. But if we attribute eyesight to a dog, so long as the meaning of "sight" is invested only with the general features of the eyesight we experience in ourselves, we stand on solid ground. We cannot adopt an insider's view of canine vision, or not exactly (we might simulate it), and so our own experience of vision is surely not an accurate model of canine vision in all its specifics, but, just as surely, a dog's sense of sight is more like our sense of sight than it is like our sense of hearing or smell.

As to the charge of incommunicability leveled against your insider's view of you, it is largely trumped up. True, your insider's view is in a sense incommunicable. You cannot open the door to your soul and give someone your experience of being you. But neither can the long-deceased English chemist William Nicholson and his surgeon friend Anthony Carlisle give me *their* experience of the electrolysis of water, which they first performed in 1800. I can't even get my hands on the particular water sample that they used. If in the land of the dead they received a letter from me complaining that I cannot find *their* water sample, and therefore I must regard their findings as unrepeatable and "subjective", I imagine they might send some such reply:

> Dear Michael,
> Find your own blinking water already.
> All the best,
> Bill and Tony

Obviously I can always get my own water and see for myself, when I do the kind of thing they claimed to have done, whether my particular water sample really decomposes into hydrogen and oxygen as they said it would. Your inside experience of yourself is a similar story. You cannot give it to me. I cannot have your insider's view of you. No matter. I can get hold of one instance of human nature in that way—namely, myself—and I can check to see whether what you said about human nature based on your inside view of it holds up in my case. I am not stuck taking your word for it. If you claim to have ESP, or telekinetic powers, and that we can all find these within ourselves by "looking within", I can only shrug and say, "Not I." But if you say you are able to grasp truths that never began to be true, and which can never stop being true, such as "3 is prime", well, when I look within myself I find the same thing. Now we can talk to one another, and know we are possessors of a common property. And even if I did not have you to talk to, or you did not have me, each of us still has his own inside view, just as Nicholson and Carlisle had their own electrolysis of water to look at as often as they liked, even if no one else bothered to repeat the experiment for themselves.

Some experiences at the root of the science of the soul are "subjective" in the sense that they are experiences of things in the experiencer, in the knowing subject, but are not "subjective" in the sense of confusing a subject with an object, nor again in the sense of being trapped in the knowing subject and being in no way revelatory of things common to us all. Much less are they "subjective" in the sense of being biased or partial. The science of the soul itself is therefore in no incriminating way "subjective" and cannot for this reason be stripped of its title as a science.

Scientists Agree a Whole Lot, Philosophers Not So Much

Another argument for scientism and against the philosophy of nature goes like this: Scientists may at times disagree, but they agree at least on their principles and methods, and consequently they agree on whole bodies of important conclusions, too. Philosophers, on the other hand, seem to agree on nothing. If philosophy were a real knowledge of things, and of the things of nature in particular, then even if philosophers could not convince nonphilosophers of their findings, they should at least be able to convince each other. But they persistently disagree, and not only about their conclusions, but even about their starting points. So it seems their philosophy is not genuine knowledge after all.

This seems to be why our universities typically divide their departments into "sciences" on the one hand and "humanities" on the other, often lumping in philosophy with the latter. The implication is that philosophy can offer no genuine knowledge of reality, but only a kind of cultural experience or a tour of various artfully crafted outlooks that we can enjoy (or not) as if they were so many works of fiction. It seems to be the implicit doctrine of most of our institutions of higher learning that if you want to learn about reality, then go to physics, chemistry, and biology, but if you just want to feel certain ways and imagine some things, or if you want to make other people feel certain ways and imagine certain things, literature is one good tool for that, and philosophy another. Since different people *want* different things, want to feel and imagine different things—for instance, you want to feel that *x* is immoral and wrong, while I want to feel that it is good and right—so it is that we find opposite philosophies in the world to serve our diverse desires. Science, on the other hand, is not about what we *want*, but about what *is*, and therefore we don't get opposed sciences the way we get opposed philosophies.

This very common view is entirely understandable. But it carries the disadvantage of being almost entirely wrong. True, there is much that goes by the name *philosophy* that is self-consciously not truth-seeking, only attitude-adjusting, or promising to enable us to get what we want. The work of Richard Rorty, late philosopher of UC Berkeley, fell into that category, for example. But that is a billion miles away from what Aristotle was up to. Aristotle did not give a hoot how we feel or what we want. He was trying to find out the way things really are. To what extent he succeeded is another question, but the first thing to notice is that, whether he succeeded or not, the word *philosopher* is said of an Aristotle and a Rorty much as the title *doctor* is given both to a physiology professor and to someone who performs purely elective surgeries. The two "doctors" have little in common beyond their title, and so too do the two "philosophers". One of them strives to illuminate, the other to empower, or else gratify. The standards for success or failure in each case are entirely different, and so it is impossible for one of them to be "better philosophy" than the other (although what "philosophy" means in one case might be an altogether better and more honest kind of thing). The philosophies of Aristotle and Kant, opposed as they are, have far more in common. Both thinkers said what they said in the service of truth, not of our wishes. The usual placement of philosophy among the humanities as opposed to the sciences overlooks this general agreement among those called *philosophers* in the truth-seeking sense. We often read the philosophers as though they were only trying to please us or get us to like the way they talk about things, not say something true and verifiable. That is simply a false reading of most philosophers. The principle that "philosophy is not truth-seeking" is also inconsistent with itself—as soon as it is said, it is seen to be a truth-seeking piece of philosophy itself. We cannot avoid having philosophical views that we claim are true and whose truth we claim to know. We can, however, avoid serious and honest thinking about our philosophical convictions.

Very well, but what should we make of the curious fact that philosophers disagree with one another more often than scientists do? One possible answer is to observe that philosophers agree more than most people think, and scientists disagree more than most people think. While that is quite true and worth saying, I will not elaborate on it here because, however true it may be, it does not explain the phenomenon of disagreement among the philosophers. There remains a marked inequality between the disagreement we find among philosophers and that found among scientists. The philosophers disagree more. What is the reason for this inequality?

The explanation that occurs to many people, and certainly to believers in scientism, is that philosophers simply don't have any real knowledge, but only think they do. This is implausible, since it is precisely the philosophers, starting before Socrates, who first and most often warned us against thinking we know something when really we don't! And philosophers are very intelligent people who have shaped the world with their ideas. If we embrace the easiest and first explanation for their disagreement that leaps to mind, we will be like those believing the earth is at rest, since that most readily explains why we do not feel it moving. Very well, but then why can't the philosophers who are right about X, Y, and Z convince all the others? If the true cause of this is not the utter ignorance of every philosopher in history—an incredible thought when put so bluntly—then what is it?

The true cause is precisely the attentiveness of philosophers to experience other than that of the empirical variety, and to conceptually evident principles. Most philosophers are ready to reckon the findings of science into their accounts of things, but if they are not themselves modern scientists, then they will also make use of the data of universal experience. They will also invoke self-evident principles, statements they take to be evident just through understanding the concepts in them, independently of seeing truckloads of instances. For example, the statement "What contains a container also contains what the container contains",[3] while a bit of a tongue twister, is self-evidently true to anyone who understands what it is saying. We don't need to see a thousand examples of the statement to become convinced—we grasp the concepts and the meaning of the statement, and our conviction is complete. Principles like this one are true, certain, accessible to us, and even possessed by all of us at least in an unreflective way. Even philosophers who have denied the Law of Non-Contradiction—the rule that "no definite statement can be both true and false at the same time"—have done so mainly because they thought they found things that contradicted it, and thus they thought they should attack the principle only because they themselves unwittingly were using it. Ironically, it is because principles

[3] For example, if Chicago is in Illinois, then it must be in the United States.

like these are so well known to us, so ever-present and effortless in all our mental activity, that we cannot notice them without special reflection. Consequently, we are used to using them in unspoken form, and for that reason might not recognize them when someone else puts them to us in words.

Here we see both the source of philosophy's great certainties, and also the cause of its great disagreements. The chief foundations of philosophy, in contrast to empirical science, are *interior certainties*, such as your interior experience of being a single being, and your conceptual certainty that no exact statement can be both true and false at once. In conversation with someone else, you cannot point to such certainties, as you can to a thermometer or to the needle of a Geiger counter, and say, "See?" The only way to get common, mutually acknowledged, explicit agreement to such certainties is through the medium of words, since the certainties themselves do not consist in externally sensible things. But the medium of words is somewhat foreign to the certainties themselves. Your native conviction about the Law of Non-Contradiction does not present itself in you in the form of an abstract formula (e.g., "No definite statement can be both true and false at the same time"), but instead you feel its force in concrete instances—when, for example, one doctor says, "You have pancreatic cancer," and another says, "No, you don't," you don't believe them both. What a face-slapping fact! And yet when some people (even some philosophers) hear the abstract formula "No definite statement is both true and false at the same time", they worry about being taken in by philosophers (or by other philosophers). The abstract generality of the formula rouses their suspicions and makes it appear subject to all kinds of counterexamples.

The very intensity and interiority of such certainties is the cause of the need to express them in words in order to achieve a meeting of the minds about them. The same intensity and interiority is the reason why the verbal expressions of them take on a foreign feel or a look not recognized at first. We know the principles of philosophy first of all in a natural, unreflective, nonverbal way, in the concreteness of very particular situations. Abstract formulas meant to describe back to us our own experience or interior understanding are liable to sound jargonish and unfamiliar, even if they are in fact faithful to what we know within. This moment of unfamiliarity with principles expressed verbally and abstractly is fraught with danger. It presents an opportunity for objections against the principles to arise (and never forget that we can raise formidable difficulties even with the existence of motion!). What we know interiorly, when put to us in unfamiliar language, can appear like an impostor.

A concrete, nonphilosophical example might serve to illustrate the strange possibility of not recognizing what is normally quite familiar to us when it comes to us in some unaccustomed context or dress. I am the oldest of nine children. My parents raised us in New Hampshire, where they still live. Our mother has always bemoaned the distances that jobs and other needs have placed between us and her. Most of us live on the East Coast, although one of us lives in Colorado, and I currently live in California. That means we don't often get together as a whole family. As a surprise gift to our mother for her seventieth birthday, we all planned to visit her together in the summer of 2015, unannounced. Plans were laid. We traveled. We met at a Starbucks. We caravanned to the old neighborhood. We pulled up in the driveway in about six different vehicles. My father reports that when he saw so many people arriving in his driveway, he called Mom over to the window.

"Marie! Something is happening!" he said.

She came and peered out the picture window in the living room. She made a funny face, like the kind you might make when you take a sip of grapefruit juice when you were expecting milk. And then she said, "I don't know these people!"

Her eyesight was not the problem. With her glasses, she sees better than I do. And although it had been twenty years since we had all been together, she sees many of us on a regular basis. And we were not wearing weird disguises. It was just us. But she did not recognize any of us. Not at first. If my mother can fail to recognize her own kids just because they are showing up at an unexpected moment and in an unannounced ensemble, you had better believe that even philosophers who love the truth, and who in most ways know it quite well, better than other people do, can sometimes fail to see it when it takes on an unaccustomed look—even if it bites them on the nose.

Philosophical agreement requires mutually acknowledged agreement on the fundamental truths of philosophy as expressed in words. It therefore requires that any listeners whose agreement we seek not be put off by the seeming strangeness of the words we might be forced to

use in order to say back to them what we think they already know—
and also that they not be prejudiced against the fundamental truths
by their awareness of difficulties they do not yet know how to solve.

An empirical observation, on the other hand, makes no such
demands. Although it is a nonverbal certainty, it is also something
exterior that needs no verbal expression to turn it into common
ground for two or more people. If we disagree about the temperature in the room, you can point to a thermometer. If I doubt the
thermometer, we can get another one. If I doubt all thermometers,
you can safely ignore me. If I am reasonable, however, you settle the
argument by pointing to that instrument, to an externally sensible
thing we can both inspect without having to put it into words.

Not every principle of philosophy is like that. Philosophy relies
on the medium of words in order to express, and make commonly
available, what I am calling its "interior certainties", those of internal
experience and of conceptually evident truths. And the very putting
of them into words makes it difficult to recognize them, and easy
for them to appear subject to difficulties. And philosophers are more
sensitive than most people, not less, to philosophical difficulties. This
is to their credit. Zeno showed himself more subtle than most people
when he discovered some of the major problems about motion (even
if he was not as wise as those who were able to solve them and to see
that his paradoxes were mere problems after all, and not refutations
of the existence of motion). Nonetheless, their intelligent sensitivity
to problems and their reliance upon the medium of words also means
the philosophers have more obstacles standing in the way of their
universal agreement than the scientists do—not because philosophy
is not real knowledge, but because it is in this respect more difficult
than empirical science in its beginnings.

The argument for scientism based on philosophical disagreement,
then, fails because it assigns a false (indeed farfetched) cause to that
disagreement. Philosophers do not disagree because they are a bunch
of know-nothings. They disagree because philosophers avail themselves of experiences, concepts, and principles even when it is difficult to get large numbers of people to agree to them in words.

It *is* possible to get a fair number of philosophers to agree on the
correct principles, to understand the difficulties about them and also
the solutions. When this happens, philosophers tend to agree on
their conclusions as well. Philosophers, for example, who admit the

human experience each of us has of his own substantial unity also tend to agree that nature acts for the sake of an end, since that is a consequence of the fact that a human being is a single substance. At the risk of disagreement among philosophers, philosophy gains the power of understanding truths that a purely empirical science by itself can never reach, such as the existence of god and the immortality of the human soul. By restricting itself to the experiences, principles, and methods on which it is possible to get great numbers of people to agree, empirical science must remain silent about many of the most important questions we have about ourselves and the world, but gains the authority and the power of progress that only a large and cooperative work force can supply.

Can Common Experience and Common Notions Produce Anything besides Common Knowledge?

For some people, another intellectual impediment to the acceptance of any philosophy of nature is the suspicion that common experience and common notions cannot produce anything beyond common knowledge. In order to deserve the name *science*, it is not enough for some particular understanding of the natural world to be true and certain—it must also be uncommon, and the product of rigorous procedures. Self-evident statements, such as "Whatever moves has speed", or "What contains a container contains what the container contains", or "Things that coincide are equal", don't qualify as scientific knowledge. And it is not easy to see how we can get past such trivialities without the aid of new experience, especially the time-consuming and exacting experience known as empirical observation.

In the service of real advances in our knowledge, most people appreciate the need for a new brain-imaging machine, a new particle accelerator, a manned mission to Mars—even if they don't want to pay for these things. What is not so obvious is how our ordinary experience, the kind of experience everyone already has, can possibly contribute anything new or significant to anyone's knowledge. We easily believe that whatever experience we all continuously possess must, without any special effort on our part, lie fully transparent to us, and contain no new secrets worth finding out. Try telling people that their own ordinary day-in, day-out experience of themselves and of the world contains an untold wealth of astonishing, life-changing truths that few people know because of the effort required to coax those truths out into the light. It is rather like telling them there are billions of dollars' worth of gold coins hidden throughout their own house, under the sofa cushions, in the backs of drawers behind the socks, and the only reason they have not noticed these in all the years they have lived in their house is that they have not looked carefully enough.

This can put a strain on the powers of belief. This is exactly the problem that Socrates encountered long ago. People then as now possessed a day-to-day familiarity with justice, friendship, courage, and the like, and quite naturally assumed that they understood these things through and through. They thought they thoroughly understood the definitions and implications of the contents of their own vocabulary and experience. Socrates showed that such thorough understanding of familiar things does not come for free, but only, if at all, after the careful work of sifting and inferring that is philosophy.

You, of course, know better. If you have not begun reading this book with this very chapter, but have been through the preceding ones, you know quite well that from ordinary facts about ourselves it is possible to deduce extraordinary ones, and that doing so is often an arduous and unusual sort of business that precious few people undertake.

Are you at all worried about how to convince other people that this is so, that the data of their ordinary experience is truly a mine containing deep implications that need to be dug out, but which do not require any additional experience for their verification? If so, you might try carrying out an experiment like the one Socrates conducted with the help of a certain slave boy in Plato's dialogue called *Meno*. Socrates wanted to show that all of us already know a great number of profundities. He wished to show that without any new experience beyond that of thinking, we can uncover significant truths not explicitly known to us before, just from what is already lying dormant in our minds. To show this, he proposes to get an uneducated slave boy to explain how to double a square. Did I promise I would drag no more mathematics into our discussion? Well, if I did, this exercise will be so straightforward and short and sweet that it will hardly feel "mathematical". It will feel more like picking out tiles for the kitchen.

Let us substitute for the slave boy some acquaintance of yours who, in his zeal for empirical methods, denies the possibility of advancing our knowledge in any significant way without recourse to new experience—particularly, if we are in search of new knowledge that is quantitative and exact, we might add, since that especially might seem to require scientific methods of measurement. A person of this description, I promise you, cannot be a mathematician, and so is very unlikely to know how to double a square. Draw for him a square on a sheet of paper, like this:

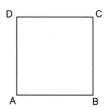

Next, we ask our friend how to draw the square that has exactly double the area of this square ABCD. How long will the side of the double square be? (If he says, "The square root of two," he is savvier than many, but we will persist and ask him to tell us how long that is exactly, and how to draw it. Otherwise, he has only given a fancy name for "the length which is such that the square on it is double", which gets us nowhere.) Many people will guess that we simply double the length of the *side* AB, and the square on that double side will have the double area.

So we do as we are told and extend side AB to E so that AE is double the length of AB. We then draw the square on AE, as AEGK, and ask our friend whether this square is in fact double the original square ABCD, as he said it would be.

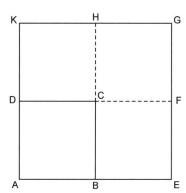

Our friend will surely see right away that AEGK is not double ABCD, but is in fact quadruple. When he says so, we follow his lead, and extend DC to F and BC to H, showing the four squares composing AEGK, each of which is equal to our start-square ABCD. Now we join DB, BF, FH, and HD by straight lines and ask what sort of figure DBFH must be.

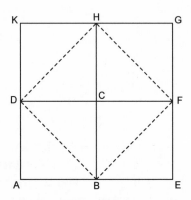

Our friend will have no difficulty recognizing it as a square. And how big is it compared to our original square? He will most likely see, without our assistance, that DBFH is composed of four congruent triangles, while ABCD is composed of two such triangles. Hence, DBFH is exactly double ABCD. So the answer to our question about how to draw the square that is exactly double ABCD is just to draw the square on its diagonal, BD. Lovely!

The point of the demonstration is this: Our friend came to know something universal, exact, and necessarily true, something he did not know before, and which most people do not know, all without any new kinds of objects being introduced into his experience. Surely he had seen squares before, and even the pattern of our final diagram. None of that was new. Only we asked him to consider those familiar objects now in a new light, with a view to a question he had not explicitly considered before. If, by chance, doubling the square is something our friend already knows how to do, or if he finds it insufficiently impressive and too trivial to count as a real advance in his knowledge, we can easily replace it with any number of other mathematical problems with pretty solutions that he is unlikely to know.

The general point stands. It is possible to increase our knowledge not only by acquiring new experience, but also by newly exploiting our prior experience, and thus to advance in a nontrivial way from things everyone knows to things very few people know, and to do so with exactness and certainty.

That is the very purpose of philosophy.

Science Gives Us Control over Nature, Philosophy Gives Us None

Just before the dawn of modern science, Francis Bacon complained that the old way of understanding nature, chiefly exemplified in Aristotle, was "barren of works".[4] It did not give us *control* over nature, so we should not rest satisfied with it. We should seek out a knowledge that, to use Descartes' famous phrase, would make us "masters and possessors of nature".

That is all well and good as far as it goes. Who would have us still living in the Stone Age, or stuck in the preelectricity and prepenicillin days of Bacon and Descartes? It is all very well to romanticize about the simpler times of days gone by, to wax nostalgic for the quietude and clean air prior to the Industrial Age. But a simple toothache will jerk us back to a reality in which we need not live in abject fear of medieval dentistry. Why should we be slaves to Mother Nature's every whim? If our god-given reason can discover a way to tame nature a bit, and subject her now and then to our needs and wishes, well then, so long as we can do so without doing her (and hence ourselves) irreparable harm, more power to us.

It is another thing, though, to say that only that knowledge of nature which places it at our disposal, which drives technological innovation and drug design and all the rest of it, is knowledge of nature at all. Believers in scientism would have it so. If what was said in the prior chapters of this book, for example, does not bear

---

[4] Bacon says that the ancient Greek thinkers "have that which is characteristic of boys: they are prompt to prattle, but cannot generate; for their wisdom abounds in words but is barren of works". Francis Bacon, *The New Organon*, Aphorisms, book one, LXXI, ed. Fulton H. Anderson (New York: Macmillan/Library of Liberal Arts, 1960), 70.

technological fruit of any kind, if it leads to no inventions, no patents, no way of predicting earthquakes or hurricanes, then it is pure poetry,[5] not real understanding.

The true connection between knowledge and power over nature is subtler than that, however. When theory gives us control over nature, this proves only that there is something to the theory. It does not prove the theory is the truth. For centuries, sailors successfully navigated the seas by Ptolemaic astronomy, which served the purpose as admirably as Copernican theory could, even though the Ptolemaic system was further adrift from the truth. Newtonian physics, though antiquated, serves admirably for many practical purposes. The Ptolemaic system and Newtonian physics do of course share some elements in common with reality. If they did not, they could not be useful. Where a theory affords us some power over nature, there must be at least some grain of truth to it, or some likeness or approximation to the truth.

The converse statement is untrue. It is a mistake to suppose that where there is any truth, there must also come with it some degree of power over nature.

There can be no doubt that much of our knowledge does give us power over what we know. And much pseudoknowledge is exposed for what it is precisely by its inability to produce results or to predict. But why should we believe that all knowledge of nature ought to give us power over it? The real question is when we should expect our knowledge to give us power over nature and when we should not.

The general rule seems to be something like this. The more a knowledge of nature is (1) a knowledge of nature's means—of parts, components, materials, or movements and processes and the quantitative rules they obey—and the more it is (2) a knowledge ignoring what belongs to natural things as natural, attending instead to features (especially quantitative ones) common to natural and artificial things, and the more it is (3) a knowledge of what nature does after we have done something to it, the more probable it becomes that such knowledge of nature will bear technological fruit, and give us new control over matter or new prediction power.

---

[5] The disparaging implication that poetry contains no real understanding is not my own, but just another scientistic idea.

Materials are for the sake of substantial forms in nature, as your organs and cells and their constituents are at the service of your soul and its life. Modern science largely ignores substantial form, however, which implies that it is concerned more with nature's materials, nature's means. Modern science also frequently abstracts from the distinction between the natural and the artificial. This is truest and clearest in mathematical physics. Newton's Law of Inertia, for example, applies to a stone, a horse, and a piano equally well—launch any of these far enough into the empty reaches of space, and it will tend to keep going with the final velocity you gave it. Modern science, moreover, is in large part a knowledge of what nature does after we do something to it. We send particles through bubble chambers and study the paths they trace out. We combine substances to learn how they will react. We put rats in mazes after injecting them with a trial drug, or after conditioning them or genetically altering them. By all accounts, then, we should expect much of modern science to bear technological fruit, even if not all of it does.

On the other hand, we have no reason to expect technological fruit from a knowledge of nature that (1) pays special attention to nature's ends, to whole and individual substances and their forms, and which (2) takes special interest in what belongs to natural things as natural, as distinct from artificial things, and which (3) does not do anything special to nature in order to learn from it, but only gathers up the concepts of nature that we all form just by living in it and then infers things from these. This is an apt description of the part of natural science I have been calling the philosophy of nature, and a fair description, too, of the path we have followed throughout this book.

The objection to the philosophy of nature on the grounds that it does not produce technologies is therefore without foundation. We should not expect new technologies from natural philosophy, nor even from all modern science.

This does not mean that the philosophy of nature is entirely irrelevant to practical matters or to the work of modern science. A knowledge of ourselves from within, for example, is indispensable in neurosurgery, neuroscience, neurology, and empirical psychology. We cannot associate diverse brain acts empirically observed with their corresponding powers in us without first knowing from within what those powers are. You experience "hearing music", "seeing yellow", "feeling relief about the election"—all of which, no doubt, are accompanied by more or less specific brain events in you. But no outsider's experience of the brain events themselves, however crisply and beautifully they might be displayed in real-time images of your brain, will ever reveal what "hearing music" is, or "seeing yellow" or "feeling relief about the election". We cannot derive these notions from terminology based wholly on an outsider's experience of things any more than we can derive them from the naked concepts of algebra. Understanding what we are looking at from the outside, in these cases, requires a previous understanding of what is going on as experienced from within. And a refined understanding of what is going on in the mind, as experienced from within, is the work of the philosophy of the soul.

More significantly, a knowledge of our souls and of the innate inclinations we possess as human beings is the only nonreligious source for common standards of human action, of right and wrong. In general, what makes anything a good thing of its kind—a good pencil, a good eye, a good concert pianist—is that it does well the activity for the sake of which it exists. Why should "a good human being" be an exception to that general rule? While strictly empirical science tries to ignore "that for the sake of which" in nature, including human nature, the philosophy of nature specializes in that sort of thing. Small wonder, then, that modern science provides us with no moral direction. It is famously amoral, in fact. (I don't mean modern scientists are amoral, of course—just that when they moralize, they are drawing on knowledge other than their science.) Even when modern science tells us how to produce some technological innovation, it is silent on the question whether we should produce it, and whether we should use it, and for what. The science that can tell us whether human cloning is possible cannot tell us whether it is right or wrong. It would of course be unfair to condemn such a science for failing to answer questions it was never meant to answer. It is no wiser, though, to condemn philosophy for refusing to tell us how to produce a cell phone or cure cancer.

15

Know Thyself: An Integral Knowledge of Nature

We came into the world like brother and brother; And now let's go hand in hand, not one before another.

—William Shakespeare, *The Comedy of Errors*

The Rarity and Necessity of Natural Philosophy

All five rationales for scientism, while containing some elements of truth, also contain fatal errors and overlook crucial distinctions. Scientism hasn't got a leg to stand on. By far the greater part of our knowledge of nature rests on specifically empirical foundations. But all our knowledge, including the empirical type, rests also on ordinary experience, which holds important secrets of its own to reveal to those who have the care and the patience to unearth them. The part of the science of nature that does this I have been calling *natural philosophy*. It may seem that this way of knowing nature, this entrance hall to natural science, based on ordinary experience and asking questions not yet demanding special empirical methods, has been largely neglected in the last few centuries. For every one practitioner of the philosophy of nature today there are perhaps hundreds of scientists.

Why should that be? If, as the foregoing considerations imply, natural philosophy is a genuine part of the science of nature, and if it is so certain and its conclusions (such as the immortality of the human soul) so momentous, then why is it hidden from public view and not a mainstream enterprise in our universities? Is there some kind of conspiracy going on?

It would be exciting if there were, but that is not really the case. Instead, it is just a natural consequence of what the philosophy of nature is that it receives relatively limited attention. There are three principal reasons for this.

The first reason for the rarity of the philosophy of nature is that it bears little or no technological fruit, and for that reason cannot attract venture capital. That is clear enough to stand without further ado.

The second reason is that the philosophy of nature is in certain respects a specialization like any other. Specializations can be so specialized that their names are not commonly known, and some of them are largely unheard of outside their own circles. (I confess I did not even know there was such a thing as a "physical chemist" until I became friends with one in 2007.)

For what reason should we call the philosophy of nature a specialization? At first this may seem an odd thing to say. Devoting one's whole intellectual life to understanding the mating instincts of the Tsetse fly, now *there's* a specialization for you. It takes a special person to make that a primary focus. But the nature and immortality of the human soul? The spirituality of the human mind? The inherent purposefulness of natural things? These are hardly provincial concerns.

While that is true, we must remember that the philosophy of nature is not the only road to such things. There is religious faith, too, whether of a reasonable type or not, and there is also humble opinion. We are free to believe in immortality and an afterlife in the absence of coercive evidence to the contrary, and that method is much faster and easier than going through all the labors of love in a book like this one. Desire for a kind of immortality in ourselves and our loved ones is far from rare, but it is not by itself sufficient motivation for undertaking the mental labors of philosophy. Not when shorter, faster, easier paths lie open to us. Sufficient motivation therefore requires one thing more: the desire to know. If faith in the word of another or common opinion satisfies us, if we do not positively suffer from the need to understand for ourselves whatever we can of such deep things, then we will not turn philosopher. Philosophical wonder is not an idle curiosity, a desire to know something as long as the knowledge comes practically for free. It is a powerful urge to know, driving the sufferer to undertake enormous mental toil—under many teachers and through many books and over many, many years, if need be—in order to come to understand.

And one can feel this way about a great many things, even if we stick to natural things in particular. We can feel this way about black holes, or the metamorphosis of caterpillars into butterflies, or the size and shape of the universe, or human embryology, or magnetism, or the formation of crystals—the list goes on forever. Any one of these things can capture our imagination and compel those of us thirsty for knowledge to make it our whole life's pursuit. A good thing, too. This division of interests enables us to divide and conquer all things and know much more of reality than we would had we all the same degree of interest in the same things. Philosophical wonder and scientific curiosity, an all-consuming passion to know that compels us to endure many wants, to struggle through many long hours of work and through many disappointments and dead ends, is a fairly rare thing to begin with. Divide it now by the number of other things that can thus attract us, and it is no great marvel that there are so few philosophers of nature among us. If anything, it is a marvel there are so many.

Natural philosophy nonetheless persists, even thrives. There is a fair number of very fine minds engaged in it these days, some of them formally trained in the empirical sciences as well, and the number seems to be growing. This is probably in part a response to scientism. Scientism in some respects is more credible these days than it was in the eighteenth and nineteenth centuries when it first became prominent, and it is currently blessed with a number of famous, respected, eloquent (even if loud and misinformed) prophets. The cure is the philosophy of nature, and so some scientists have begun to explore it, and a few philosophers have been roused from tranquil pursuit of their own work into saying some things in public that they did not hitherto think it necessary to say to anyone but their colleagues.

Two Parts, One Whole

We now see in outline the true relationship of the philosophy of nature to modern science. The two form complementary parts of one whole body of knowledge: natural science. The whole science of nature (or of you in particular) is neither the empirical part alone, nor philosophy alone, but an organic unity of the two. They are not equal parts, quantitatively or qualitatively. Quantitatively, the empirical branches of modern science outnumber the parts of the philosophy of nature by far, which fits with the power of empirical methods to get into questions as detailed as we like, unhampered by the generality of our common experience and common conceptions of nature. Qualitatively, they complement and depend on each other in various ways. With its nearly unlimited scope for particular questions (it can ask about whatever we can devise empirical tests for), modern science satisfies our desire to explore, and lends ever-finer resolution to our picture of the universe. It magnifies for us the very small, the ultimate parts of ourselves and all familiar things, and brings near to us the very far, revealing the ultimate wholes of which we are parts. It infers the distant past and predicts the distant future. It even goes beyond the good of knowledge and puts food on our tables and clothing on our backs, places means of transportation and communication at our disposal, and cures some of our ills. What natural philosophy lacks in these departments, it makes up for by its own unique advantages, which the special methods of modern science alone cannot supply. Where empirical methods bring us detailed understandings and new discoveries, philosophy brings us a wealth of universal, certain, and stable truths. Where modern science can place the reins of nature in our hands, philosophy can discern the ends that must govern our use of nature if we are to better ourselves rather than self-destruct. Where purely empirical methods must fall silent before the greatest questions about ourselves—about god, our mortality and immortality, our ultimate origin and destiny— philosophy has things to say.

Natural philosophy and the empirical way of doing science are thus distinct parts of one whole knowledge of you and of nature, like cooperative parts of one organism. Each completes the other and leads us to the other. Each emphasizes and exploits different kinds of experience, principles, and methods in the study of nature, with complementary advantages and limitations. A sign of their unity is that they were both born together, most conspicuously in ancient Greece, although their maturation rates were quite different. Natural philosophy rose to a great height as early as Aristotle, but empirical science was a lisping toddler even in the great Archimedes. It would not come into its own until Galileo and those after him, partly because its true power could not be known, even suspected, until fairly sophisticated instruments such as telescopes had been invented. So it is that we speak of empirical science as *modern* science.

Upon the portal at the oracle of Delphi, in accord with instructions handed down from the Seven Sages, there was inscribed the two-word exhortation "Γνῶθι σεαυτόν" ("Know thyself"). This advice may seem strange. In certain ways, we cannot help but know ourselves and need hardly be advised to do so. But the ways in which we inevitably know ourselves tend to be superficial, and thanks to our nearness and our partiality to ourselves, we also tend to get a good deal wrong about ourselves, sometimes with disastrous results. So the advice is wisely given. Human beings, unlike animals, are capable of knowing their own nature, and need to know themselves in order to know how to conduct themselves. But unlike god, we are also capable of failing to know ourselves as well as we ought to—hence the exhortation.

This book has been about one form of self-knowledge we can hardly afford to ignore. It is about what we are, and about our origins. Modern science has a great deal to say in answer to both of these questions. We are everything that modern science can genuinely discover us to be. But we are much more besides. We must know ourselves to be the possessors of immortal souls, and the offspring of god.

Our nature comes in two parts, an organic body and a spiritual soul, so that we straddle the worlds of purely material and purely nonmaterial beings. These parts of us were fashioned and fitted together by a mind who has the interests of mind in mind, which is the ultimate reason why our bodies automatically, unconsciously, naturally serve the needs of our intellects and wills. These are the main lessons of this book.

We can now draw one final lesson about ourselves. Not only does our human nature automatically form our organs of knowing, but it also gets us started in the actual work of knowing the world. Our minds of their own accord form our first thoughts for us, without conscious effort on our part. We do not get to select what features of the world to notice first and from which to construct all our subsequent understanding of it. Instead, human nature, common to us all, chooses what volumes will make up our library of elementary notions. That is why we all have access to the very same primary ideas: *motion, time, length, whole, part, one, many, substance, quantity, quality, relation, cause, effect, same, other,* and so on. Many questions cannot be answered in terms of these ideas alone, but no question can be answered without them. And it turns out that common concepts such as these, and the ordinary experience that gives rise to them, do suffice for answering the all-important questions about ourselves that this book has been about. There is something of the democratic in that, and of the providential, too. When it comes to the deepest truths about ourselves, those of interest to us all, nature provides us all with the initial means of knowing them.

"Know Thyself" exhorts us, among other things, to know what riches of knowledge we possess, to recognize their worth, as well as to acknowledge our ignorance—to know, in other words, what we really know, and what we really don't. Socrates showed that many things we easily suppose ourselves to know, we really do not know. We have in these last three chapters focused mainly on the other side of the problem. Conscious of the spectacular successes of modern science, we are in danger of despising what all of us really know about nature and ourselves just by being human beings—in danger, too, of holding cheap the implications of our common knowledge. In truth, the deepest import of our ordinary experience is neither totally obvious to us without effort nor totally closed off to our inspection and discernment—nor are its contents all trivialities and truisms.

Our "ordinary" knowledge is therefore "ordinary" only in the sense that all of us have it and use it. But really it is extraordinary in content. The fact that all of us share it does not make it ordinary, but makes us extraordinary.

Let no one tell you otherwise.

EPILOGUE

Afterlife

Nothing can harm a good man in life or after death, and his fortunes are not a matter of indifference to the gods.

—Socrates, in Plato's *Apology*

The undying thing we call the soul departs to give account to the gods of another world, even as we are taught by ancestral tradition—an account to which the good may look forward without misgiving, but the evil with grievous dismay.

—Plato, *Laws*

We must not follow those who advise us, being men, to think of human things, and, being mortal, of mortal things, but must, so far as we can, make ourselves immortal, and strain every nerve to live in accord with the best thing in us.

—Aristotle, *Nicomachean Ethics*

The young man lay asleep in an unforgiving chair. A steady blast of air conditioning hushed the intermittent beeps and chirps of the monitoring equipment on a nearby cart. The man stirred. He grew dimly aware of a voice gently rousing him in a tone of imperfectly suppressed urgency. It was his wife. The man sat up, blinking in the darkness of an unfamiliar room. His wife was now clutching his wrist—hard. Then he remembered. It was time again. He held his wife's hand, and with his other hand pushed the "Indiglo" button on his watch. "One," the man whispered, "... two ... three ... four ...," he continued, counting off the seconds. He felt useless. But his wife had said that his counting like this helped her. She knew, listening to his voice, that the pain would subside around "thirty", that only a faint glimmer of it would remain by "forty", and all would be over by "forty-five". As he counted, the man watched the needle on a machine trace a sharply climbing line on a moving strip of paper. When the line finally peaked and began to drop again, he breathed easier. "OK," she said soon afterward; "it's OK again." Her grip on his hand relaxed. The two of them dropped off to a dream-less sleep for a few minutes more—the man from mere fatigue, his wife due to exertion and the influence of something called Stadol. How long these rituals actually continued the young man could not tell. It seemed a lifetime. According to his watch, it was only some hours later that he and his wife saw their first child for the first time face-to-face.

"He is purply-pink," thought the man, "like an eraser on a pencil."

"He's a *Leo!*" cried one of the nurses for sheer joy (the hospital was in California). She laid the baby on the young mother's bosom, and the father found himself suddenly overcome with emotion. At first sight, the child had been a stranger, but when he saw his wife caressing him, he recognized him. This was his son. Tears started in his eyes.

"Do you want to cut the cord?" asked another nurse. It took a moment before the father realized she was speaking to him.

"Oh," he said, "all right," not at all certain he wanted to cut the cord.

She handed him a pair of rather heavy and funny-shaped shears, and showed him where to make the cut, just there, not far from a little clamp near the baby's navel-to-be. The cord was thick as rope and strangely twisted and semitranslucent, an alien thing that looked more like an internal organ than like anything meant to see the sun. The first-time father bravely took the cord in hand and gave the shears a gentle squeeze, expecting the cord to give way like an over-cooked noodle. To his great surprise, the stout little thing withstood this first effort and required three more earnest squeezes before it came apart. This bond to embryonic life did not easily let go. Come to think of it, the baby must have found it difficult to leave that snug little world, the only one, till now, that he had ever known.

What must being born be like to a baby? Babies come from a dark, warm place of muffled sounds with a continuous mother's heartbeat somewhere above them. In this place they feel no need to eat or drink or breathe, and there is little difference between sleeping and waking. To the unborn baby, the womb is pretty much the whole universe, suggesting very little of life outside it. What was it like then to be forcibly evicted from that place, from one's natural abode, from absolutely everything one knows, and to see light and breathe air for the first time?

The young father found it hard to believe that he himself had once been just such a creature as that, and that he, too, had undergone the same violent transition. He retained no memory of that first life in the womb. Now he could understand it only as an outside observer.

Presumably, you also retain no accessible memory of being born, or of your first days of life in the light. Those are matters you mainly hear about from others and take on trust, although if you are willing to go through the trouble you might be able to confirm a few parts of the story yourself. For the most part our lives consist in a vivid present trailing off into the fog of the past. Years go by after we are born before we begin to form memories accessible in the long term. Years more go by before we wonder about our own beginning, about how our parents brought us into existence. As a race, we have yet to understand our own reproduction fully. Human embryology holds many secrets for us still, and perhaps will never disclose them all.

If temporal beginnings and natural causes continue to elude our full comprehension, all the more must the eternal origin of all things, our supernatural origin, exceed our understanding. We catch glimpses of god in science and philosophy. We can also get some sense of him, of his presence and causal power, in the ordinary experience of having and raising our own children. Where did I come from? My parents, I am told. And that is true. But I did not clearly perceive the inadequacy of that answer just from the experience of being their child. I saw it much better in having children myself.

My understanding of what goes on inside the womb is vague at best. If I knew all that doctors, nurses, and embryologists know, I certainly would not have been surprised by my first child's eraser-pink skin, or by the resilience of his umbilical cord. In any case my knowledge or lack thereof was entirely irrelevant to my son's coming-to-be. His conception and growth were not applications of any human science, primitive or advanced. As time passed, and he grew, and then acquired a sister, and later a brother, and they grew, it became more and more apparent that these astonishing little beings were nonetheless the offspring of someone's knowledge. Amy and I often eavesdropped on our young children when they were engaged in conversation. When Max was eight and Ben was four, and they were playing together with a pile of stuff called "Bionicle" (a series of robotlike toys put out by the Lego company), I overheard this discussion:

BEN: Where does Bionicle come from?
MAX: China.
BEN: Oh, so it's Japanese.
MAX: No, it's *Chinese*.
BEN: What's the difference? Aren't Japanese and Chinese the same?
MAX: *No*, Ben, Japanese people are a *kind* of Chinese people.

Where did they get these ideas? Granted, they were riddled with misconceptions. But they were *their* misconceptions, made in the course of their own efforts to form a picture of the world. Their mother and I had never sat them down to teach them about cultures on the other side of the world, but here they were, theorizing about them. Countless episodes like these in a very concrete way brought home what philosophy had taught me—that human beings are intellectual creatures not to be fully explained by their nonintelligent causes, nor even by those imperfectly intelligent causes of the same species, their parents. Watching my children play and listening to them speak, I felt how inadequate an explanation I was of these wondrous creatures, and found myself wondering where exactly they had come from. I experienced myself more as their steward than as their author.

Our own temporal beginnings and natural origins, and our experience of the birth and growth of children, can thus bring home more immediately what philosophy reaches only through a long series of inferences—namely, the need to admit a superhuman intelligence behind the scenes, an author of human parenthood, an inventor of the very idea of human birth and infancy.

If the birth and growth of our children can so strongly suggest their divine origin, can the prospect of death similarly shed light on the fates of our souls?

Your soul is immortal. We have learned that much by sitting at the feet of the philosophers. The apparent parallels and symmetries between birth and death are therefore quite real. Birth is the end of our prelife in the womb. It is probably traumatic in some degree for the child being born. And it is of course not only an end, but also a beginning of new life, ordinarily a longer, fuller, and more perfect life, for which the previous one had been a physical preparation. In its new life, the child will see others face-to-face for the first time, most significantly its parents, and it will from then on share life with them rather than remain cut off from them. Death bears striking similarities to these aspects of birth. Our death is the end of our life on Earth. It is usually traumatic in some degree, often to a significant degree, not only for those dying, but also for their loved ones who must let them go. And it is not only an end, but also a beginning of new life, a longer, fuller, and more perfect life, for which life on Earth had been a spiritual preparation. In that new life we will see others for the first time since their death, and others for the first time ever, and most significantly, it is likely we shall see god.

God, the author of all life, invented human eyesight, a gift that no child in the womb could imagine or predict, although it was developing in that child from the very beginning in its invisible way. Such a gift can be used only after birth, after a painful separation from prelife. And then! Then our world, at first no bigger than ourselves, in a flash opens up to include the faces of other selves, and not too long afterward pushes out to the stars, and our souls expand to make room for all that grandeur. Could this first gift of new and larger life be a sort of pledge to us? Once we know there is a being who exercises providence over all things, who acts out of generosity and for the sake of what is good and beautiful, we can hardly conclude otherwise. The opening of our eyes in this world is a foretaste, then, of an opening of our minds in the next. The world outside the womb, to the child inside, is a mere murmuring beyond an opaque barrier. The world beyond the grave to most of us is all inference or rumor or a trust in the word of others. But the time for such dark and muffled perception is finite. We will one day find ourselves thrust beyond our current limitations and dazzled by the brightness and undreamt-of palpability of a world that dwarfs our prior concept of the universe. Our lives inside our mothers prepare us for life outside them. In similar fashion, our lives within matter prepare us for life outside it. (It is no accident that the word *matter* is so similar to *mater*, the Latin word for *mother*.)

Parallels between birth and death in this way illuminate the nature of death. Contrasts between birth and death teach us still more. Birth is not a destruction of the one being born. Death is a destruction of the one dying—not a total destruction, to be sure, since the soul lives on, but a destruction of the dying person nonetheless. The newborn is in a new condition outside the womb, but is no longer incomplete without it. The departed human soul is unlike a newborn in that respect. The soul is not merely in a new condition outside the body, but is somehow incomplete without it, more the main ingredient of a person than a complete person in its own right.

The destructive nature of death moves us to wonder about our own deserving, a point of illuminating difference between birth and death. We did not deserve to be born into this world, or to be born into such a life as we happened to be born into, whether we were rich or poor, healthy or sick, well cared for and loved, or neglected and abused. Since we did not exist before our birth, we could not have done anything to deserve to be born, or to be born into good circumstances or bad. The situation is different for our afterlife. By the choices we make with the hand we are dealt in this world, we will deserve the life into which we will be born by dying. There is a god who is not indifferent to the welfare of his creatures, least of all the rational ones capable of knowing and loving him by a part of themselves he made to live forever. There is nonetheless very little justice to be had in this life. The good often go unrewarded or even punished, while the wicked and the cruel go largely unpunished or even rewarded and praised. Perfect and final justice there must be, if god is just. We do not find such justice in this life. We therefore find it—or it finds us—in the next.

Putting the pieces together, we discover a fresh reason for hope. Death is a destruction—not an annihilation, but nonetheless a separation of a soul from its body, without which it is bereft and incomplete. In itself, the condition is neither good nor desirable. It is more like a punishment, or a somehow necessary evil, and can form no part of immortal happiness. Good souls who die, even if they enjoy a new kind of life and find relief from bodily suffering, are not rightly left for all time separated from their own bodies, even as the injustices of this world are not rightly left for all time unredressed. The demands of justice and the goodness of god compel us to admit that the good, at least, will one day be made whole again. The details are impossible to determine by mere philosophy. But it stands to reason that the dead, at least those to whom god will impart some share in his own immortal blessedness, should one day, when the time is right, live in their bodies once more.

They will not have mortal bodies, though, to die again, and then again and again. That would be like returning to the womb as a grown-up. A grown-up body does not return to the womb, which is only the first preparation, not the final destination, of a mature body. A grown-up soul does not return to mortal life, which is only the first preparation, not the final destination, of a mature soul.

We are mixed creatures, we humans—half-mortal by the natural condition of our bodies, half-immortal by the nature of our souls. It fits our two-part constitution to live not just one life, but two, one for each component in our nature. One life is temporary, in keeping with the natural mortality of our bodies. The other is eternal, in accord with the immortality of our souls. Obviously we must live the temporal one first if we are to live it at all, and so it is preparatory for the eternal one.

In this first life in our mortal skins, our soul is largely subjected to the condition of the body. The soul, by its nature immortal and made to understand and savor immortal things, much of the time gets dragged away from these pursuits in order to serve the mortal needs of the body. The human soul yearns for the true, the good, and the beautiful, not only in this or that particular true, or good, or beautiful thing—this dear friend or relative, this fine food and wine, a great moral victory, an amazing discovery of science, a sublime piece of music or transporting sonnet—but it wants any and all truth, goodness, and beauty, to see the whole nature of these, not just to sample them as they haphazardly come along piecemeal in various and limited representatives. The ongoing dissatisfaction of our souls in finite and temporary goods proves its inner nature can derive no complete happiness except from the possession of all goods. "All goods", however, exist together only in one single being, the source of all goods, the infinite good, god. Every soul therefore instinctively seeks god in seeking any good, whether it understands this about itself or not.

Poor soul. In this life, it is largely distracted from its chief desire, laboring instead to race through a succession of short-lived goods, often mere bodily goods, in a finite time. The soul is always *preparing* to be happy and only rarely and briefly and incompletely *is* happy. Even when we are at our happiest, in the very pink of health and prime of life with wealth and success and family and friends, we spend a third of our lives asleep. Our greatest happiness is punctuated with periods of oblivion, not because the nature of happiness demands it, but because our bodies do. Young children usually rebel at bedtime. Each night is a temporary halt of life, like a death in miniature. Life must cease for a time, and that is a thing to be lamented. Nor do we find our waking lives to be just what we would wish them to be. The greater number of us are not independently wealthy, but spend most of our lives earning our daily bread, clothing ourselves, repairing the roof over our head. The majority of us, too, suffer from health problems or bodily complaints to one degree or another. We would rather be enjoying the company of family and friends, but instead lie in bed nursing a recalcitrant migraine, unable even to think. The body is like an infant crying incessantly for the soul to provide for it, and when in rare moments it grows quiet, the soul knows it has precious little time to see to its own needs before it will be summoned again to play servant to the body.

Christopher Hitchens opened his book *Mortality* with these lines:

> I have more than once in my time woken up feeling like death. But nothing prepared me for the early morning in June when I came to consciousness feeling as if I were actually shackled to my own corpse.[1]

That was the beginning of his discovery that he had esophageal cancer. Even before some such moment comes for us and we *feel* the closing grip of our mortality, we might say all of us are born shackled to our own corpses. Our souls are indentured servants to our bodies, and live this life in the body under a strictly enforced time limit. Socrates went so far as to describe our mortal bodies as prisons for our souls. If it is right that god is just and therefore rewards the just, it cannot be into bodies such as these that he will restore their souls.

[1] Christopher Hitchens, *Mortality* (New York: Twelve, Hachette Book Group, 2012), p. 1.

Human bodies they must have, since human souls form human bodies, but mortal bodies they need not have, since the human soul is not mortal. The soul was subjected to the body during the mortal life of the body. Then the body must be subjected to the soul during the immortal life of the soul. The body will serve and obey the whims of the soul, no longer burdening or restricting it.

Even so, not a few of us worry about what such a life would be like. Many a sci-fi or fantasy novel has been written on the theme of immortality, and more often than not the lesson is that we should not want it. Such stories usually invite us to imagine immortality in this life, but just for one character or a few and not for their family and friends. Then those cursed with immortality are sentenced to watch all their loved ones die, of course. No thanks. Or else we are made to imagine what it would mean if all people could be prevented from aging and dying, and yet we must all continue to share the finite resources of one planet. Surely that is not blessedness. Just as surely, it is not the afterlife. This sci-fi immortality is nothing other than *this* life made permanent, like a child condemned to live forever in the womb.

Shedding this misconception, we may still labor under another. We might worry that, after sufficient time, we will have run out of things to do in the hereafter. After a hundred million years of immortal living, we will be able to say with a stretch and a yawn, "Been there, done that," to absolutely everything. There will be nothing left to do to make life worth living. We will be eternally bored, sick to death of living, wishing we could die. Images of little harp-strumming babies with wings do not much improve the picture. Really, though, this idea of a boring afterlife is just another version of the first misconception. It is a mental substitution of this life for the afterlife. It allows for an immortal body for ourselves and others, for our freedom from concern about resources, but only while disallowing any new kinds of activity for our souls that would suit an eternal existence in which we do not need to eat or sleep.

If god is not the most bored, but the most blessed of all beings, there must be something absolutely good enough for him (let alone us) to make his endless life worth the living. And this absolutely good-enough something is nothing other than his own infinite wealth of being all things in one. If all good things, actual and possible, lie within his power to produce, then he must contain all their perfections in himself in some superior and unlimited way. We cannot in this life, this dark womb, imagine or conceive that infinite goodness and beauty, but can only infer its existence as the source of all the partial and imperfect reflections of it that constitute the universe.

If finite goods satisfy for finite time, an infinite good satisfies for infinite time. All our experience is of finite goods, and all these in the end we find dissatisfying, cloying, in many cases attractive only once or for a time, and dull or repetitive thereafter, like a dime novel. It would be a great mistake for us to presume the infinite good suffers from these same limitations that belong to other goods precisely because they are limited. I dearly love *The Lord of the Rings* (hardly a dime novel). But after reading it three times myself, then twice out loud to my kids, and seeing the movies countless times, both the animated versions and the live-action ones—well, I've had enough of it for a good stretch, or at least until I have forgotten some of it. There are other books waiting to be read that have something to offer that *The Lord of the Rings* does not. Sometimes I grow tired of reading altogether, partly because I'm just tired, and partly because there are other things to do in life that have something to offer that cannot be gotten out of any book. Such is the nature of finite goods. But god is not a finite good. With bodies reconditioned for immortal life, our souls cannot get tired of communing with god.

We have arrived now at one of the frontiers of philosophy. It is natural to want to know more. Reason itself induces us to look for sources of truth uncramped by the limits of reason. Has god had anything to say to us in words about these enormous questions? Or is mute creation and our own reason, our spark of the divine intelligence, his only manner of communicating with us in this life? If he has had something to say to us in words, that path runs beyond the borders of philosophy, so I will say no more about it in this book. One thing we can be sure of, however, is that our souls are of greater consequence than our bodies. We must be very solicitous for the welfare of both, but if it ever comes down to a choice between them, we should be willing to give up our bodies in the pursuit of what is truly good for our souls, as even Socrates did, to say nothing of a Joan of Arc or a Thomas à Becket.

The knowledge of our immortal souls is no idle curiosity from which we can safely quarantine our day-to-day living. It should teach us to set priorities. Here the major monotheistic religions and philosophy itself speak with a single voice. If it seems impractical to devote much time and energy to the pursuit of wisdom, to moral excellence, to the frequent examination of our souls as we wend our way through this fleeting life, this can only be because we are deceiving ourselves into thinking we are already immortal, and in full control of our lives. This is to live in ignorance or forgetfulness of that future appointment when we will be called to account for all we have done and left undone.

If you were given two houses for your own, but only one of them in perpetuity, and the other irrevocably slated to be demolished within the year (although you had to live in it for the present), which one would you invest yourself in more? Immortal life to come and the present mortal life are like that. We must beware of investing ourselves in things at the expense of others that deserve our attention more. When I was younger, I had often heard that buying a house was a sound investment. I learned the hard way that this is not always true. The first house my wife and I bought was an old one into which we dumped truckloads of money ("truckloads" for us, that is), and out of which we received little return because we had to sell it in 2009 when the housing market was imploding. It was a lovely colonial that had been built in the 1920s, which meant old-house charm—and old-house headaches. Within the first year, we had to replace the roof. Then we had to replace the furnace. Then, when the doctor found unacceptably high levels of lead in Ben's blood, Amy and the kids had to go away to live with my in-laws while I undertook a massive and expensive lead-abatement project.

It wasn't all bad, though. Far from it. The house came with an unfinished, spacious, walk-up attic with windows on the gable ends and plenty of headroom because of the steep pitch of the roof. I covered the rafters and studs in tongue-and-groove pine boards, laid down a hardwood floor, and installed my own built-in, homemade bookcases of red oak, decked out with fluted moldings standing on handsome plinths. The bookcases stood just where the roof started to get too low for anyone to stand and so served as knee walls. I had venting roof windows put in. In winter they were covered in snow and cast a strange, cool, agreeably moody glow throughout the place. In other seasons of the year, they let in light and fresh air and the sound of rain in the trees. Sometimes in the evenings, when I grew

weary of books, I would lie down on the carpet in this attic sanctu-
ary of mine, gaze up through a roof window, and count the stars. It
became my refuge, my ivory tower, a quiet study doubling as an art
studio. And in all the decade in which I painted and read and wrote
in that peaceful retreat from the world, the invigorating and Christ-
massy scent of the pine boards never faded.

Then along came a sudden need to relocate the family, to take a
teaching job back in California, where our first child, Max, had been
born. When we broke the news to the kids, they were understandably dismayed. We tried to tell them that we had no real choice in
the matter, that we knew just as many people in California as in New
England, that we were really just returning to where we used to live,
that many of their relatives were planning to go out there to school in
the near future, that they would adjust. These things did not resonate
with them. All they could hear was that pretty much their entire life
as they knew it was coming to an end. The five of us would remain
together, yes, but it was good-bye to cousins, to grandparents, to
aunts, uncles, friends, to New England itself, and in all likelihood the
good-bye was permanent, except for short visits few and far between.

The house, too, had to be left behind—the house that for eleven
years we had called "home", a word for which the children knew no
other meaning. We were going to be *homeless*, as far as they could
see. And it certainly felt that way for a while. I have a vivid memory
of sitting on the floor of my beautiful study, tired after sealing up
the last box of my books. Except for a layer of light dust, the shelves
were now bare; the whole office was empty and echoed, containing
only a table and a desk, a rolled-up carpet, and stacks of taped-up
boxes. Everything was going into storage for an as yet undetermined
amount of time, until we could find a new house in California—*if*
we could find one. How long would it be till we saw all our familiar
belongings again? In what strange house would we open those boxes?
How long before we felt at home once more? So many happy memories lived in every room of our first house. Forlorn, I looked around
at my attic refuge, which would no longer be mine now, but someone else's. All that work I had done. So much of my money, time,
and planning had gone into it. I looked at my two hands. How much
work had these two hands done on this house, this house I now had
to leave behind? And then for some reason the thought crashed into

me like a thunderbolt: a day was coming when I would have to leave behind not only the work of my hands, but my hands themselves.

Of course I had always known this in an abstract way. But somehow it became much more real at that moment. And it continues to become still more real as I get older and see more and more people I know and love depart from this life. I thank heaven for the consolation of philosophy. I thank heaven more that I have not only the relatively cold lessons of philosophy to lend me the courage and hope to live for a life hereafter, but also a living faith in God's assurance that once I see it, I will laugh at myself for having feared the transition, that final cross-country move. I need fear nothing but my own undeserving. I need only conduct my life like the pilgrimage that it is, carry out my assignment as captain of the little ship that is my family, and with every turn of the rudder make for the everlasting shores.

ACKNOWLEDGMENTS

I am extremely grateful to my old friend Matt McSorley, and to his dear mother, Cecilia, who not only gave their generous permission to mention them in this book, but who also in many ways inspired it.

As always, I am deeply indebted to my wife and children for letting me spend countless hours behind a closed door, hacking away at a manuscript, and also for letting me use their sayings and doings to make a point now and then. (I also drag their good names into the classroom, and sometimes my students laugh and accuse me of performing philosophical experiments on my children. I remind them that this is still legal in most states.)

Thanks, too, to my brothers David and John. Through conversations and email exchanges they helped me gain greater clarity about certain ideas that otherwise would have remained vague in my mind.

Others helped shape this book without knowing it, especially my students, who never tire of teaching me the difference between what makes sense and what doesn't. I must also thank all my present and former colleagues and associates—especially Tony Andres, David Appleby, Joe Audie, Travis Cooper, Glen Coughlin, Sean Cunningham, Carol Day, Chris Decaen, Brian Dragoo, Katherine Gardner, Patrick Gardner, Tom Kaiser, John Keck, Jack Neumayr, John Nieto, Chris Oleson, Paul O'Reilly, and Elizabeth Reyes—for their many insights into the nature and powers of the soul that they have shared with me in conversation.

My teachers are particularly responsible for anything good in this book. Special thanks must go to Duane Berquist for guiding me and some friends through the commentary of Thomas Aquinas on Aristotle's book *On the Soul*, in a series of Wednesday night seminars that ran for three years in the early 1990s. For this and many other services to me (and to many others) he has been entirely unrewarded in every earthly way, so far as I can tell. Thanks also to his wife, Rosalie, for putting up with the seminars, and for certain words of encouragement she probably does not remember saying to me, but which I have never forgotten.

If this book is at all readable, it is not my fault. I did everything I could to put the whole thing in what seems to be my native tongue: hyperabstract, unreadable, philosophical jargon. But my two greatest, wisest, most indefatigable critics, my father and my brother Paul, thwarted many of my efforts. They gleefully attacked the first manuscript with all kinds of instruments, both blunt and sharp, and I made changes accordingly, just to quiet them. Then they did the same to a second manuscript. They even, in some cases, subjected a third or fourth draft of a chapter to their slash-and-burn methods. The sheer quantity of their marginal comments and emails (always brilliant, often hilarious, never too gentle) nearly equals the length of the book itself. These two merciless revisers were absolutely determined that the thing should be readable. They seemed to think that was important, somehow. What lies before you is largely the result. For those portions of the book that read like modern English to you, these two behind-the-scenes editors are to blame. If at times you have found some tangled knots, some dry-as-dust deserts, some tough slogs, some chewy paragraphs you could make nothing of, you may write me a thank-you note. Those were the bits I managed to smuggle back in.

APPENDIX

Chapter Summaries and Related Passages in Aquinas

In this book are many twists and turns, principal points and subordinate points, arguments and counterarguments, and illustrative material besides. There is some danger of losing sight of the forest for the trees in any given chapter, and in moving from one chapter to another. So I thought it might be helpful here to name the forests—that is, to state in brief and plain language the main point or points each chapter was about. It is not really possible to squeeze all that into a chapter title, I find. Under each chapter title below, I supply the main question the chapter is meant to address, a short description of the chapter content, and references to some places where Thomas Aquinas makes related points in his own writings.

Chapter 1: Your Insider's View

Does Your Insider's View Have Anything Important to Say about You?

There are two views of you, one from within, and another from without. You have both. Other people have only the outside view of you, as you do of them. In order to find out what kind of being you are, this book consults both views of you, but especially your insider's view. Neither view of you, the insider's view or the outsider's view, says everything we can know about you, but both together form a more complete picture than either one alone.

In Aquinas:

- *Commentary on Aristotle's* On the Soul 1.1
- *Summa Theologiae* I–II, q. 112, a. 5 ad 1

Chapter 2: Hidden Powers

Do You Possess Any Knowing Powers Not Known to Most People?

We now put your insider's view to work. Consulting your sense experience, we find that you possess hidden knowing powers not known to most people. In particular, we discover your "universal sense", which can know the objects of all five senses and can compare, contrast, and correlate them.

In Aquinas (who calls this power of yours the *sensus communis*, or "common sense"—an infelicitous phrase in English, since it bears quite another meaning):

* *Commentary on Aristotle's* On the Soul 3.2–3
* *Summa Theologiae* I, q. 78, a. 4

Chapter 3: Introducing: Your Intellect

How Does Your Intellect Differ from Your Imagination?

By means of your insider's view, you can distinguish between your ability to form universal ideas (e.g., your idea of "what a triangle is") and your ability to form images of particular things (e.g., an image of "this triangle"). Your power of forming universal ideas is called your intellect, and your power of forming images is called your imagination.

In Aquinas:

* *Commentary on Aristotle's* On the Soul 2.12
* *Commentary on Aristotle's* On the Soul 3.4–5

Chapter 4: Paragon of Animals

How Do You Differ from Animals?

Thanks to the sharp distinction between imagination and intellect, you can now draw a clear line between yourself and the other animals, even though they may be called "intelligent" in some sense. Their intelligence does not include the power to understand universal ideas, whereas yours does. You are also a nobler and more complete kind of being than any of the irrational animals, which are in turn nobler beings than plants.

In Aquinas:

- *Commentary on Aristotle's* On the Soul 2.5–6
- *Summa Theologiae* I, q. 78, a. 1

Chapter 5: Beyond the Brain

Is Your Intellect a Power of Your Brain?

Interference with your brain (physically, chemically, or in other ways) can alter, inhibit, or halt your acts of understanding. This proves that your intellect depends on your brain in some way. Does this mean your brain is the organ that carries out the act of understanding? No, since its ability to grasp universal ideas proves your intellect is nonmaterial and incorporeal. Your intellect depends on your brain only because it depends on your imagination (which is in your brain) to present it with images and symbols of things about which to form universal ideas.

In Aquinas:

- *Commentary on Aristotle's* On the Soul 1.2
- *Summa Theologiae* I, q. 75, a. 2 ad 3
- *Summa Theologiae* I, q. 75, a. 5
- *Summa Contra Gentiles* 2.49–50

Chapter 6: A Life-and-Death Question

What In Your Body Is Primarily Responsible for It Being Alive?

After seeing that a part of you is nonmaterial, we naturally wonder how your nonmaterial mind and your material body are unified in a single you. Since it is one and the same you who both understands in the mind and lives in the body, what gives you the power to understand must also cause your body to be alive. What is it in your body that causes it to be alive? Considering certain candidates leads us to the answer: it is a certain form in your body's materials. This "form" of yours is not your body's organization, but something even more fundamental than that.

In Aquinas:

- *Summa Theologiae* I, q. 75, a. 1
- *Summa Theologiae* I, q. 76, a. 1

Chapter 7: Black Birds and Blackbirds

Are You an Individual or a Collective?

To grasp the nature of your form better, we must understand in what way it unifies the parts of your body in making them to be you. Does your human form make you a single collective of many beings (such as your molecules), or a single individual? Both the external view of you and your insider's view of you confirm that you are not a collective of many distinct entities, but a single individual being. Your parts (both macroscopic and microscopic) are many and diverse, and retain their qualitative diversity within you, but they are only diverse parts of one being (you), not diverse beings in their own right.

In Aquinas:

- *Commentary on Aristotle's* Nicomachean Ethics 1.1
- *Summa Theologiae* I, q. 76, a. 1
- *Summa Theologiae* I, q. 76, a. 3

Chapter 8: What Growth Says about You

Is Your Essential Form Divisible into Parts?

To understand the nature of your form still better, we must learn whether or not it is divisible into parts. As you grew up, your human form preserved the unity of you throughout your many different sizes, and therefore it is something more fundamental than your body's dimensions. And since your form unifies your many parts into a single you, it cannot itself have many parts that need unifying, or else we wind up in an infinite regression. Your form therefore has no parts, but is instead whole in every part of you. In this chapter, your form gets its name: *soul*.

In Aquinas:

- *Commentary on Aristotle's* On the Soul 2.1–4
- *Summa Contra Gentiles* 2.56
- *Summa Theologiae* I, q. 76, a. 8

Chapter 9: Your Immortal Soul

Is Your Soul Immortal?

Whatever is destructible is either a composition of materials and a form, or else it is a form that depends on the thing it forms in order to exist. Your soul falls into neither category, since it is a pure form, not a composition of matter and form, and since, thanks to its intellectual nature, it has a life outside your body and therefore does not depend on your body to exist. Your soul, therefore, is naturally immortal.

In Aquinas:

- *Summa Theologiae* I, q. 75, a. 6
- *Summa Contra Gentiles* 2.55

Chapter 10: Eyes Are for Seeing

What Is a Living Thing? Is Purpose Inherent in the Parts of a Living Thing?

On our way to asking where your immortal soul comes from, this chapter inquires about the distinction between living and nonliving things in order to bring to light a certain kind of purposefulness that exists in nature. A thing is alive if it is a single natural being that is made of tools for itself. The parts of living things are truly "tools", and not just things that happen to be useful as though they were tools. A tool implies a purpose, and living things, including human beings, have purposes, definite self-beneficial tendencies, naturally built into their parts and powers, even apart from their conscious desires.

In Aquinas:

- *Summa Theologiae* I, q. 18, a. 1–3
- *Summa Contra Gentiles* 3.2
- *Commentary on Aristotle's* Physics 2.8 (his most general book on the philosophy of nature)

Chapter 11: The End of Evolution

Does Evolution Logically Exclude Purpose from Nature?

The theory of evolution, whatever its strengths and weaknesses, is not only compatible with natural things acting for the sake of various ends, but presupposes this fact about them. Cosmic evolution too, or the development of the universe, is toward life, and intelligent life in particular, as its target or end.

In Aquinas we will not find much of anything about evolution, of course, but we do find some general principles that bear on how to understand it. For example, in *Summa Contra Gentiles* (3.22), he explains why he thinks that the ultimate end of all natural forms and processes in nature is the human soul, and why matter tends to this as to an ultimate form. Aquinas sometimes opposes the view of the pre-Socratic philosopher Empedocles that the parts of animals and plants first arose by chance and those that worked stuck around—a very early view roughly similar to that of Darwin. When Aquinas opposes this idea, he opposes it not simply as an idea about how new natural things might come to be in nature, but only as an alternative to and substitute for the idea that natural things act for the sake of certain goods (see, for example, his commentary on Aristotle's *Physics* 2.8).

Chapter 12: A Totally Original Thought

Why Does Mindless Nature Naturally Serve the Needs of Mind?

The maker and end of the universe is an intellectual being, god. He is the first origin of your soul, and the reason why natural things unconsciously and mindlessly serve the needs of consciousness and mind.

In Aquinas:

- *Summa Theologiae* I, q. 2, a. 3
- *Summa Contra Gentiles* 1.13

Chapters 13–15: Know Thyself

Is Your Self-Knowledge Trustworthy?

The main modern objection to all the foregoing results is not that the reasoning behind them is bad, but that the first premises they start from are not to be trusted, since they arise out of ordinary experience. Ordinary experience, say such objectors, should be completely replaced by scientific observations whenever we really want to know the truth about the world and ourselves. Accordingly, this chapter examines the chief thesis of "scientism", that all genuine knowledge of nature and of human nature in particular must arise out of empirical methods that reduce entirely to the language of chemistry and physics. The reasons behind this common but largely unspoken and unexamined assumption, while understandable and enlightening to consider, are invalid. Common sense, universally shared experiences and ideas of the world, and the self-evident truths that arise from these are in fact a sure and irreplaceable foundation not only for the philosophy of nature, but also for modern science.

In the time of Aquinas, modern science as we think of it today did not really exist, and natural philosophy was almost universally respected among the educated. Scientism, therefore, was not a problem.

CORRIGENDUM CONCERNING
AN ELECTRIC SHARK

When my father gave me his feedback on an early version of the chapter now titled "Introducing: Your Intellect", he noted that I had gotten some things wrong. My mother had not really wanted him to encourage me in my plans to build an electric shark, and he had not in fact stifled any laughter at my drawing. Here was his comment in the margin:

> Actually Mom challenged me for humoring you in this matter. Why encourage the boy in a project so impossible? My answer was, "Every kid has the right to a dream, and I'm not going to be the one to burst his."

My historically false account of these details was not a deliberate deception. It was a confusion, I think, of the electric shark memory with another one—my first "novel". This early, illustrated oeuvre, written in the mid-1970s, ran on for twenty-seven pages of single-spaced type from an old manual typewriter. I recently discovered that I still have a copy in my possession. It is some sort of fantasy story—hilariously bad. If memory serves, it was when my father read this little book of mine (his first feedback!) that he reacted as described in chapter three, and my mother gave him a scolding look.

Wishing to avoid overworking things, I have retained the inaccuracy in the narrative in chapter three. My chief goal in providing personal anecdotes is not to render an exact account of my little doings, but to set the tone for whatever is to come, and maybe to illustrate a philosophical principle or problem. I have drawn often from early memories because these are more likely to contain elements common to the memories of everyone else, and to communicate something of the fresh and unglossed contact with reality from which philosophy should begin, so far as possible.

In the interests of historical accuracy, however, I have included this corrigendum.

INDEX